And We All Fall Down

And We All Fall Down

Ben Shapiro

Creators Publishing
Hermosa Beach, CA

A Note From the Publisher

Since 1987, Creators has syndicated many of your favorite columns to newspapers. In this digital age, we are bringing collections of those columns to your fingertips. This will allow you to read and reread your favorite columnists, with your own personal digital archive of their work.

Creators Publishing

Contents

Book One

The Left's Phantom Wars

What to Expect in 2014

January 1, 2014

2013 was a year of revelations, a year of possible turning points. For nearly two decades, since Ronald Reagan left office, America moved steadily in the direction of the left, both culturally and politically. When the Soviet Union fell, optimistic scholars believed the world had shifted inexorably in the direction of free markets and liberal democracy. Instead, the West gradually embraced bigger government and weaker social bonds, creating a fragmented society in which the only thing we all belong to, as President Barack Obama puts it, is the state.

All battles for the soul begin with culture. And while the battle against Obama's unprecedented growth of government started with the tea party victories of 2010, the cultural battle against the left didn't truly take until 2013. The seeds were planted for this cultural battle in earnest in 2012, when Obama and his Democratic Party allies put race, sexual orientation and abortion at the core of his reelection campaign. Americans were told by the media that Obama's competence mattered less than the fact that half the country was mean, nasty, racist and homophobic. Todd Akin's absurd comments on conception via rape were the issue, Americans were told, not the imminent takeover of the health care system; Obama's sudden support for same-sex marriage was the issue, not his devastating regulatory state; George Zimmerman and Trayvon Martin were the issue, not the destruction of entire swaths of the United States via leftist governance.

And it worked. Conservative Americans, bludgeoned into silence on cultural battles, decided to focus entirely on Obama's economic buffoonery. Unsurprisingly, it didn't work; culture, as my friend Andrew Breitbart was fond of stating, is upstream of politics.

2013 marked a turning point. From Chick-fil-A to "Duck Dynasty," conservative religious Americans found their footing: Whether you are for or against same-sex marriage, it is plainly un-American to override someone's religious beliefs in the name of your politics. Conservative Americans seemed to realize, for the first time in a long time, that the battle over same-sex marriage came wrapped in a larger battle over religious freedom. And they fought back, and won.

Meanwhile, conservatives began to fight back against the left's uncorroborated assertion of right-wing racism. While MSNBC focused laser-like on one Confederate flag at an anti-Obamacare rally, those same MSNBC hosts laughed at Mitt Romney's adopted black grandchild (Melissa Harris-Perry), suggested that someone ought to "p***" and "s***" in Sarah Palin's mouth (Martin Bashir), used anti-gay slurs (Alec Baldwin), shook down businesses over race (Al Sharpton) and labeled words like "black hole" and "Chicago" racist (Chris Matthews). Race, the right realized, was an obsession only for the left.

And in the aftermath of the left's successful 2012 "war on women" meme, the right began to fight back, too. Beginning with the left's attempted deification of amoral Texas state Sen. Wendy Davis, who filibustered for 11 hours on behalf of the murder of 21-week-old fetuses, the right refused to be cowed. Abortion is a real moral issue with real lives at stake, and no amount of leftist badgering could back conservative Americans off their attempts to protect the unborn.

The cultural battles gradually made their way into the political arena, too. Freed from the burden of the beige and blundering Romney campaign, conservatives stood up against the growth of government on moral, not merely practical, grounds. Obama's signature program began to collapse the moment Americans awakened to the deep immorality of government-controlled medical care. Sen. Ted Cruz's government shutdown strategy, right or wrong, highlighted conservative opposition to the state as cradle-to-grave caretaker. American distrust of government, for the right reasons, soared.

This does not mean the battles are over for conservatives. They're just beginning. The media have already geared up toward nominating Hillary Clinton in 2016 (The New York Times whitewash of Benghazi this week was only the beginning). The DC-run Republican Party has a disheartening way of crippling its own conservative base in order to cut deals. But 2013 could go down as the year that conservatives moved beyond standing athwart history shouting "stop," and began shoving in the opposite direction, which could make 2014 historic.

Why Socialism Is on the Rise

January 8, 2014

It took capitalism half a century to come back from the Great Depression. It's taken socialism half that time to come back from the collapse of the Soviet Union. In New York City, avowed socialist Mayor Bill de Blasio has declared that his goal is to take "dead aim at the Tale of Two Cities" -- the gap between rich and poor. In Seattle, newly elected socialist city Councilmember Kshama Sawant addressed supporters, explaining, "I wear the badge of socialist with honor." To great acclaim from the left, columnist Jesse Myerson of Rolling Stone put out a column telling millennials that they ought to fight for government-guaranteed employment, a universal basic income, collectivization of private property, nationalization of private assets and public banks.

The newly flowering buds of Marxism no longer reside on the fringes. Not when the president of the United States has declared fighting income inequality his chief task as commander in chief. Not when Senate Majority Leader Harry Reid, D-Nev., has said that America faces "no greater challenge" than income disparity. Not when MSNBC, The New York Times and the amalgamated pro-Obama media outlets have all declared their mission for 2014 a campaign against rich people.

Less than 20 years ago, former President Bill Clinton, facing reelection, declared "the era of big government" over. By 2011, Clinton reversed himself, declaring that it was government's role to "give people the tools and create the conditions to make the most of our lives."

So what happened?

Capitalism failed to make a case for itself. Back in 1998, shortly after the world seemed to reach a consensus on the ineffectiveness of socialist schemes, economists Daniel Yergin and Joseph Stanislaw wrote that the free market required something beyond mere success: It required "legitimacy." But, said Yergin and Stanislaw, "a system that takes the pursuit of self-interest and profit as its guiding light does not necessarily satisfy the yearning in the human soul for belief and some higher meaning beyond materialism." In other words, they wrote, while Spanish communists would die with the word "Stalin" on their lips, "few people would die with the words 'free markets' on their lips."

The failure to make a moral case for capitalism has doomed capitalism to the status of a perennial backup plan. When people are desperate or wealthy, they turn to socialism; only when they have no other alternative do they embrace the free market. After all, lies about guaranteed security are far more seductive than lectures about personal responsibility.

So what is the moral case for capitalism? It lies in recognition that socialism isn't a great idea gone wrong -- it's an evil philosophy in action. It isn't driven by altruism; it's driven by greed and jealousy. Socialism states that you owe me something simply because I exist. Capitalism, by contrast, results in a sort of reality-forced altruism: I may not want to help you, I may dislike you, but if I don't give you a product or service you want, I will starve. Voluntary exchange is more moral than forced redistribution. Socialism violates at least three of the Ten Commandments: It turns government into God, it legalizes thievery and it elevates covetousness. Discussions of income inequality, after all, aren't about prosperity but about petty spite. Why should you care how much money I make, so long as you are happy?

Conservatives talk results when discussing the shortcomings of socialism. They're right: Socialism is ineffective, destructive and stunting to the human spirit. But they're wrong to abandon the field of morality when discussing the contrast between freedom and control. And it's this abandonment -- this perverse laziness -- that has led to socialism's comeback, even though within living memory, we have seen continental economies collapse and millions slaughtered in the name of this false god.

Negotiating With Space Nazis

January 15, 2014

On Tuesday, the Iranian government announced that it had reached a secret agreement with the West on its nuclear development. The details of the agreement were not released, but suffice it to say that the Iranians could not contain their glee. Iranian President Hassan Rouhani celebrated the deal with an English-language tweet claiming that the "world powers surrendered to Iranian nation's will"; Iranian Army Commander Maj. Gen. Ataollah Salehi said the diplomatic breakthrough resulted from American military "weakness"; and the Iranian foreign minister laid a wreath at the tomb of the Beirut Marine barracks bomber.

Meanwhile, President Barack Obama urged the United States Congress to "give peace a chance." After weeks of sending out his pacifist minions, including faux pro-Israel group J Street, to tell Americans that support for sanctions meant support for war, Obama himself echoed that message. "My preference is for peace and diplomacy," the apparent flower-child-in-chief stated. "And this is one of the reasons why I've sent the message to Congress that now is not the time for us to impose new sanctions. Now is the time for us to allow the diplomats and technical experts to do their work." He said that a rational, reasonable Iran would be "willing to walk through the door of opportunity that's presented to them."

Only Iran is not rational or reasonable. It is delusionally anti-Western and anti-Semitic, which means that America is now in negotiations not just with a terror-supporting state but radicals with more than a hint of insanity.

To prove this point, on Sunday, the Iranian semiofficial news agency FARS, which bills itself as independent but is effectively regime-run, ran a news article explaining that since the end of World War II, America had been run by a shadow government of Nazi space aliens. Seriously.

Basing its report on documents supposedly culled from National Security Agency leaker Edward Snowden, FARS reported that there was no "incontrovertible proof" that the American foreign policy agenda was driven by an "alien/extraterrestrial intelligence agenda."

Not "alien" as in foreigner. "Alien" as in little green men from Mars. FARS quotes Snowden as stating that there "were actually two governments in the U.S., one that was elected, and the other, secret regime, governing in the dark." This shadow regime had been run by space aliens -- also known as "Tall Whites" -- who were operating their regime from Nevada after emigrating from Nazi Germany after World War II. These space aliens, FARS stated, built the Nazi war machine's submarines.

This would be hilarious were it not part of a piece. Large swaths of the Islamic world also buy the myth that Jews use the blood of non-Jewish children in both their Passover matza and Purim hamentashen. "The Protocols of the Elders of Zion" remains a best-seller throughout the Islamic world. Iranian television routinely broadcasts Holocaust denial, while Iranian press outlets proclaim that the Zionist regime is producing another Hitler.

Assume for a moment that the Iranian regime actually believes the propaganda it spouts. Why, then, would it negotiate in good faith with space alien Nazis who drink Muslim blood?

Many pacifists in the West, including Obama, apparently assume that no one rational would continue to develop nuclear weapons in the face of world opposition, especially when offered a way out. What Obama fails to recognize is that Iran is far from rational -- and, more importantly, Obama's own assumptions about Iranian intentions put America and the West in a position of weakness. This weakness will be on display for all the world to see when Iran goes nuclear.

Abortion and the Suicide of the West

January 22, 2014

Jenelle Evans, 22, had an abortion this year. Originally featured on MTV four years ago as a pregnant teenager, Evans, who loves to party, had a son, gave the son to her mother to raise, got into heroin, got married and went to jail; her husband ended up in jail as well on drug charges. They got divorced. He didn't know that Evans was pregnant. She got an abortion. He found out about it on the commercials for "Teen Mom 2."

Now she's pregnant again. With a third guy. Who may or may not be seeing another woman on the side.

Since the legally and morally despicable decision of the Supreme Court in Roe v. Wade in 1973, American women have aborted some 56 million children. The vast majority of these children have been aborted for reasons that have nothing to do with rape, incest or the health of the mother. We have destroyed an entire generation of children purely for self-worship. Children are difficult; therefore, they can be done away with. Children are burdensome; therefore, they don't exist in the womb. Or, as President Barack Obama once put it regarding his own daughters, "If they make a mistake, I don't want them punished with a baby."

Meanwhile, the same society that has busily anesthetized millions to the murder of the unborn casually pushes social costs onto the next generation -- a generation that, increasingly, does not exist. According to the 2010 census, just 24 percent of the American population is under age 18, compared with 39.4 percent that is 45 and older. America is aging, and aging quickly.

And what of the young? Their chief concerns these days are legalization of marijuana, state-sponsored same-sex marriage and provision of birth control. If we think the demographics and economics of the country look bad now, wait until America relies on a generation of overprivileged, underachieving Americans convinced of their own moral rectitude based on a puerile libertarianism freed of libertarianism's consequences. Sex and drugs have replaced building for the future; abortion and the welfare state have replaced consequences.

In the end, this philosophy will lead to the dominance of the state. There are only two types of society that can survive. First, there is the heavy-entitlement, heavily regulated society, in which compulsion takes the place of free choice. Second, there is the free society, in which individual actions carry individual consequences. America used to be the second type of society. As we realize that there is no next generation to foot our bills, we will transition more toward the first.

So, how can we solve all of this? Not through the law -- the law follows culture. The only way to restore an American future is to restore the social and religious institutions that fostered genuine American values. This means fighting back against the tyranny of those who conveniently proclaim to "live and let live" while simultaneously demanding that Americans with traditional values shut the hell up. This means emboldening our churches and synagogues to once again speak out on behalf of virtue. This means treating family as a priority rather than an afterthought or punishment.

Evans is a victim of the society that built her -- a society that has enabled her misdeeds and rewarded her sins. But she cannot be the basis of America's future. If she is, America will, quite literally, have no future.

How Hollywood Is Killing
Same-Sex Marriage

January 29, 2014

In May 2012, Vice President Joe Biden floated a political trial balloon: He came out in favor of same-sex marriage. In the process, he stated that the way had been paved for the same-sex marriage movement by Hollywood. "I think 'Will & Grace' probably did more to educate the American public than almost anything anybody's ever done so far." Biden, of course, was absolutely right: Hollywood's personalization of the societal issue of same-sex marriage has shifted millions of minds.

Now, unfortunately for same-sex marriage advocates, Hollywood is busily shifting those minds back.

On Sunday, the Grammys tooted its self-proclaimed righteousness by trotting out Queen Latifah to officiate the mass wedding of 33 couples, including gay couples. She did so as new Grammy winner Macklemore shouted cloyingly sanctimonious antireligious slogans into his microphone: "The right-wing conservatives think it's a decision / And you can be cured with some treatment and religion ... Playing God, aw nah, here we go / America the brave still fears what we don't know / And God loves all his children is somehow forgotten / But we paraphrase a book written 3,500 years ago." To top off the marriages, Madonna then staggered out to warble "Open Your Heart."

This wasn't an argument for same-sex marriage. It wasn't even attractive image-making on behalf of same-sex marriage. It was hatred of Biblical values cloaked in pietistic nonsense.

Begin with the marriages themselves. The only rationale for getting married on the Grammys en masse would be either attention-seeking or spite toward Americans with traditional values, or both. Neither of these rationales scream "love," "commitment" or "societal building block."

Move on to the cheering audience -- a group of anti-marriage Hollywoodites who largely see the institution itself as patriarchal. The same folks standing up for same-sex marriage at the Grammys largely scorn the institution of marriage itself. The only time they embrace marriage is when it is being mocked, undermined or perverted. That's not a cuddly case for same-sex marriage.

Finally, look at the artists: Macklemore, who rages against religious Americans for cash and Grammys; Madonna, who is happy to glom onto the marriage bandwagon after selling her body for decades, and running through a raft of unsuccessful marriages and relationships of her own; Queen Latifah, acting as a stand-in for the government, offering up salvation via paper licenses from the state. None of this warms hearts or changes minds.

But this is Hollywood unmasked: angry, vindictive, self-righteous, anti-Biblical. The case for same-sex marriage rests on an application of Biblical principle -- monogamy and commitment -- to actions condemned by Biblical text. For years, Hollywood was able to get away with perverting the Bible by ignoring it. But in its rush to congratulate itself for overthrowing Biblical values without a shot, Hollywood spiked the football and revealed its true agenda. And that agenda is not the agenda of tolerance for individuals, but an ugly agenda of unearned moral superiority via destruction of traditional values.

Letter to My Newborn Daughter

February 5, 2014

Last Tuesday evening at 6:19 p.m. PST, my wife gave birth to our first child, a 7-pound, 9-ounce, 21-inch little girl named Leeya Eliana. The labor was long, approximately 26 hours, and my wife endured it heroically. Before, we were a married couple; now, we are a family.

On the sixth day of her life, I wrote my little girl a letter to memorialize our hopes for her at the dawn of her life. With my wife's permission, here it is:

Dear Leeya Eliana,

This is Daddy and Mommy writing to you. You are now six days old, and you are tiny and cute, and you poop a lot -- and you get really mad when anybody tries to change you. But you are also sweet and calm, and you look at us with your huge blue-gray eyes, and we love you so much because we know that not only are you a manifestation of how much Mommy and Daddy love each other, but you are the future of the Jewish people and the American people, and that we are preserving God's word and His freedom for the next generations. That's why we gave you your name: Leeya -- in Hebrew, "I Belong To God."

And you were our answer, Leeya. After Mommy and Daddy prayed very hard to Hashem to give them a healthy little baby, God answered them: Eliana. So your first name is about your relationship with God, and your middle name is about how thankful we are for you.

We hope you grow up to be the best, most principled, most joyful person in the entire world. We want you to be a leader for God, no matter what you choose to do -- to live with His justice and

His compassion, with His standards and His kindness. And we want you to love your family as much as we love you, and to carry forward our mission as a family and as a people. We will do our best to train and guide you. We promise to always take you seriously and to always listen to you. And we promise to never leave you.

You are the best thing that has ever happened to us, and that's what makes all the poop and the crying and the late-night feedings and the sleep deprivation worth it. You may not always agree with everything we do -- you're going to be a teenager, and you're going to realize that Daddy and Mommy are just human beings trying their best. But we will do our best to ensure that you understand that we love you more than anything, and that it is our mission to help you find the best path to serving God.

Love you forever,

Daddy and Mommy

Why Democrats Hate Work

February 12, 2014

Last week, the Congressional Budget Office released a report discussing the ramifications of Obamacare. The report revealed that the work-hour equivalent of approximately 2.5 million jobs would disappear from the workforce, thanks to Obamacare, in a voluntary process in which employees would simply dump out of their jobs, knowing they could get health care through expanded Medicaid and federal subsidies they would lose by working.

Sen. Charles Schumer, D-N.Y., an ideological leftist thought leader, spun the report as a massive positive for Obamacare: "The single mom, who's raising three kids (and) has to keep a job because of health care, can now spend some time raising those kids. That's a family value." And Senate Majority Leader Harry Reid, D-Nev., celebrated the report as a defeat for the dreaded condition known as "job lock" -- the situation in which you have to stick at a job you don't like for the benefits. "We have the CBO report," Reid stated, "which rightfully says, that people shouldn't have job lock. If they -- we live in a country where there should be free agency. People can do what they want."

But, of course, people can only do what they want by taxing other Americans, borrowing from foreign creditors, and burdening future generations with unsustainable debt. And unfortunately, Schumer's proclamation that the greatest beneficiaries of Obamacare will be single mothers turns out to be false: One of the studies relied upon by the CBO stated that those who benefit from the end of job lock are disproportionately white, single and of work age.

In reality, the Democratic vision of the world centers on the notion that work itself is a great evil to be avoided, and that any program allowing people to free themselves of work -- whether to finger-paint or start a garage band -- is an unmitigated good. "Job lock," according to the definition Reid gives, goes by another name, according to those who live in the real world: "having a job." There are times that everyone hates his or her job. Were they freed from the economic consequences of having these jobs, they'd drop out of the workforce.

There are only two problems with this strategy: First, someone has to pay for it; second, it is not the recipe for human fulfillment. Leisure time is only leisure time when it is earned; otherwise, leisure time devolves into soul-killing lassitude. There's a reason so many new retirees, freed from the treadmill of work, promptly keel over on the golf course: Work fulfills us. It keeps us going.

This doesn't mean every job fulfills us, naturally. But we have all worked rotten jobs in order to get to jobs we like. Capitalism doesn't mean, as my grandmother used to say, that you don't have to walk through some manure to get to the roses. It just means that if you walk through enough manure, you'll likely get to the roses sooner or later. In the leisure-first world of the left, however, wallowing in mire is a preferred road to happiness over the hard work that brings true fulfillment.

The European style of living is seductive: fewer hours worked, more hours at the cafe, less concern over self-betterment. But that style of living does not produce a purposeful life. Perhaps we'd all be happier in the short run were we somehow freed of our job lock. But we certainly would not contribute to the betterment of ourselves or the community around us. We'd leave the world worse than we found it. The opt-out society opts us out of societal happiness.

The Left Preaches the Great Apocalypse of Global Warming

February 19, 2014

This week, Secretary of State John Kerry announced to a group of Indonesian students that global warming was "perhaps the world's most fearsome weapon of mass destruction." He added, "Because of climate change, it's no secret that today Indonesia is ... one of the most vulnerable countries on Earth. It's not an exaggeration to say that the entire way of life that you live and love is at risk."

Meanwhile, Hollywood prepared to drop a new blockbuster based on the biblical story of Noah. The film, directed by Darren Aronofsky, centers on the story of the biblical character who built an ark after God warned him that humanity would be destroyed thanks to its sexual immorality and violent transgressions. The Hollywood version of the story, however, has God punishing humanity not for actual sin, but for overpopulation and global warming -- an odd set of sins, given God's express commandments in Genesis 1:28 to "be fruitful, multiply, fill the earth, and subdue it."

This weird perspective on sin -- the notion that true sin is not sin, but that consumerism is -- is actually nothing new. In the 1920s, the left warned of empty consumerism with the fire and brimstone of Jonathan Edwards; Sinclair Lewis famously labeled the American middle class "Babbitts" -- characters who cared too much about buying things.

In his novel of the same name, Lewis sneered of his bourgeois antihero, "He had enormous and poetic admiration, though very little understanding, of all mechanical devices. They were his symbols of truth and beauty." Lewis wrote, through the voice of his radical character Doane, that consumerism has created "standardization of thought, and of course, the traditions of competition. The real villains of the piece are the clean, kind, industrious Family Men who use every known brand of trickery and cruelty to insure the prosperity of their cubs. The worst thing about these fellows it that they're so good and, in their work at least, so intelligent."

Lewis, of course, was a socialist. So were anti-consumerism compatriots like H.G. Wells, H.L. Mencken and Herbert Croly. And their brand of leftism was destined to infuse the entire American left over the course of the 20th century. As Fred Siegel writes in his new book, "The Revolt Against The Masses," this general feeling pervaded the left during the 1950s, even as more Americans were attending symphony concerts than ballgames, with 50,000 Americans per year buying paperback version of classics. That's because if the left were to recognize the great power of consumerism in bettering lives and enriching culture, the left would have to become the right.

Of course, consumerism is not an unalloyed virtue. Consumerism can be utilized for hedonism. But it can also be utilized to make lives better, offering more opportunity for spiritual development. It's precisely this latter combination that the left fears, because if consumerism and virtue are allied, there is no place left for the Marxist critique of capitalism -- namely that capitalism makes people less compassionate, more selfish, and ethically meager. And so consumerism must be severed from virtue (very few leftists critique Americans' propensity for spending cash on Lady Gaga concerts) so that it can be castigated as sin more broadly.

In a world in which consumerism is the greatest of all sins, America is the greatest of all sinners, which, of course, is the point of the anti-consumerist critique from the left: to target America. Global warming represents the latest apocalyptic consequence threatened by the leftist gods for the great iniquity of buying things, developing products, and competing in the global marketplace. And America must be called to heel by the great preachers in Washington, D.C., and Hollywood.

Piers Morgan Is the American Left

February 26, 2014

This week, CNN's Piers Morgan announced that "Piers Morgan Live" would be coming to an ignominious end sometime in March. His replacement has not yet been chosen. But his television demise came not a moment too soon for millions of Americans who had tired of his sneering nastiness.

The New York Times chose not to see it that way. Instead, the Times insisted, Morgan's problem sprang from his British accent and heritage: "Old hands in the television news business suggest that there are two things a presenter cannot have: an accent or a beard ... Mr. Morgan is clean shaven and handsome enough, but there are tells in his speech -- the way he says the president's name for one thing (Ob-AA-ma) -- that suggest that he is not from around here." Morgan himself attributed his downfall to his foreignness: "Look, I am a British guy debating American cultural issues, including guns, which has been very polarizing, and there is no doubt that there are many in the audience who are tired of me banging on about it."

No doubt the notion of a British entertainer coming to America, clearing millions of dollars, and then lecturing Americans on their fundamental rights galled many. But what truly galled so many Americans was Morgan's underlying perspective -- a perspective shared by the Times, as well as most of the left. Morgan, unfortunately, believes that Americans are typically racist, sexist, homophobic bigots clinging to guns without regard to the safety of children. We, in his world of unearned moral superiority, are the bad guys.

Which is why Morgan had nothing to say when I appeared on his program in the aftermath of the Sandy Hook Elementary massacre, handed him a copy of the Constitution to remind him of the Second Amendment, and then told him that he was a "bully ... demoniz(ing) people who differ from you politically by standing on the graves of the children of Sandy Hook." His only response: "How dare you."

It's why Morgan had nothing to say when I suggested a few months later that his gushing response to gay basketball player Jason Collins' coming out sprang from his disdain for the American people: "Why do you hate America so much that you think it's such a homophobic country, that when Jason Collins comes out it is the biggest deal in the history of humanity, and President Obama has to personally congratulate him?" Again, Morgan had no answer.

As the left has no answer. The left's perspective on the role of government is inextricably linked to its view that Americans, free of government strictures, are brutally discriminatory, selfishly violent. Without the guiding hand of our betters, we would all be Bull Connors (a government employee), hoses at the ready. Without the sage wisdom of our leftist superiors, we would all be shooting each other at shopping malls.

The countervailing perspective -- that America is a pretty damn great place filled with pretty damn great people -- has little currency for the left. But when their hate-Americans perspective is repeatedly exposed, Americans begin to find it tiresome. That's what happened with Morgan. That's what will happen to the American left if the American right somehow finds the stomach to call out the left's snobby scorn for everyday Americans.

The Faculty Lounge Administration

March 5, 2014

On Sunday, Secretary of State John Kerry appeared on CBS's "Face the Nation" to respond to Russia's invasion of the Crimea region of Ukraine. "You just don't in the 21st century behave in 19th-century fashion by invading another country on completely trumped up pretext," Kerry stated. He added, "It's an incredible act of aggression. It is really a stunning, willful choice by President (Vladimir) Putin to invade another country."

So, what would the United States do about Russian aggression? America would consider dropping its scheduled attendance at the G8 meeting in Sochi, Kerry said: "He is not going to have a Sochi G8, he may not even remain in the G8 if this continues." And on Monday, the Obama administration got truly tough: It announced that it would not send a presidential delegation to the Paralympic Winter Games in Sochi.

Which, of course, had Putin quaking in his boots. Because if there's one thing a Russian autocrat fears, it's faculty lounge-style sneering about his unsophistication followed by symbolic withdrawals from meaningless events.

But this sums up the Obama administration in its entirety: When it comes to dealing with America's enemies, the Obama White House simply assumes that there is no true conflict. After all, who could disagree with an America that has spent five years on bended knee to the rest of the world, that has minimized its influence in the world, and that is planning to slash its military by 30 percent over the next several years? Who could oppose an administration so dedicated to harmony that it is willing to undercut its own allies for the sake of a humbler America on the global stage?

This complete incapacity to understand America's geopolitical enemies dominated the 2012 election cycle. With the help of the media, the Obama campaign scoffed its way to victory by tut-tutting Mitt Romney's designation of Russia as America's chief geopolitical challenge. That acidic jeering, which cloaks a pathetic naivete, underscored America's unwillingness to place armed troops in Benghazi.

And that same desperate and ironical urbanity reared its ugly head last week when National Security Adviser Susan Rice blithely informed David Gregory, "It's nobody's interest to see violence return and the situation escalate." When Gregory asked whether Putin sees the world "in a Cold War context," Rice ignored the question entirely: "He may, but if he does, that's a pretty dated perspective."

But that's the point: If Obama and his staff disagree with a perspective, that doesn't mean it isn't real. Wishful thinking won't make the Palestinians an Israeli peace partner, no matter how much President Barack Obama pressures Israel to make concessions; caustically mocking Putin's worldview won't make it any less real or mitigate the Russian threat.

In the ivory tower inhabited by the great intellects of the Obama administration, however, no problem is too big to be thought or talked or surrendered away. If Russia won't change its perspective, we will simply cut our military more to convince them we mean well; if the Palestinians or Iranians don't change their perspectives, we will force Israel to negotiate with them in order to prove our goodwill.

Meanwhile, our enemies laugh. And they should. The global battlefield is no place for the Kennedy School political science grad students who inhabit our White House and believe that a well-aimed, snooty barb is a substitute for a muscular foreign policy presence.

The Entertainment President

March 12, 2014

For years, conservatives have puzzled over President Barack Obama's continued personal popularity in the face of his dramatically uninspiring performance as commander in chief. Obama seems to inspire a bizarre personal loyalty among his advocates, particularly among young people who should by all rights be concerned with their fading futures and collapsing prospects. Why do his numbers remain so stubbornly mediocre?

The answer came Tuesday in the form of a ridiculous video cut by Obama with the help of "The Hangover" star Zach Galifianakis and the online outlet Funny or Die. Funny or Die is in the viral video business; it often features celebrities in bizarre skits designed to draw clicks. But Funny or Die also has a political agenda: In September, the Los Angeles Times reported that Funny or Die honcho Mike Farah had become an integral part of "the campaign to ensure the success of President Obama's healthcare law." Obama enlisted Farah in July 2013 during a meeting with Hollywood bigwigs in which Obama recruited his arts team to rally to the Obamacare cause.

The video, the latest in an ongoing series of episodes of a faux talk show titled "Between Two Ferns," has Galifianakis interviewing Obama about Obamacare. The portly actor, best known for playing a moron in movies, asks Obama questions about whether he will miss winning at basketball when he is no longer president. Obama, on script, answers by getting testy with Galifianakis before pushing Obamacare with his usual lack of verve: "Healthcare.gov works great now. And millions of Americans have already gotten health care plans. And what we want is for people to know that you can get affordable health care."

That wasn't Obama's only major media appearance this week. Obama also introduced the Fox reboot of the miniseries "Cosmos," explaining to Americans that hope and change could still be attained through science: "America has always been a nation of fearless explorers who dream big and reach farther than others might imagine." Which sounds better than "America has always been a nation of close-minded bigots requiring the intervention of government to force them into tolerance and diversity."

Obama's pop-cultural focus may seem demeaning to the office of the presidency. It may be mockable. But it is also tremendously effective. In the first 24 hours alone, the "Between Two Ferns" segment received almost 8 million views; approximately 20,000 people visited Healthcare.gov directly from the watching the segment. That's not bad for a pure propaganda effort.

Conservatives must understand that culture is the lifeblood of politics. Most Republicans have no idea what Funny or Die is, let alone why people watch it. BuzzFeed is a dirty word to most conservatives, even though their sons and daughters read it regularly for its cat lists -- and some of them stay for the leftist politics. Obama gets culture, or at least does a serviceable job of pretending he does. His shock troops in the entertainment industry are willing to do the rest on behalf of the Obama agenda.

Why No One Minds His Own Business Anymore

March 19, 2014

When I was a kid -- which wasn't that long ago, given that I just turned 30 in January -- I recall hearing a popular phrase on the playground: "Mind your own business." MYOB reared its head whenever somebody threatened to rat out a fellow student for anything from harmless roughhousing to juvenile delinquency. The phrase is sometimes attributed to the First Epistle to the Thessalonians, a rough translation of which states: " ... make it your ambition to lead a quiet life: You should mind your own business and work with your hands, just as we told you, so that your daily life may win the respect of outsiders and so that you will not be dependent on anybody."

Unfortunately, the phrase "mind your own business" has lost all meaning. After all, you don't get to mind your own business in America today. If you're a religious business owner, the government can force you to serve a same-sex wedding and cover your employees' abortion-inclusive health care plan. If you're a landowner, the government can simply seize your property and hand it over to another private party in order to increase tax revenue. If you're an entrepreneur, the thicket of government intervention weighing you down, from minimum wage to tax regulation, stifles innovation and stymies creativity.

Today, Americans are only told to mind our own business when we're not, in fact, engaging in business. Concerned about the societal fallout from sexual promiscuity? Mind your own business. Worried about the rise of single motherhood? Mind your own business. Upset about an epidemic of young people seemingly willing to trade the responsibilities of adulthood for an infantilized freedom? Mind your own business.

Societal problems are now personal; personal problems are now societal.

That shift in the American mindset reflects a deeper shift in the nature of our relationship with government and each other. This week, Michelle Obama released a video explaining to us that we needed to sign up for Obamacare now -- for the sake of our mothers. "We nag you because we love you," the first lady said.

But, of course, she doesn't love us. She doesn't even know us. Nonetheless, too many Americans have been convinced that individuals exercising personal choice are a societal problem; government, our Great Mother, can care for us personally. If we believe, as Hillary Clinton does, that it takes a village, then those who insist on personal privacy and freedom are obstacles to happiness and accomplishment. Only the collective is good. Any manifestation of individuality that poses a threat to that collective is by necessity evil.

We no longer live in a nation in which we can mind our own business. My business is your business, and vice versa -- unless, that is, we are engaged in activity that tears down family, church and community. If I'm a business owner rejecting service to a same-sex wedding, I have no right to invoke "mind your own business." Conversely, if I'm a member of a same-sex couple, I can invoke "mind your own business" all day long -- even if I'm making my business your business by engaging your services.

The obliteration of the distinction between the personal and the collective marks the end of American rights. But if you're worried about it, you should probably mind your own business.

Time for Congress to Telecommute

March 26, 2014

Few Americans have ever met their congresspeople. They don't see them at the grocery store; they don't meet them at the bowling alley. They're more likely to see their representatives in photographs from the Daily Grill in Washington, D.C., than at a local town hall. Constituents' closest contact with those they elect comes on Election Day, when they punch a chad next to a name.

This is precisely the opposite of how government was supposed to work.

In Federalist No. 46, James Madison posited that members of Congress would "generally be favorable to the States" from which they sprang, rather than toward the federal government. The federal government had to be part-time, given the distances between the states and the time required to travel. Politicians generally ended up in Washington, D.C., for just a few years in the early days of the Republic. That part-time government led to smaller government. Representatives showed up to vote on issues of major import to their constituents; then they went home to live among those who voted for them.

With the dramatic increase in ease of transportation and the incredible decrease in the amount of time required to travel between far-flung areas of the United States, representatives began spending more and more time in Washington and less and less time in their home districts. The first session of Congress, which lasted from March 4, 1789, to March 3, 1791, ran a grand total of 519 days. During the 109th Congress, lasting from Jan. 4, 2005, to Dec. 8, 2006, Congress was in session for a whopping 692 days.

And congresspeople spent more of that time in D.C. Many congresspeople spend their weeks in Washington and fly home on weekends, if that often. Approximately 8 in 10 congresspeople spend more than 40 weekends per year in their districts, according to the Congressional Management Foundation and the Society for Human Resource Management.

This has a predictable impact: Congresspeople do not fear their constituents. They simply don't see them often enough to fear them. That's why Democrats crammed through Obamacare in the dead of night over the Christmas holiday -- they hoped to escape the wrath of their constituents. Members of Congress have more in common with the people they hobnob in Washington, D.C., than they do with the people they're supposed to represent.

But now there's an easy solution: telecommuting. Why should congresspeople have to visit D.C.? Thanks to Skype, meetings are possible across the country. Thanks to email, communications are simple. And we've had the technology to vote from afar for decades. Why should we have backroom deals made over cigars thousands of miles distant from those who are affected by those deals? Instead, let's put congresspeople among those who must choose them -- and let's let them live with the consequences of their decision-making.

If Washington is the problem, then telecommuting could be the solution. It's time to make our representatives answerable to their communities rather than their dinner buddies. And the way to do that is to keep them close, rather than allowing them to roam free with our tax dollars far from home.

Why Hillary Clinton Will Win in 2016

April 2, 2014

On Tuesday, House Budget Committee Chairman Paul Ryan, R-Wis., presented his 2015 budget proposal. The Senate Democrats did not provide any such proposal; President Barack Obama's proposal posited an unending federal deficit and massive tax increases. Ryan's proposal, by contrast, lowered the rate of increase of spending moderately (by $5.1 trillion over the next decade), struck Obamacare from the rolls, and suggested revamps to Social Security and Medicare.

This was possibly the dumbest thing Ryan could have done.

Senate Majority Leader Harry Reid, D-Nev., immediately jumped on the budget proposal, suggesting that Ryan's budget came from "Kochtopia," and that it had been produced in reality by the nefarious Koch brothers. The former Clinton administration secretary of labor called the budget "cruel and unusual punishment." Ryan, Democrats claimed, was mean, nasty, heartless, brutal.

The same day Ryan laid out his blueprint for spending, Obama and his minions claimed victory for Obamacare, trumpeting their fudged sign-up numbers for the Affordable Care Act. "7.1 million Americans have now signed up for private insurance plans through these market places! 7.1! Yep!" Obama blustered. Never mind the fact that Obama had canceled some 5 million health care plans and then threatened people with fines for failing to repurchase under Obamacare; never mind the fact that the administration would not release numbers on how many Americans had paid for Obamacare; never mind that well under 1 million Americans who previously lacked health insurance took advantage of the Obamacare exchanges to get into the market. Obama had wanted his 7 million; now he had his 7 million.

Republicans reacted with predictable confusion and outrage. They suggested -- rightly -- that Obama had "cooked the books." They complained that sign-up numbers did not justify the entire overthrow of the health insurance system. And Obama, the man who canceled plans, doctors and drugs for millions of Americans, responded thusly: "Why are folks working so hard for people not to have health insurance?"

This is why Republicans will lose in 2016.

Democrats understand the art of narrative. Republicans do not. Republicans would rather have Ryan wave around a 100-page budget backed by all the stats. Democrats would rather point at Ryan and say he hates children. Americans don't have time to read 100-page budgets. Case closed.

Republicans would rather complain about each and every aspect of Obamacare. They enjoy debunking Obama's falsified statistics and singling out his corruption of data. Democrats would prefer to point at those Republicans and suggest that they don't care enough about poor, sick children. Americans don't have time to wade through media falsehoods or read beyond the headlines. Case closed.

In 2016, the Democratic Party will nominate Hillary Clinton. Her narrative has already been written by the media: starry-eyed young Republican turned disenchanted leftist seeking honesty and accountability in government; wronged woman married to a charming rogue, victimized by a viciously sexist right-wing conspiracy; first lady, senator, jet-setting secretary of state; elderly grandmother called once more to public service by her ailing country. You can all but hear the music swell and the slow clap begin as she steps to the microphone.

What, precisely, is the Republican narrative? Is it Ryan's CPA-style approach to government management? Is it Chris Christie's government-as-huggable-friend Hurricane Sandy routine? Is it Jeb Bush's riches-to-riches story?

Republicans continue to lose because Republicans get distracted from story by information. Democrats continue to win because they never let information get in the way of a good story. Until

Republicans figure that simple truth out, no amount of truth will put a Republican back in the Oval Office.

The Rise of American Totalitarianism

April 9, 2014

Last Thursday, Mozilla, the company that's home to the web browser Firefox, forced the resignation of CEO Brendan Eich. What, precisely, had Eich done wrong? Back in 2008, Eich had donated $1,000 to the Proposition 8 effort backing traditional marriage in California. Dating website OKCupid posted a ban on Firefox traffic, issuing a message to Firefox users instead: "Those who seek to deny love and instead enforce misery, shame, and frustration are our enemies, and we wish them nothing but failure." That ban reportedly prompted the action at Mozilla.

Of course, it was the people pushing for Eich's ouster who were enforcing "misery, shame, and frustration." Eich had never brought his politics into the workplace. Mozilla had no history of treating homosexuals differently, and no single instance of Eich doing so could be documented. Nonetheless, he had violated the dictates of the Thought Police. And thus he was ousted.

It's a disturbing story, to be sure. But it's also just the tip of the iceberg: Unfortunately, the same folks administering the private Thought Police would love to extend their control into the realm of government. These are not libertarians arguing for the right to hire and fire as you see fit in the private market. These are power brokers seeking to use whatever means necessary to quash opposition.

That's why gay couples have sued photographers, bakeries and florist shops, attempting to shut them down if they refuse to cater to same-sex weddings. That's why the Obama administration has attempted to fine businesses that do not wish to pay for health coverage they deem sinful. The underlying idea: If the left dislikes what you do, the left can compel you not to do it. As Kevin

Williamson of National Review writes, American society is quickly morphing into a system governed by T.H. White's totalitarian principle: "Everything not forbidden is compulsory."

Freedom is secondary to the yays and nays of the governing few in this vision. Freedom is merely that which the government allows -- and the government should only allow you to do the bidding of the left. If you, recognizing that sometimes people will take action with which you disagree, believe that government should stay out of people's business, you must therefore be an advocate for discrimination and brutality. To allow Eich to work is to discriminate against gays. To allow religious businesses to reject contraceptive mandates is to push women into back alley abortions. Forget the notion of disagreeing with your opinion, but defending your right to say it -- in the view of the leftist totalitarians, such a notion is inherently unworkable.

When fascism comes, it will come not with jackboots but with promises of a better world. The jackboots come later, when we've all been shamed into silence -- when we've been taught that to allow that with which we disagree is to agree with it, and when we've accepted that the best method of preventing such disagreement is government power. We're on the verge. All it will take is the silence of good people -- people on all sides of the political aisle -- who fall prey to the ultimate temptation in a republic: the temptation to force their values on others utilizing the machinery of government. We're already more than halfway there.

Why Conservatives Win Elections and Lose the War

April 16, 2014

On April 1, 2014, President Barack Obama triumphantly announced that 7.1 million Americans had selected a health insurance plan through Obamacare. In doing so, he nastily labeled his political opposition uncaring and unfeeling. "Why are folks working so hard for people not to have health insurance?" Obama asked. "Why are they so mad about the idea of people having health insurance?"

That night, Comedy Central's Stephen Colbert sat behind his desk at "The Colbert Report," playing his version of a conservative: vicious, mean and cruel. "I wish I could come to you with some good news, but the worst imaginable thing has happened: Millions of Americans are going to get health care."

This is why conservatives lose. They lose because while they proclaim that Obama's signature legislation fails on the merits, raising costs and lowering access to vital services, the left surges forth with a different message: Conservatives are rotten to the core.

This message doesn't just emanate from politicians in Washington. Entertainers like Colbert parrot back White House talking points in the guise of mockery. For many young people who get their news from Colbert, the only conservatism they see comes out of the mouth of a hard-core leftist playing a conservative who doesn't exist. There is no conservative sitting up nights wondering how to deprive Americans of health insurance. But many young people don't know that. They simply assume that the person Colbert is parodying must exist -- otherwise, his satire isn't satire at all, but a political smear job, an ugly and stereotypical blackfacing of conservatives.

For Colbert to be funny, one of two alternatives must be true: Either his repulsive character must be based on a core reality -- conservatives are evil -- or his audience must believe in that core unreality. With the help of Obama and an entertainment industry dedicated full time to the defacing of conservatives' character, the latter has certainly become the case. Too many Americans now perceive conservatives as morally deficient. All it has cost is hundreds of millions of dollars and several decades of consistent attacks springing from Hollywood and the political world.

That's why so many Americans now seem comfortable giving the government power to violate freedom of conscience for conservatives: Evil people don't deserve freedom and therefore, can be deprived of it. People who consider themselves civil libertarians suddenly find their inner totalitarian when it comes to Christian-owned bakeries. That can only happen when those people become convinced that Christian-owned bakeries are fronts of hatred and darkness. And that can only happen when they are falsely maligned as such, over and over again.

Conservatives can win short-term political fights and lose the war for hearts and minds. And that's precisely what has happened, thanks to the lack of moral clarity on the right. It's not enough to be good on policy. Americans must think of you as good. By neglecting that deeper battle, conservatives sow the seeds of their own destruction -- and the destruction of American freedoms, as well.

Why Bundy Ranch Is Just the Beginning

April 23, 2014

This week, Nevada rancher Cliven Bundy, whose standoff with the federal government over taxes and land-use rights has captivated the nation, announced, "I don't believe I owe one penny to the United States government. I don't have a contract with the United States government." His legal case is problematic; the Bureau of Land Management certainly has jurisdiction over the federal lands on which his cattle graze. But his moral case is significantly stronger: paying taxes to a government that uses those tax dollars to restrict your activities on land your family has worked since the 19th century -- over a turtle, no less -- is sickening stuff. A government squeeze is a government squeeze.

Bundy's position on the federal government itself is unjustifiable. He stated in a recent interview: "I believe this is a sovereign state of Nevada. I abide by all of Nevada state laws. But I don't recognize the United States government as even existing." Obviously, the federal government does exist, and if the state of Nevada exists, it only does so because it was formed with the permission of the feds under the Constitution.

In fact, the Constitution of the of Nevada explicitly denies Bundy's interpretation of the law: "no power exists in the people of this or any other State of the Federal Union to dissolve their connection therewith or perform any act tending to impair, subvert, or resist the Supreme Authority of the government of the United States."

So Bundy's wrong on the legal and constitutional merits of his anti-federal case. But he does represent a growing problem in the

United States: the problem of a seemly omnipotent federal government running roughshod over local rights.

As America's federal government grows, and as its unelected bureaucracy extends its reach over nearly every aspect of American life, more and more Americans will justifiably believe that their government no longer represents them. They will show up to Bundy Ranch-type standoffs believing that the government is not their government.

When American colonists plotted revolt against the British government, they did so on the pretext that they were being taxed without representation. James Otis, the firebrand leader of the early anti-British movement, famously wrote: "no parts of His Majesty's dominions can be taxed without their consent ... every part has a right to be represented in the supreme or some subordinate legislature." But the simple reality was that the colonists likely would not have accepted representation in the Parliament as a justification for taxation; Congress stated in 1765 that the colonies "are not, and from their local Circumstances, cannot be, represented in the House of Commons of Great Britain." The impracticality of directing representatives thousands of miles away on complex legislation in a time without instant communication precluded the possibility of America becoming part of a British federation.

We have instant communication today, but a no more responsive government. Resistance to the Stamp Act killed its implementation in the United States but paved the way for war; resistance to the BLM's enforcement of federal law in the Bundy Ranch situation ended in federal withdrawal, but is merely the first step in a far-larger conflict. Like Bundy or not, his situation will not be the last of its kind, so long as the federal government insists on its ever-growing authority, and so long as states and localities refuse to stand up for their citizens.

Of Donald Sterling's Racism and the Rise of Thoughtcrime

April 30, 2014

In November 2009, Los Angeles Clippers owner Donald Sterling settled a lawsuit in which the Department of Justice alleged that Sterling had discriminated against Hispanics, blacks and families without children in his rental properties. The lawsuit contained testimony that Sterling had suggested Hispanics were poor tenants because they "smoke, drink, and just hang around the building," and that "black tenants smell and attract vermin." The settlement cost him and his insurers $2.73 million.

The NBA and the national media said virtually nothing. That same year, the NAACP gave him a Lifetime Achievement Award.

In 2005, Sterling signed a check for more than $5 million to settle a lawsuit alleging that he had attempted to prevent non-Koreans from renting in his facilities in Koreatown.

The NBA and the national media said virtually nothing.

This week, Sterling's 31-year-old girlfriend, V. Stiviano, released a tape of the 80-year-old racist being an 80-year-old racist. Sterling apparently told Stiviano he didn't want her posting pictures of black men on her Instagram account and didn't want her bringing black men to Clippers games.

The entire media establishment suddenly went insane. Colin Cowherd of ESPN idiotically called for the league to void all of Sterling's contracts with his players and agents -- a violation of basic contract law. Magic Johnson declared that the NBA should force Sterling to sell his team -- a violation of basic contract law. President Barack Obama, determined never to let an opportunity pass to label America racist, took to the microphones to declare Sterling's racism a symptom of America's "legacy of race and slavery and segregation."

This is, at the very least, hypocrisy. Last year, Sterling signed coach Doc Rivers, who is black, to a contract worth $7 million per year. Chris Paul, who is black, is slated to make nearly $19 million this season. Blake Griffin, who is black, is slated to make $16 million. DeAndre Jordan will make $11 million. The coach, these players and their agents surely knew about Sterling's legacy. So did Cowherd, Johnson and Obama. They all said nothing.

But the big problem here isn't hypocrisy. The big problem is that the market is turning on Sterling not over action, but over words. Sterling's a pig, and that's been no secret for decades. But what triggered America's response? Sterling's thoughts. American society now considers expression of thought to be significantly more important than action. Sterling got away with actual discrimination for years. But now he is caught on tape telling his gold-digging girlfriend he doesn't like blacks, and that's when the firestorm erupts?

This is the thought police at work. Feelings matter more than action. Words matter more than harming others. That sets a radically dangerous precedent for freedom of thought and speech, particularly for those whose thought and speech we hate. Freedom of speech and thought matters especially when it is speech and thought with which we disagree. The moment the majority decides to destroy people for engaging in thought it dislikes, thoughtcrime becomes a reality.

Sterling's career should have been ended by public outrage based on his established patterns of discrimination years ago. To end it based not on such disreputable action but on private musings caught on tape demonstrates America's newfound disregard for the rights of those whose thought we find despicable.

The Left's Phantom Wars

May 7, 2014

On Monday, as Vladimir Putin waged an actual war in Ukraine, Bashar Assad waged an actual war in Syria, and a Nigerian terror group waged an actual war on underage girls, President Barack Obama announced his own war on "climate disruption." White House adviser John Podesta explained on Monday afternoon that Obama would be acting alone to push new regulations under the Clean Air Act to combat climate change. That announcement came in the wake of an 840-page report from the federal government suggesting that the globe is on the verge of a meltdown: "Climate change, once considered an issue for a distant future, has moved firmly into the present."

That's hardly the only war in which the left is currently engaged. The left is fighting a war on racism -- a war in which the declared enemy is America, given that America is apparently plagued by "hidden bias." That's the newest term trotted out by MTV, which has launched its "look different" initiative, in coordination with shakedown groups like the Council on American-Islamic Relations, the NAACP, the National Council of La Raza and the Gay and Lesbian Alliance Against Defamation. The goal: to convince young people that while they aren't overtly racist, they hold secret racist beliefs that can only be cleansed by embracing the leftist agenda. The war must go on, after all, even if the enemy has been largely vanquished.

There's the left's phantom war on sexism, too, in which Democrats claim women are victimized by a male patriarchy. Women, leftists say, earn significantly less than men, despite studies showing that in most major cities, young women without children and with the same jobs as men earn significantly more. Women, leftists say, are victimized by a conservative religious minority that doesn't want to pay for their birth control. Again, the enemies of women remain faceless -- but we are told they lurk behind every corner. The winning strategy, once again: embrace leftism.

The war on poverty continues apace, as well. The latest incarnation: the war on income inequality -- a war specifically geared toward endlessness. After all, sans Communist revolution, income inequality will always exist. And according to the left, it will always require rectification.

Today's leftism tilts at windmills rather than fighting real opponents. It ignores actual conflict in favor of broader, amorphous battles with shapeless opponents and no clear measures of victory. After all, how will we know if we defeat climate change? There is no way to tell whether we did it, or whether the global temperature was set to drop anyway. How will we know if we defeat sexism? Clearly, the left believes that women in the workplace in record numbers and achievement of equal pay for equal work doesn't do the trick. How will we know if we defeat racism? The left has already moved the goalposts from equal opportunity to equal result, an unachievable pipe dream in the absence of totalitarian control.

And so the wars go on -- endless, expensive, draining. They sap America of our vitality, our strength and most importantly, our core values. But at least, the left tells us, we have gained heaven: an everlasting unearned moral superiority over our fellow nonracist, nonsexist, non-poverty-hating Americans.

How the West Won the Great Hashtag War of 2014

May 14, 2014

This week, a picture emerged of Islamist terror group Boko Haram's leader Abubakar Shekau holding a machine gun in one hand and a piece of paper in the other. On that paper was scrawled: "#WeSurrender."

Thus came to an end the Great Hashtag War of 2014.

Led by the bravery of First Lady Michelle Obama, former Secretary of State Hillary Clinton and the Democratic women of the United States Senate, the West tweeted Boko Haram into submission. When Obama released the H-bomb of Twitter -- a sad duck-faced picture of herself in an empty room holding a sign reading #BringBackOurGirls -- total victory was achieved: 276 Nigerian girls who had been kidnapped and converted to Islam avoided sale into sex slavery, and the 150 Nigerians murdered by Boko Haram just last week suddenly sprang back to life.

No wonder the Obama State Department has saluted the Power of Hashtag. If only we'd discovered it earlier, we could have saved tens of millions of lives. If the French had only utilized the #MaginotLine instead of the Maginot Line, the Nazi jackboots never would have clip-clopped along the Champs-Elysees.

Now, there were those who argued that hashtagging by world leaders was not merely useless but counterproductive. They argued that hashtag foreign policy projected a sense of Western impotence combined with an overweening sense of unearned moral superiority that comes from sounding off in public. They said that when a former secretary of state neglected to label Boko Haram a terrorist group during her tenure, but tweeted out #BringBackOurGirls, that demonstrated the pathetic weakness of the Obama administration. They opined that it was one thing for powerless people in Nigeria to push a hashtag campaign in an attempt to prompt action from authorities, but quite another for the authorities themselves to ignore action in favor of hashtagging.

But that missed the point: Awareness was raised. People in authority demonstrated their outrage at kidnapping and sex slavery. Not enough to actually do anything useful, of course, but enough to publicly express that outrage. And now that we all know their feelings on the subject, we can go home happy.

As it turns out, the proper solution to a plea for help is to amplify that plea rather than to help. By doing so, awareness is raised, consciousness is increased, chakras are released. The Power of Hashtag reigns supreme.

The best news of all: You were there. You were part of the Hastag War. We will be thankful for that years from now, when we're sitting by the fireplace with our grandchildren on our knees, and they ask us what we did in the great Hashtag Wars, we won't have to cough, shift them to the other knee, and say, "Well, I tweeted about Solange and Jay-Z."

Will Detroit Be Healed by Searching for 'Subtle Racism'?

May 21, 2014

Just off of the James C. Lodge Freeway in Detroit is Eight Mile Road. The stretch near the freeway is just east of the famed area that provided the basis for the Eminem film of the same name. To its north lie predominantly white suburbs -- over 77 percent of those who live in Oakland County are white -- with median family income in excess of $65,000. Married couples comprise approximately half of households, with fewer than 15 percent of households led by a single female. Since 1990, the population of Oakland County has jumped from 1.083 million to 1.202 million.

South of Eight Mile Road lies the city of Detroit, with a nearly 83 percent black population and a median household income of under $27,000. Almost 74 percent of households in Detroit are led by single parents, nearly all women. The population of the city has dropped from 1,027,000 in that same period to approximately 713,000.

Eight Mile Road itself paints a bleak picture. In the middle of a weekday, the streets are sparsely populated; old, solid-structure brick houses with rotten roofs dot the side streets; beaten-up Pontiacs from the early 1990s sitting forlornly in driveways. Hair salons, liquors stores and rim stores are open for business, but they're located between defunct hair stores, liquor stores and rim stores.

What happened in Detroit? Horrific governance destroyed the industrial infrastructure that created the growing mixed-population base of the city; it centralized employment in the government while devastating the business and tax base. Businesses fled to the suburbs, as did whites. The bulk of the black population, trapped in a cycle of poverty and government dependence, sold a bill of goods by Detroit's politicians, stayed behind. Those politicians covered their mismanagement with racially charged rhetoric, from former Mayor Coleman Young to jailed former Mayor Kwame Kilpatrick. When Detroit went bankrupt in 2013, it was the final result of decades of failed policy decisions based on central planning.

When financial analysts look at Eight Mile Road, they see the tragedy of a once-proud city separated. On one side of the road, Detroit; on the other side, Detroit without the mismanagement. To fix the situation would require good governance -- slashing regulations, lowering taxes, attracting business, creating jobs.

Instead, politicians offer more of the same. This week, Attorney General Eric Holder stated that America's racial disparities are a result of continued racism and suggested that neutral laws had reinforced an enduring "subtle racism" throughout the country. Holder cited particular disciplinary practices in schools and sentencing guidelines as repositories of racism.

None of this will heal Detroit or places like it. Economic health requires a dedicated workforce, a free entrepreneurial climate, protection against crime. Those, in turn, require solid two-parent families, a competitive educational environment and a dedication to equal application of the law rather than equal results under it.

Eight Mile Road is a blot on a once-beautiful city. It will remain a dividing line so long as America's politicians continue to use it as one.

Does Obama Care About the Troops?

May 28, 2014

On the day before Memorial Day, President Barack Obama secretly flew into Afghanistan for a surprise visit to the troops. "We're going to stay strong by taking care of our wounded warriors and our veterans. Because helping our wounded warriors and veterans heal isn't just a promise, it's a sacred obligation ... I'm here to say that I'm proud of you," he stated.

But he wasn't in Afghanistan out of mere pride for the troops. As usual, Obama was using the troops for political purposes. Whether he's taking credit for their successful missions ("Today, at my direction, the United States launched a targeted operation against that compound in Abbottabad, Pakistan") or portraying them as victims of brutal, hawkish foreign policy (we "have seen over 3,000 lives of the bravest young Americans wasted" in Iraq), the troops are but implements in Obama's quest for political victory.

And so Obama headed for Afghanistan when news broke that hospitals with the Veterans Affairs had falsified waitlists, resulting in the deaths of dozens of veterans. Because he cares.

This follows a long pattern for Obama. In April 2009, Obama flew to Iraq for a surprise visit. The press dutifully recorded accounts of cheering throngs of troops eager to get a picture of the president with their cameras. They did not, however, report on allegations at the time that soldiers were pre-screened for placement at the Obama event, and that cameras were handed out to the troops.

In October 2009, Obama got up early -- earlier even than he usually does for his tee times -- to visit Dover Air Force Base, Delaware, and watch the coffins of fallen soldiers come home, amid accusations that the war in Afghanistan was spiraling out of control.

The New York Times reported, "The images and the sentiment of the president's five-hour trip to Delaware were intended by the White House to convey to the nation that Mr. Obama was not making his Afghanistan decision lightly or in haste." That sentence disappeared from the original report shortly after it hit the internet.

The following month, Obama visited Osan Air Base in South Korea, where he stood before troops and stated, "you guys make a pretty good photo op." He used that perspective to its full advantage one month later, when he announced his short-term, midlevel surge in Afghanistan at West Point (New York).

And, of course, when push came to shove during his re-election campaign, Obama showed up -- surprise! -- in Afghanistan, on the one-year anniversary of the killing of Osama bin Laden, where he stated, "The goal that I set -- to defeat al-Qaida and deny it a chance to rebuild -- is now within our reach."

Obama has slashed military funding at historic levels; he insisted that sequestration cuts come largely from the Defense Department. His Veterans Affairs is a shambles, yet he won't fire his top man, Eric Shinseki. Iraq is collapsing. Afghanistan will soon follow.

But he routinely claims that he loves the troops.

Do you believe him?

Barack Obama, Judge of Life or Death

June 4, 2014

On Sept. 30, 2011, two American Predator drones based out of a Saudi Arabian CIA facility swept into Yemen and fired Hellfire missiles at a car containing terrorist and American citizen Anwar al-Awlaki. He was killed. So, too, was terrorist buddy Samir Khan, an American born in Saudi Arabia. President Barack Obama promptly announced the kill: "The death of Awlaki is a major blow to al-Qaida's most active operational affiliate. He took the lead in planning and directing efforts to murder innocent Americans ... and he repeatedly called on individuals in the United States and around the globe to kill innocent men, women and children to advance a murderous agenda." Nowhere did Obama mention that either man was an American citizen.

Last Saturday, Obama announced that the United States had traded five Taliban terrorist leaders in exchange for American Sgt. Bowe Bergdahl. As the days passed, it became clear that Bergdahl was no American hero: he was, in fact, a deserter. He left a note at his base in Afghanistan on June 30, 2009, stating that he hated the military; he emailed his father stating that he hated America. Reports a year later from the U.K. Daily Mail stated that Bergdahl was teaching the Taliban bomb-making and had converted to Islam.

When asked about these problematic issues, Obama immediately signaled that Bergdahl's status as an American was an overriding factor in bartering terrorists for his release. "Whatever those circumstances may turn out to be, we still get an American soldier back if he's held in captivity. Period. Full stop," Obama lectured. Former Secretary of State Hillary Clinton also jumped into the act: "This young man, whatever the circumstances, was an American citizen -- is an American citizen -- was serving in our military. The idea that you really care for your own citizens and particularly those in uniform, I think is a very noble one."

The point here is not that Bergdahl should have been droned, or that al-Awlaki shouldn't have been. The point is that the president of the United States now has the apparent authority to determine whether or not someone deserves to live -- indeed, whether he deserves to be hit with a Hellfire missile or whether we should exchange high-level terrorists for him. And no one can stop the president in such decision-making. He is the judge, jury, and either executioner or savior. He is all-powerful.

This should be frightening to anyone with a modicum of common sense. American citizenship is now, apparently, a malleable commodity. Vice President Joe Biden believes that immigrants here illegally are citizens. Obama believes that some Americans who join Islamist groups are citizens, while others are not. Who is an American? Whomever the executive branch deems an American. Who isn't? It depends on whether Obama ate his Wheaties or not.

Either American citizenship counts for something, or it does not. Either joining America's enemies strips you of your rights, or it does not. But when the president of the United States can arbitrarily decide whether or not those rights have been stripped, all of our rights have been stripped.

Prosecute the President

June 11, 2014

President Barack Obama believes he is above the law.

That's because he is.

This week alone, Obama announced that he would unilaterally change student loan rules, allowing borrowers to avoid paying off more of their debt; he signaled that he would continue his nonenforcement of immigration law, even as thousands of children cross the border; he defended his nondisclosure of a terrorist swap to Congress.

And, he said, more such actions were in the offing. "I will keep doing whatever I can without Congress," Obama explained.

This is not just executive overreach. In many cases, Obama's exercise of authoritarian power is criminal. His executive branch is responsible for violations of the Arms Export Control Act in shipping weapons to Syria, the Espionage Act in Libya, and IRS law with regard to the targeting of conservative groups. His executive branch is guilty of involuntary manslaughter in Benghazi and in the Fast and Furious scandal, and bribery in its allocation of waivers in Obamacare and tax dollars in its stimulus spending. His administration is guilty of obstruction of justice and witness tampering.

And yet nothing is done.

Impeachment, which has been suggested as a solution by many, is a nonstarter. In the entire history of the republic, the House has impeached just 19 officials, and just eight were actually removed from office after Senate trial. Impeachment is a political solution to a criminal problem -- and politicians are far too fearful of blowback to use it as a tool in upholding law.

Thanks to presidential immunity and executive control of the Justice Department, there are no consequences to executive branch lawbreaking. And when it comes to presidential lawbreaking, the sitting president could literally strangle someone to death on national television and meet with no consequences. As Professor Akhil Reed Amar of Yale Law School has written, "a sitting President is constitutionally immune from ordinary criminal prosecution -- state or federal."

So what can we do? We can tell Congress to delegate its power to check the executive branch. The Racketeer Influenced and Corrupt Organizations Act creates a broad capacity for prosecution of criminal conspiracies; it also provides for civil lawsuits against such conspiracies, turning American citizens into, as the Supreme Court puts it, "'private attorneys general' on a serious national problem for which public prosecutorial resources are deemed inadequate." Minor changes to the law should allow citizens to sue federal officials within the executive branch under RICO, unmasking criminal enterprises within the Obama administration and future administrations.

The checks and balances of the Constitution have failed. The result has been, for a century, the nearly unchecked growth of the power of the executive branch. That growth has created an executive tyranny, unanswerable and inescapable under law. Our legislators have proved themselves too cowardly to fight back using the tools at their disposal. They are obviously happy delegating their power to the executive branch. Now it's time for them to delegate their power to the people.

How Fatherhood Made Me a Better Person

June 18, 2014

My baby daughter has ruined me.

I'm not typically known for being the most openly emotional person. On the incredibly rare occasions in which I find myself crying -- typically when the last track of "The Many Adventures of Winnie the Pooh" pipes through the car stereo (why would you leave the Hundred Acre Wood, Christopher Robin, you dolt?!) -- my wife revels in it. The first time it happened, she turned to me, grinning gleefully, and exclaimed, "You do have feelings!"

At least, that's how it was until Leeya was born.

Now I'm a wreck.

Last week, my 4-month-old began crying when we put her down to sleep at night. I put my hand on her chest and began rocking her back and forth. Her crying gradually reduced to cooing, and then finally she dozed off.

Maybe she wasn't crying anymore, but I was. I found myself tearing up because I couldn't help but think of a time, decades from now, when she's in pain, and I won't be there to help. I won't be there to rock her to sleep or to put her head on my shoulder or to tell her everything will be all right.

Every so often, we all gaze into the abyss. It's a depressing fact of life that eventually the clock expires, eventually the sand in the hourglass runs out. It's the leaving behind of everything that matters to us that hurts the most.

Which is why what we do now matters.

In his weekly internet address, President Barack Obama tackled Father's Day by repeating a line from his 2013 State of the Union address: "what makes you a man isn't the ability to have a child -- it's the courage to raise one." But, of course, it doesn't take courage to raise your child; it takes common decency. Only reprobates father children and then abandon them.

What really makes you man, I've realized, is not merely providing for and defending your wife, or even raising your child -- it's the action that lies in the realization that the future matters, even if you won't be here to see it. In an era in which immediate gratification and self-discovery are now given moral priority over delayed gratification and moral action, our children show us the barrenness of such a view. The words of Beyonce and Pepsi at the Super Bowl -- "Live for now!" -- ring false when you look at your crying child and understand that decades hence, your life won't have mattered a damn if you didn't live it for her.

Having children truly ends adolescence. We are all either parents or children: responsibility-takers or those who demand from others. Which is why it's such a human tragedy that Western civilization has now prized endless childhood as the ultimate ideal. When the president of the United States characterizes fatherhood as some sort of act of bravery, but the capacity to murder the unborn as a human right, society itself comes unmoored.

But we can anchor it again. Every time we rock our babies in the night, we bring order back to a disordered world. Every time we look down at our children and cry, we make the world one shade brighter. That's what children do to us -- and for us. That's what Leeya has done for me.

Welcome to the Executive Dictatorship

June 25, 2014

The Constitution is dead.

Long live the executive dictatorship.

There is almost nothing the president of the United States cannot do. This week, we found out President Barack Obama's IRS not only targeted conservative nonprofit applicants with impunity but then destroyed the emails that could have illuminated the process behind such targeting. Meanwhile, the attorney general -- the executive officer charged with fighting government criminality -- continues to stonewall an independent prosecutor, maintaining along with his boss that there is not a "smidgen of corruption" in the IRS.

On the southern border, Immigration and Customs Enforcement has been converted from a policing agency to a humanitarian-aid agency, as the Obama administration encourages thousands of unaccompanied minors to flood Texas and Arizona. Those immigrants here illegally are being shuttled around the southwest and released into the general population, and told by activists that they are just months away from amnesty.

Across the seas, Obama is unilaterally destroying America's anti-terror infrastructure. Iraq has become the preserve of the al-Qaida offshoot ISIS and the Iranian-connected Shiite government -- the specific outcome the United States originally wanted to avoid in the country. Afghanistan will soon devolve back into a Taliban-led cesspool for terror. And the Obama administration continues to fund a Palestinian government that includes terrorist groups Hamas and Islamic Jihad, and that has now kidnapped an American citizen, along with two other Israeli boys.

Nobody in the executive branch has been punished for Benghazi, Libya, Fast and Furious, serious national security leaks to major news outlets, violations of civil rights by the National Security Agency or any other major scandal. The Obama administration has seized authority to regulate health care, carbon emissions and labor relations in unforeseen ways.

And no one will stop the executive branch. Impeachment will not solve the problem of a 3 million-strong regulatory branch in which accountability is a fantasy. The legislature has no interest in stopping the growth of the executive, given that legislators seek re-election by avoiding responsibility, and granting more power to the executive avoids such responsibility. And the judiciary seems unwilling to hem in the executive branch at all, given its decisions on the Environmental Protection Agency and Obamacare.

So what's left? An elected tyranny in which the whims of the president and all of his men decide the fate of millions. The founders would have fought such a government with every fiber of their being -- and, in fact, they did fight such a government. The question now is whether state governments, elected officials and the people themselves will be willing to take the measures necessary to do the same.

The Jew-Hating Obama Administration

July 2, 2014

On Monday, three Jewish boys were found dead, murdered by the terrorist group Hamas: Eyal Yifrach, 19; Gilad Shaar, 16; and Naftali Frenkel, 16. Frenkel was an American citizen. The three were kidnapped while hitchhiking some three weeks ago. In the interim, President Barack Obama said nothing about them publicly. His wife issued no hashtags. His State Department maintained that $400 million in American taxpayer cash would continue to the Palestinian unity government, which includes Hamas.

Presumably Frenkel did not look enough like Barack Obama's imaginary son for him to give a damn. Or perhaps Frenkel hadn't deserted his duty in the American military, and therefore his parents didn't deserve a White House press conference. Maybe Michelle Obama was too busy worrying about children's fat thighs to spend a moment tweeting out a selfie to raise awareness.

Or maybe, just maybe, the Obama administration didn't care about Frenkel because he was a Jew.

Jewish blood is cheap to this administration. That seems to be true in every administration, given the American government's stated predilection for forcing Israel into concessions to an implacable and Jew-hating enemy. But it's particularly true for an administration that has now cut a deal with Iran that legitimizes its government, weakens sanctions, and forestalls Israeli action against its nuclear program. It's especially true for an administration that forced the Israeli government to apologize to the Turkish government for stopping a terrorist flotilla aimed at supplying Hamas. And it's undoubtedly true for an administration that has undercut Israeli security at every turn, deposing Hosni Mubarak in Egypt, fostering chaos in Syria and by extension destabilizing Jordan and Lebanon, and leaking Israeli national security information no less than four times.

Now the corpse of a 16-year-old Jewish American is found in Hebron.

The Obama administration's first response: to call on the Israeli government for restraint. State Department spokeswoman Jen Psaki said on June 2, "Based on what we know now, we intend to work with this government." Now, just a month later, that government has murdered an American kid. And now she says that the Obama administration hopes "that the Israelis and the Palestinians continue to work with one another on that, and we certainly would continue to urge that ... in spite of, obviously, the tragedy and the enormous pain on the ground."

To which the proper Israeli response should be: go perform anatomically impossible acts upon yourself.

The Obama administration had the opportunity to stand clearly against Jew-hating evil. Not only did it fail to do so but it funded that evil, encouraged that evil, militated against fighting that evil. But that's nothing new. Jew hatred is as old as the Jewish people. It's just found a new home in the White House.

Never Let a Self-Produced Horror Show Go to Waste

July 9, 2014

"You never want a serious crisis to go to waste," President Barack Obama's former chief of staff, Rahm Emanuel, once infamously stated. He never bothered to spell out the unspoken corollary to that appalling statement: And if there is no serious crisis available, manufacture one.

The American left has followed that pattern for generations. The left destroyed the nuclear family by incentivizing women to give birth out of wedlock. When out-of-wedlock births exploded, they used that as an excuse to elevate federal spending, elevate taxes and disestablish marriage between a man and a woman as a moral standard. The left crafted a health care crisis by instituting price and wage controls that led to employer-sponsored insurance, and then undercut that insurance with excessive regulation and easy lawsuits. They used elevating costs as an excuse to push Obamacare and elevate taxes.

Now, the left, under Obama, has crafted the mother of all crises: an influx of tens of thousands of unaccompanied minors crossing America's southern border. Some of these minors carry disease. Virtually all carry wounds, either physical or psychological, from their criminal coyote guides. That crisis is not Obama's Hurricane Katrina, as some have speculated. Katrina was an act of God, and its botched handling the act of men. This entire situation is an act of Obama. And he couldn't be happier as he watches frustrated Americans take to the streets in Murrieta, California, to protest his lawlessness.

Obama created this situation, and he certainly knows how to exploit it. Obama wants to campaign based on the suffering of these children. He wants to push for higher taxes based on their unequal economic status. He wants their eventual votes for the left. He wants the federal government to punish American citizens tired of watching their government abandon them.

It's all part of the agenda.

Obama and the media maintain the absurd fiction that Obama was thunderstruck by this crisis. Obama himself has assured the public that he wants all of the new arrivals sent home forthwith and that they were foolish to believe they could stay.

Foolish?

Four years ago, the Obama Justice Department sued the state of Arizona for daring to enforce federal immigration law, and sanctuary cities across the country remained unscathed. Two years ago, Obama declared that all immigrants here illegally between the ages of 16 and 30 who had not committed criminal felonies -- the so-called Dreamers -- would remain in the country. This week, the Ninth Circuit Court of Appeals ruled that Arizona would have to hand out driver's licenses to the Dreamers, and the city of Los Angeles announced it would no longer cooperate with Immigration and Customs Enforcement in holding requested illegals for 48 hours after their jail terms expired.

Those desperate to come to America would be fools not to jump at the chance. And their dangerous decisions to send their own children across thousands of miles of desert in the company of likely drug cartel associates underscores their certainty: They're willing to risk the lives of their children, knowing that so long as the children get to the border, Obama will legitimize them, and then, by extension, their entire families.

This, of course, is precisely what Obama wanted them to think. Now he has his crisis. And he'll exploit it for everything it's worth, no matter how much blood is spilled in the deserts of Mexico or the streets of Murrieta.

Bloodguilt Over Jews Leads to Blood Libels Against Jews

July 16, 2014

If there's one place on Earth that should understand the danger of Jew hatred, it is Frankfurt, Germany. In 1933, boycotts targeted Jews; by 1938, Germans were burning synagogues down. Between 1933 and 1945, the Jewish population of the city was decimated, dropping from 30,000 to 602. Few Jews, most of them Soviet expatriates, live in the city now.

So Frankfurt seems an odd place for a new blood libel against the Jews. Nonetheless, this week, 2,500 protesters, including Muslims and neo-Nazis -- allied once again -- showed up downtown to scream about Israel's defensive action against Hamas in the Gaza Strip. Police reportedly helped out the protesters, allowing them to utilize a loudspeaker and a vehicle to shout anti-Israel diatribes. "You Jews Are Beasts," read one sign.

Meanwhile, in Paris, Muslims attacked two Jewish synagogues, including one in which 150 Jews had gathered to mourn the deaths of three Jewish boys, who were murdered by Hamas operatives. Those Muslims, brandishing bats and chairs, attempted to break into the synagogue and ended up injuring several Jews. In recent years, thousands of Jews from France have emigrated to Israel, amid shocking reports of beatings, stabbings and an ax attack.

The Europeans, it seems, are becoming increasingly comfortable with old-fashioned Jew hatred in their midst, whether homegrown or imported.

There's a reason for that. In much of Europe, bloodguilt over the Holocaust still hangs over the heads of the population. According to a 2012 Anti-Defamation League survey of European countries, 45 percent of Austrians, 35 percent of French, 43 percent of Germans, 63 percent of Hungarians and 53 percent of Polish citizens felt that it was "probably true" that "Jews still talk too much about what happened to them in the Holocaust." Many of those who wish to move beyond the Holocaust, therefore, look for a rationale to relieve national guilt -- and what better way to relieve national guilt than to label the Jewish State an aggressor? After all, if the Jews have become the villains, then why spend too much time thinking about their victimization?

Of course, the labeling of Jews as bloodthirsty villains led to the Holocaust in the first place. Adolf Hitler saw the Jews as bloodsuckers driven by greed and dual loyalty. So did much of the rest of Europe. In the minds of those who murdered Jews en masse, Jews had it coming, because, in the words of Hitler: "The struggle for world domination will be fought entirely between us -- between Germans and Jews. All else is facade and illusion."

Those who today label Israel the font of all evil use Hitler's rationale to relieve guilt over Hitler. That's why the same protesters in Frankfurt threatening Jews carried posters comparing Israel to the Nazis: If Jews are the new Nazis, fighting the Jews becomes an obligation.

Every Passover, Jews recite a paragraph: "in every generation they rise against us to destroy us; and the Holy One, blessed be He, saves us from their hand!" The names change, but the rationale does not. And the God of Israel is always watching, even if those who attack the Jews have convinced themselves that He will turn a blind eye.

Why Vladimir Putin Is Kicking Barack Obama's Behind

July 23, 2014

On Monday, four days after Vladimir Putin's minions in Ukraine shot down a passenger airliner carrying 298 people, including an American citizen, President Barack Obama emerged from the White House to issue a statement. Scowling at the camera, Obama stated: "Russia has extraordinary influence over these separatists. No one denies that. Russia has urged them on. Russia has trained them."

Finally, after fulminating for several minutes about the nastiness of the Russian government, Obama approached the predictable climax: threats of action.

Except that there were none.

Instead, Obama explained that if Russia were to ignore his warnings, it would "only further isolate itself from the international community, and the costs for Russia's behavior will only continue to increase."

To which Putin's only rational response would be laughter.

This is a Western humiliation on an epic scale. Obama and Europe could wrongly and weakly pass off the invasion and annexation of Crimea as a historical anomaly brutally corrected. They could ignore the further invasion of eastern Ukraine, focusing instead on those naughty Israelis busily defending themselves against rocket attacks from Hamas terrorists.

But now, the West has told Putin, in no uncertain terms, that his people can hit a civilian aircraft with a missile, and that there will be no costs.

How can a second-rate power hold the United States and NATO over a barrel?

Vice President Joe Biden gave the answer in an interview with The New Yorker, albeit unwittingly (though that should go without saying, given Biden's witlessness). While bragging about his gung-ho, macho political attitude, Biden related a story about meeting Putin -- a story he pledged was "absolutely, positively" true, meaning there is a three in four chance it is complete fiction.

But, taking the vice president at his word, the story went like this. Biden met Putin at the Kremlin in 2011. They found themselves standing face to face. "I said, 'Mr. Prime Minister, I'm looking into your eyes, and I don't think you have a soul," Biden related to interviewer. "And he looked back at me, and he smiled, and he said, 'We understand one another.' This is who this guy is."

The last line from Biden is the key to the story: He sees Putin's response as a defeat for Putin somehow, a denial of his humanity. Putin, Biden seems to be saying, is an inhuman James Bond villain -- and for some reason, Biden thinks this widespread perception of Putin makes him weak.

But that's Putin's entire goal : He wants the West to believe he has no soul. While the West, like Biden, seeks to demonstrate its bigheartedness to Putin, with "reset" buttons and U.N. resolutions and G8 summits and Olympic Games, Putin seeks to demonstrate that he has no heart. He wants to be seen as cruel and inhuman. He wants everyone to know that he will never bluff and that he will always shoot first.

Obama, Biden and the European Union somehow believe that handwringing and moral proclamations will bring Putin into line. Putin knows strength -- or, at least, the impression of intransigent steeliness -- will bring the West into line. In a game of chicken, the man who openly puts a brick on the accelerator will always win.

Putin's got the brick on the accelerator. He's had quite a hot streak: Georgia, Syria, Iran and now Ukraine. The result will be a far more dangerous world, as potential Russian targets seek nuclear weapons to deter the bear, and as Putin speeds to consolidate his gains. Obama's nuclear-free world, his multipolar United Nations geopolitics, spirals the toilet, thanks to his own utopian wishful thinking.

This is what happens when children play against adults on the world stage. This is what happens when starry-eyed post-Americans are given charge of Western leadership. Putin rolls on, evilly manipulating, grossly murdering. And Obama makes peeved faces as bodies smolder in Ukrainian fields.

Obama: Troll Hard With a Vengeance

July 30, 2014

This week, as I have been predicting for months, President Barack Obama announced that he would be considering unprecedented executive action to provide legal status for millions of immigrants here illegally. His goal is not to solve the immigration crisis -- you don't grant legal status to 5 million people, and then leave the back door wide open if you're interested in solving the problem. His goal is not to help immigrants here illegally -- he instead leaves them in limbo by granting them temporary work permits, rather than blanket amnesty.

His goal is trolling.

Trolling is a practice whereby a person takes a deliberately indefensible position simply to draw passionate excess from an opponent. That is Obama's goal here: He hopes for extreme language, impassioned opposition and eventually, impeachment.

This administration is hungry for impeachment. While no Republican leader in Congress has given even a smidgen of credibility to impeachment talk, the Obama administration has been fundraising off impeachment rumors. Last Friday, the White House said that it was not dismissing the possibility of a House impeachment; senior adviser Dan Pfeiffer said that Obama "would not discount the possibility." Two weeks ago, Obama brought up the possibility of impeachment in order to mock it to his supporters. As Politico noted, "Who's talking about impeachment? Barack Obama."

Joe Trippi, a Democratic consultant, explained why Democrats love impeachment talk: "The more they talk about it, the more it has a red hot effect on their base. So if you can get the temperature just right, you're turning out all your base voters, and Democrats don't take it seriously, and it's a good year for you. If that stove gets just a little too hot, and you lose control of it, you're going to have every Democrat on the planet turning out to stop it."

Obama trolls because he recognizes that trends cut against Democrats in 2014. If he believed that Democrats were well-positioned to win back the House of Representatives, he would threaten executive action and then call on Americans to give his party a majority. Instead, he seeks to gin up outrage on the right and enthusiasm on the left. And he'll use the lives of millions of Americans and non-Americans to do it. It's a desperation play, but it's his only play.

That's because Obama has no capacity for compromise. His strategy has always been simple: govern when you have a majority; campaign when you don't. And so, for the last several years, he's spent significantly more time doing fundraisers than being president -- and even when he's being president, he's simply setting up the next stop in his endless campaign.

So what should conservatives do? First off, they should stop talking impeachment. It's a waste of time and effort. It serves no purpose. It is not principled to talk impeachment; it is idiotic. There are zero Democrats in the Senate who would vote to convict Obama and few Republicans.

Second, conservatives should point out that Obama does not have the country's best interests in mind. He does not care about the fate of immigrants here illegally -- if he did, he'd stop incentivizing children to travel thousands of miles in the hands of coyotes, then offering uncertainty as to their status, incentivizing thousands more to do the same. He obviously does not care about the political climate of the country -- if he did, he'd stop manipulating and start governing.

Finally, conservatives should ignore Obama. His rhetoric is unimportant. It is a distraction. They should focus instead on his actions, which are deliberately designed to undermine the country for his own political gain.

How the Media Craft Victory for Hamas

August 6, 2014

On Tuesday, CNN's Wolf Blitzer hosted Hamas spokesman Osama Hamden. The week before, Hamdan labeled Israeli Prime Minister Benjamin Netanyahu "a new image of Hitler" on the network. But now, for some reason, Blitzer stumbled into a random act of journalism: He asked Hamdan about comments he had made suggesting that Jews used Christian blood in matza. Hamdan stumbled around and blamed the Jews for their action in Gaza.

Blitzer called Hamdan's comments an "awful, awful smear."

The very fact that this represented a unique moment in the media coverage of the Israel-Hamas Gaza war demonstrates the malpractice of the media. The first questions on the media's collective tongue should have been: What does Hamas stand for? What are its goals? Why does it use women and children as human shields? Why does it hide military resources in civilian areas?

But that had to wait for a month.

In the meantime, CNN viewers saw an unending stream of dramatic images from Gaza of Palestinian Arab suffering: heavy blasts from Israeli ordinance, screaming women, bleeding children. Every so often, CNN punctuated its coverage with death toll statistics -- never mentioning that it received those statistics from the Palestinians themselves, and neglecting to mention the Palestinians' regular practice of classifying dead terrorists as civilians. Then CNN asked questions about Israeli "proportionality" and wondered aloud about whether Israeli strikes were sufficiently "targeted."

If you want to know why the conflict between the dramatically overpowering Israeli military and the sadistically brutal Hamas has continued for weeks, look no further than CNN and its like-minded media brethren. Hamas' goals in this conflict did not include military victory; Hamas may be evil, but it is not stupid. Its main goal was to shore up its base by achieving small concessions from Israel and Egypt, as well as the Palestinian Authority; those concessions could only be achieved if Israel could be portrayed as an international aggressor against a terror group.

And that's where the media manipulation came in. Hamas placed heavy restrictions on journalists and even threatened them. Hamas put women and children and mentally ill people in harm's way for the cameras, and as a deterrent to Israeli military action.

And the media went right along with it, proclaiming balance all the way. When I was on CNN this week with Alisyn Camerota, she maintained that CNN provided balance by presenting "both sides," to which I responded that presenting both sides in a battle between Hamas and Israel is not balance, but anti-Israel bias. No Western media member would, in 1944, have assumed that balance meant quoting both Winston Churchill and Julius Streicher. To do so would have been to forward propaganda.

But that is precisely what the media have done. They have turned balance into a synonym for amorality. In doing so, they have handed a propaganda victory to evil.

Let's Get Serious About Mental Illness

August 13, 2014

Robin Williams' suicide this week shook up people across the political spectrum -- and for good reason. When a highly successful, incredibly popular figure from our culture decides to take his own life, it feels as though suicide could happen to anyone.

It can't.

Robin Williams reportedly suffered from mentally illness. He stated during an interview in 2006 that he hadn't been formally diagnosed with depression or bipolar disorder, but stated, "Do I perform sometimes in a manic style? Yes. Am I manic all the time? No. Do I get sad? Oh yeah. Does it hit me hard? Oh yeah." He added, "I get bummed, like I think a lot of us do at certain times. You look at the world and go, 'Whoa.' Other moments you look and go, 'Oh, things are OK.'" That same year, according to the Huffington Post, he explained the temptation of alcoholism -- he had famously admitted to drug and alcohol addiction problems -- to Diane Sawyer. "It's the same voice thought that ... you're standing at a precipice and you look down, there's a voice and it's a little quiet voice that goes, 'Jump.'"

Williams' death has spurred multiple writers and celebrities to announce their own struggles with such issues; virtually every family has suffered through the horrors of mental illness. My grandfather was diagnosed with bipolar disorder decades ago, and routinely battled suicidality until his introduction to lithium.

Raising awareness is praiseworthy -- the stigma attached to getting help for mental illness should be wiped away as soon as possible.

By the same token, we ought to ensure that normalizing mental illness helps no one, and damages those who truly are mentally ill. The lack of awareness surrounding mental illness comes from two directions: first, those who pretend that mental illness represents a lack of willpower or dedication; second, those who pretend that serious mental illnesses are not mental illnesses at all, but representations of free thought and behavior. Forty years ago, the first group predominated; today, the second does.

Forty years ago, men and women feared career destruction should rumors spread that they were seeing psychologists or psychiatrists. That fear has largely dissipated. But a new threat to the well-being of those suffering from mental illness has replaced the original threat: the threat of diversity campaigners leaving those with mental illness to suffer in the name of heterogeneity.

This is not to suggest that all of those who are "different" are mentally ill, or vice versa. But it is meant to suggest that we ought to consider the mental health of those who are homeless, rather than labeling them, in blanket fashion, advocates for free living spaces. It is meant to suggest that those who suffer from gender dysphoria may not be suffering from societal bigotry, but from something far deeper and more dangerous, and that physical mutilation and stumping for tolerance will not solve their problems.

In other words, if we are to recognize the importance of mental illness as a society, the left must stop papering over mental illness with platitudes about diversity, and the right must stop treating mental illness as a moral problem rather than a medical one. Those racked with mental anguish are crying out for our help. If we don't hear them, it may be because too busy pushing political viewpoints rather than listening.

The Great Racial Disconnect on Police

August 20, 2014

On Monday, Rasmussen released a poll of Americans regarding the guilt or innocence of Officer Darren Wilson, the police officer who shot unarmed 18-year-old black man Michael Brown six times in Ferguson, Missouri. Those polls show that 57 percent of black adults think that Wilson should be found guilty of murder; 56 percent of whites, by contrast, are undecided on the matter.

The latter position is the correct one. Witnesses, including one Dorian Johnson, claim that Brown was pulled over by Wilson, attacked by him and pulled into the car, ran, stopped when told to freeze by Wilson, held up his hands, and was then shot. Other witnesses -- more than a dozen of them, according to local media -- say that Brown attacked Wilson, went for Wilson's gun, fled before being told to stop, and then charged Wilson before being shot.

Here's what we do know: Despite original media reports labeling Brown a "gentle giant," Brown and shooting witness Dorian Johnson did participate in a strong-arm robbery of a local convenience store. We know that despite original witness reports suggesting that Brown was shot in the back, he was not. We know that contemporaneous witness accounts caught on tape suggest that Brown charged at Wilson. And we know that a young black man is dead with six bullets in him at the hands of a white cop.

And to huge segments of the black community, that last fact is the only one that matters. The full facts do not matter to extremists in the black community and to their white leftist enablers, particularly in the media. A full 41 percent of black Americans believe that riots and looting represent "legitimate outrage." Not protesting -- riots and looting. Just 35 percent of blacks think that looters and rioters are criminals taking advantage of the situation.

There is a pattern here: a widespread belief in the black community that the justice system is rigged against them. That belief is not without basis -- there is no question that America has a history of racism within the criminal justice community. By the same token, there is also no question that American law enforcement is the least racist it has ever been, by a long shot, and that racism within the law enforcement community is broadly considered unacceptable and vile.

But the belief in a racist justice system seems to have maintained its stranglehold inside the black community. That belief, taken to its extreme, means support for black criminality. It is no coincidence that during the O.J. Simpson trial, 60 percent of black Americans did not believe O.J. was guilty. It is also no coincidence that many white Americans perceive black support for murderers like O.J. Simpson and riots in Ferguson as support for lawlessness, and therefore pooh-pooh charges of police racism. When crying racism becomes crying wolf, it is hard to take such charges seriously.

The solution, however, lays neither in knee-jerk accusations of racism from the black community nor in immediate dismissals of individual accusations by the white community. It lies in continued targeting and prosecution of individual racists in the police community, of course -- and far more importantly, it lies in less criminality within the black community. The high levels of crime in the black community contribute to heavier policing, which in turn reinforces perceptions of racial targeting; those perceptions then create resentment against police than ends too often in violent encounters and failure to report crime. And so the cycle starts anew.

It's time to break the cycle. The only way to do that is to focus on the fact that police have no excuse to shoot anyone unless those people are committing criminal acts. On that we can all agree. Yes, we must arduously insist that police hold to that standard, and we must prosecute those who do not to the fullest extent of the law. But by the same token, we must insist that criminal acts stop -- and to do that, we must move beyond simple anti-police sentiment.

Those Who Go Unsung

August 27, 2014

The vast majority of Americans have never met Phil Weinberg. But that isn't because he's unimportant. It's because he is important. Like millions of Americans who toil largely in anonymity, participating daily in acts of courage and generosity, Phil has never been on CNN or Fox News; while he subscribes to The Wall Street Journal, he's never had his picture dot pixelated. That's because he, like so many other Americans, is too busy making the country work.

Phil was born at the Beth Israel Hospital in Boston in 1951, just down the block from Fenway Park, and grew up a diehard Red Sox fan (of course). He began working as a kid, selling papers on a street corner for eight cents a pop, shoveling snow for neighbors. He headed his junior congregation while still a kid at Hebrew school -- where his future wife, Cheryl, saw him, although she had no clue she'd end up marrying the tall, goofy guy who was leading services.

Phil knew early on he wanted to be a teacher. He majored in education at Boston University, got another bachelor's in Jewish education simultaneously at Hebrew University, and then studied Jewish history at Jewish Theological Seminary. He worked his way through college on work study as a janitor, flipped burgers and sold Drake's cakes to other starving students. Phil actually met his wife, Cheryl, when they were both students at Hebrew College. They were best friend for six years. Then they realized what they had, and decided to get married. Their life was just beginning.

Phil and Cheryl moved down to Tampa, Florida, where Phil taught at a Hebrew day school. His teaching career took him back to Boston, and then to El Paso, Texas, and finally to California -- he earned two more master's degrees in Texas and California. That's where he got out of Jewish education and into general education at the Los Angeles Unified School District. One of the roughest school districts in the country, LAUSD is perennially underperforming; its student population includes some of the most poverty-stricken areas in the United States.

Phil jumped in with both feet. He taught special education, a self-contained class for children with specific learning disabilities -- but since LAUSD was badly administered, the district threw all sorts of children in Phil's classes, including autistic kids, developmental delays and emotionally disturbed children.

Despite the challenges of LAUSD's administrative chaos, Phil sought to teach these kids, many of whom had parents who either couldn't or wouldn't raise their children. He taught the children, many of whom were immigrants to the country, patriotic songs, even though the district disapproved of such political incorrectness. He read them stories, making sure to play all the parts. He created specific goals and reports for each student.

These kids were his kids.

Phil and Cheryl were never able to conceive naturally, so they adopted a son. Their son was troubled, but they poured their heart and soul into raising him, just as they pour themselves into everything they did.

Phil is my uncle -- not the brother of my mom or dad, but an adopted uncle. He is best friends with my father. And my father only has one rule for his friends: They must treat his children with kindness and generosity. Phil is the epitome of both.

My father always said as we were growing up that surrounding your children with good people is one of the chief tasks of a parent. My parents certainly did that with Phil. He is an intellectual, a brilliant man, well-read, soft-spoken. He always provides information, but he is never strident, never arrogant. He is a friend, an advisor, and a mentor. And he is never happier than when I or my sisters tell him about what we're achieving and what battles we're fighting.

I'm writing about Phil now because he's in a hospital in California. He's been battling cancer for several years; last week, he had a stroke. He's still fighting, and he'll still keep fighting. Because that's what we do as Americans. We may never get our 15 minutes of fame. We may never get our headshot on cable television. But we will make the country work, teach the next generation, and do so because we are a generous and forgiving people, willing to slog in the trenches without fame or fortune.

That's my Uncle Phil.

Of Racial Delusions and Riots

September 3, 2014

Last week, as riots in Ferguson, Missouri decrescendoed and the country held its collective breath over the question of the indictment of Officer Darren Wilson in the shooting death of Michael Brown, rappers Diddy (formerly P. Diddy, formerly Puff Daddy, formerly Sean Combs), 2 Chainz, The Game, and Rick Ross, along with 10 of their fellows, released a song: "Don't Shoot."

The Game explained why he felt the necessity to record the song: "I am a black man with kids of my own that I love more than anything, and I cannot fathom a horrific tragedy like Michael Brown's happening to them. This possibility has shaken me to my core."

The lyrics of the song speak to a perverse view of race in America -- a view reinforced day after day by a media dedicated to the proposition that American law enforcement maliciously targets black men at random. To this point, nobody knows the facts of the case in the Brown shooting. Nonetheless, the rappers label the shooting cold-blooded, first-degree murder. Because facts are unnecessary; only feelings are real. "God ain't put us on the Earth to get murdered, it's murder," says one rapper, TGT. Another, The Game, raps, "They killin' teens, they killin' dreams, it's murder."

Next, Diddy launches into a listing of various black men killed under controversial circumstances. Some, like Emmett Till, were murdered in acts of pure and evil racism. But Diddy lumps together Till with Trayvon Martin and Michael Brown -- and even Ezell Ford. Last week, the Los Angeles Police Department released the identities of the two police officers who shot Ford. One was Asian; the other was Hispanic. The Huffington Post did not even cover their races.

The Los Angeles Times buried that relevant fact in paragraph 13 of their comprehensive story. But again, facts do not matter: Only a feeling of persecution matters.

Then Rick Ross sums up the generalized view of America created by media-stoked racial conflagrations like the Michael Brown situation: "Black men, we pay the toll, the price is your life, Uncle Sam want a slice, black dress code now we looting in the night, now we throwing Molotovs in this Holocaust." A grand total of just under 100 young black men are killed by white police officers each year, according to statistics provided to the FBI by local police. To compare police treatment of young black men to the Holocaust is not only statistically idiotic, but also morally dangerous.

Nonetheless, that is the view of police for many blacks: police as paramilitary white force out to target black men. When I was recently in the CNN green room with former Obama green jobs czar Van Jones, he and I got to talking about the Ferguson situation. I asked him why he believed there was such a racial gap in the interpretation of the situation. His answer: "You're Jewish, right? Wouldn't you jump to conclusions if you heard that the Nazis or Hamas had killed a Jew?"

Of course, not even Van Jones, Diddy, 2 Chainz, and the rest truly believe what they say about the police. All those who spout about a "Holocaust" by police against blacks would call 911 in approximately 3.5 seconds if their houses were robbed. But if we truly believe that America's police forces are akin to Nazis or Islamic terrorists, there can be no decent solution. Fighting police would be a moral imperative, not a moral evil.

And therein lies the problem. The only real answer to the antipathy between large segments of the black community and police is threefold: first, taking seriously fact-based allegations of racism against the authorities, and investigating and prosecuting such allegations if well-founded; second, not jumping to conclusions about non-fact-based allegations; and third, lowering crime rates among young black men, thereby lowering interactions between police and young black men.

But those are not solutions backed by the racially delusional. Instead, they suggest an unending and circular "conversation" about race that goes something like this: Police sometimes shoot young black men; that's because police are racist; therefore, those who resist police are not morally unjustified; rinse, wash, repeat.

Sadly, America's media backs this second approach. And so we end up with damaging foolishness like "Don't Shoot" infusing our pop culture and the snarky but empty-headed racial guilting of Jon Stewart and Stephen Colbert invading our news. And nothing gets solved. We just get more hate, more rage and more violence.

The Global Map, 2017

September 10, 2014

Barack Obama pledged to radically transform America when he took office. He didn't stop at America. President Obama's greatest legacy may be the radical reshaping of the global map.

Fast forward three years. Here's where we stand.

Given Europe's failure to stand up to Russian aggression in Crimea, Russia's borders have expanded to include Eastern Ukraine, northern Kazakhstan and larger portions of Moldova. As of 2014, Russia had consolidated its hold on Transnistria, the Eastern region of Moldova, which is heavily Russian; Russia had annexed Crimea; Russia had placed troops inside Eastern Ukraine.

But it didn't stop there. Russia began squeezing Georgia again, and pro-Russian regimes are consolidating their power in Kazakhstan and Belarus. Belarus asked the Russian government to place 15 warplanes inside the country in 2014; Kazakhstan got into a tiff with Russia over comments Putin made unsubtly suggesting a possible invasion of the country, and then complied with Putin's demands when the West did nothing.

Thus far, Putin has not invaded any NATO countries. But that could change, given the high Russian population in Latvia and Estonia.

Meanwhile, in the Middle East, Jordan's kingdom has fallen, replaced by a radical Islamist regime. That Palestinian Arab regime has attempted to consolidate its power by forming an alliance with Hamas in Judea, Samaria, and Gaza. In Lebanon, the Iranians and Syrians have effectively annexed southern Lebanon. Israel's only quiet border is now its southern border with Egypt.

In Syria, Bashar Assad has retained a measure of power by essentially conceding territory to ISIS in the eastern part of the country; after a halfhearted intervention against ISIS, the international community went quiet as ISIS formed its sought-after caliphate in eastern Syria and northern Iraq. In response, Iran essentially invaded southern Iraq, and Turkey launched covert action against the Kurds in order to prevent the formation of a broader Kurdistan encompassing parts of Turkish territory.

With the withdrawal of the United States and its allies from Afghanistan, Pakistan has once again made its presence felt. The Taliban have effectively taken control of large swaths of territory, with the help of the Pakistani regime, which has shifted leadership but not position with regard to radical Islam.

In the most stunning international move, China has threatened full-scale annexation of Taiwan, barring access to the South China Sea from Western countries and cutting off Taiwan's trade routes. The West has refused to leverage China, fearing financial retaliation. China has made similar moves against the Philippines.

Come 2017, this will be President Obama's legacy: a world of redrawn borders, all to the benefit of some of the worst regimes on the planet. When America retreats from the world, its enemies expand.

The Conversation We Won't Have About Raising Men

September 17, 2014

On Thursday night, the Baltimore Ravens took on the Pittsburgh Steelers. The event carried national significance thanks to the Ravens' public-induced decision to cut running back Ray Rice after tape emerged of Rice clocking his then-fiancee in the head, knocking her out cold. CBS sportscaster James Brown utilized his pregame show to draw attention to the problem of domestic violence -- and suggest widespread culpability for domestic violence. "Our language is important," Brown suggested. "For instance, when a guy says, 'You throw the ball like a girl' or 'You're a little sissy,' it reflects an attitude that devalues women, and attitudes will eventually manifest in some fashion."

Brown wasn't the only commentator to blame "The Sandlot" for Ray Rice's horrifying Mike Tyson-esque blow to his future wife's head. ESPN commentator Kate Fagan explained, "This is behavior that is happening at the grassroots level that is born through years of our culture like raising men to want to not be like women and using language like 'sissy' and 'you throw like a girl' that demean women. ... [We need to focus on] really reprogramming how we raise men."

Naturally, this talking point was celebrated far and wide by a mainstream press more interested in perpetuating the tenets of political correctness than in actually fighting domestic abuse. The real solution to domestic abuse is twofold: punishing it to the greatest possible extent, and yes, raising young men differently. But to state that the greatest risk factor for future domestic violence is insulting other boys as "throwing like girls" is pure idiocy. No man has ever hit a woman because she "throws like a girl." But plenty of young men have hit women because they had no moral compass and did not believe in basic concepts of virtue -- and plenty of young men lack such a moral compass and belief in virtue thanks to lack of male role models.

Teaching respect for women begins with ensuring that solid male influences models fill the lives of young men -- men who respect women, cherish them, treasure them and believe in protecting them. This is an unpopular stance, because it suggests that boys require men to raise them. Which they do. But that truth doesn't fit the logic of the left, which seems to think that lack of fathers counts less than rhetorically bothersome phrases.

For leftists, the answer to domestic violence isn't to deal with any of the issues that could lead boys to become abusing men. The answer, instead, is to lecture Americans about the use of the word "sissy" -- not because that solves the problem, but because it makes those on the left feel warm and fuzzy inside. Similarly, the left will tell Americans that the name of the Washington Redskins matters far more to Native-Americans than the nearly half of Native-American youths who drop out of high school; they will explain that "microaggressions" are the true problem faced by blacks in America, not lack of education, poverty or unwed motherhood.

We extol the language police even as we castigate moral authorities. And so our problems grow worse. But at least we feel better about them.

A Moral Universe Torn Apart

September 24, 2014

"I am not ashamed," a young woman says into a camera. "I am not ashamed."

The woman is Leyla Josephine of Glasgow, and she is a self-described feminist performance artist. She is reading a poem titled "I Think She Was a She" -- a poem lauded by The Huffington Post as "unapologetic. ... She ardently declares her power over her body as she reminds us that a woman exercising her right to choose is not uncommon -- and should never be shamefully brushed under the rug."

What, exactly, is this poem? It's Josephine recounting her abortion of her unborn daughter. She notes, "I know she was a she and I think she would've looked exactly like me. I would've told her stories about her grandfather, we could've fed the swans at Victoria Park." Then, however, she reveals just what she's done: "I would've supported her right to choose. To choose a life for herself, a path for herself. I would've died for that right like she died for mine. I'm sorry, but you came at the wrong time."

You came at the wrong time. Therefore, murder is justified.

At least Josephine has the intellectual honesty to admit that her daughter was in fact a daughter, not some fictional ball of tissue. But by blithely signing away her daughter's life in the name of convenience, Josephine becomes the emissary of a deep and abiding evil. Her lie that she would lay down her life for the right of her child to choose life, when it is eminently clear that she would not even sacrifice an iota of inconvenience to avoid killing her own child, is morally sickening. Her child did not choose to die for her convenience. Her child had no such choice.

But Josephine doesn't care. "Don't you mutter murder on me," Josephine spits.

Meanwhile, an ocean away, the creator of Obamacare, Dr. Ezekiel Emanuel, has written an equally nausea-inducing piece in which he stumps for death at 75 years of age. Not merely death for himself, mind you -- death for everyone. "My father illustrates the situation well," Emanuel writes, in coldly eugenic fashion. "About a decade ago, just shy of his 77th birthday, he began having pain in his abdomen. ... He had in fact had a heart attack, which led to a cardiac catheterization and ultimately a bypass. Since then, he has not been the same." Emanuel's father is 87, and says he is happy. That doesn't matter. He's no longer useful, according to Emanuel.

Emanuel sees wondrous good for the rest of us in sending the elderly to the "Logan's Run" carousel -- after all, "We want to be remembered as independent, not experienced as burdens ... [leaving our grandchildren] with memories framed not by our vivacity but by our frailty is the ultimate tragedy."

This is the cult of death created by a society that values amusement over life. Amusement means that the death of others is second priority; amusement means that if your own capacity diminishes, your raison d'etre has ended.

If America was built on life, liberty and pursuit of happiness, today's leftist death cult devalues the first and destroys the second in pursuit of the third. And, in the end, there will be no happiness, for happiness is not ceaseless hedonism but living a moral and responsible life. Apparently, we dismissed that definition of happiness long ago. The result: an un-civilization of Leyla Josephines and Ezekiel Emanuels.

The Throat-Clearing President Versus the Throat-Cutting Terrorists

October 1, 2014

Last week, President Obama spoke to the United Nations about the growing threat of the Islamic State in Iraq and Syria. In the course of that speech, he discussed a wide variety of threats to Western civilization, ranging from Ebola to global warming, from chaos in Syria to China's incursions in the South China Sea. The speech seemed unfocused, meandering. But it held together thanks to one common thread: Barack Obama believes that words solve everything. Particularly his own.

Obama's narcissism isn't mere arrogance. It's messianism. It's pure faith that his verbiage can alter the course of history. "We are here," Obama said, "because others realized that we gain more from cooperation than conquest." Well, actually, no -- the United Nations exists because evil nations were forced through conquest to admit that cooperation might be a more advantageous strategy.

"While small gains can be won at the barrel of a gun," Obama said, "they will ultimately be turned back if enough voices support the freedom of nations and peoples to make their own decisions." Not exactly -- millions of voices in North Korea have not altered the fate of those stuck in the world's largest gulag, nor have millions of voices in Iran freed them of the tyranny of the mullahs.

"The ideology of ISIL or al Qaeda or Boko Haram will wilt and die if it is consistently exposed, confronted, and refuted in the light of day," Obama spouted. If good argument killed bad argument, Islamism wouldn't be on the march, but on the ash heap of history. Global politics, it turns out, is not a Harvard Law mock trial.

"We believe that right makes might," Obama summed up, "that bigger nations should not be able to bully smaller ones, that people should be able to choose their own future." Hogwash would be too kind a word to describe this sort of highfaluting idiocy -- if right made might, millions of Jews would still populate Europe.

In reality, right dictates that right arm itself -- right must become might in order to emerge victorious. Americans know that.

Because Americans know that, Obama must occasionally bow to reality. And so, in the same speech in which Obama called for Russian, Chinese and Syrian conflicts to be resolved through diplomacy, he uttered the most un-Obamaesque comment of his entire presidency with regard to ISIS: "The only language understood by killers like this is the language of force."

This is eminently true. It is also so far out of Obama's wheelhouse that he almost strained an oblique in making that statement. And, in fact, when polling doesn't apply to him, Obama is happy to pressure other nations not to use the language of force -- in the same speech, Obama pressured Israel to negotiate with its enemies, even though its enemies are of the exact same ilk as ISIS. If Obama does not bear a striking animus for the Jewish state, the best that can be said is that he wants Israel to be on the cutting edge of Western civilization's rhetoric-first throat-cutting. After all, Obama tells Israel, too many Israelis are "ready to abandon the hard work of peace."

Yes, the hard work of peace. With people who want to slit their throats.

That's the real Obama, not the puffed-chest commander in chief threatening to bomb virtually everyone in virtually every country in the Middle East.

And that's the problem. Lack of foreign policy comes from lack of belief in the principled use of force. And so Obama, the messianic narcissist, vacillates between two extremes: empty threats and pathetic wheedling. Neither works.

Rise of the Barbarians

October 8, 2014

On Friday night, a Huntington Beach man, 43, was walking back to his car after the Los Angeles Angels played the Kansas City Royals in the American League Division Series. Three men accosted him, and then proceeded to beat him senseless. He is currently in critical condition at a local hospital after police found him unconscious.

I didn't find the story particularly shocking, given that I took my father and two younger sisters to the Angels-Royals game on Thursday night. Throngs packed the stadium -- the team announced the attendance at 43,321. We had bleacher seats, which sold for $68. The team must have also sold standing room tickets, since behind the bleachers -- lines of fans stood three deep, watching the game.

When my family and I arrived at the game, the ushers had not cleared paths through the standing-room crowd for those who wanted to get to their seats. We gently edged our way toward the seats.

Which is when I heard a guy scream into my ear: "Why the f--- are you bumping me?"

I turned to face a young Hispanic man, wearing a long-sleeved flannel shirt (it was reportedly 93 degrees outside at the time), baggy jeans, an Angels cap cocked off at a bizarre angle, the brim unbent. He wore a close-cropped three-day stubble. He was approximately my height, but probably 20lbs. heavier than I. Two of his friends flanked him.

Though I hadn't bumped, I quickly apologized -- after all, what point is there in a confrontation at a sporting event?

My apology, however, was not accepted. "I said, why the f--- did you bump me?"

Again I apologized. When it became clear that this fellow had downed at least a few beers and had his mind set on some sort of violence, my sister grabbed my arm and we walked away. He glared at me the rest of the game. My sisters focused on reassuring me that getting into a physical fight with the dolt would have served no useful purpose, and could have ended in a 3-on-1 beating. Which didn't make me feel much better.

Unfortunately, this fellow wasn't the only beer-soaked Neanderthal in the bleachers. When a Royals fan, who happened to be black, showed up with his girlfriend, two boozy white Angels fans screamed -- with children in close proximity -- "Go back to f---ing Kansas City!"

It's unlikely any of these charming folks were involved in the beating of the Huntington Beach man after Game 2 of the ALDS. But we now live in a society where young male barbarians are growing in number, their masculinity tied into useless aggression. More and more, young men seem to channel their aggressive instinct not into building, but into destroying -- not into defending the innocent, particularly women and children, but into confrontations for no apparent reason other than demonstrating dominance.

Why?

As a society, we have robbed men of their protective missions. Men who seek to protect women and children are called anti-feminist, gender normative. Men have abandoned their responsibilities to the state. As for building things -- well, there too, men have been told that to build is to act selfishly, without concern for the community. And young men have no male role models, since many of their fathers have abandoned them or abandoned true maleness in pursuit of vainglorious brutality. All of which leads to an increase in destruction by men without purpose, hemmed in only by the power of the state and the benefits of self-interest.

None of this is an excuse for barbarianism, of course. But it does help explain why masculinity used to center around acting like a gentleman, while now it centers around acting like a boor. The more we foster the barbarian mentality, the more barbaric society becomes.

A Bowla Ebola Idiocy

October 15, 2014

On Monday, The Daily Mail reported that NBC's chief medical correspondent, Nancy Snyderman, had a hankering for a bowl of soup from Peasant Grill in Hopewell Boro, New Jersey. So she hopped in her car with one of her crewmembers and headed over to the Grill. When she got to the restaurant, she had her crewmember run inside, grab the soup, and run back out.

There was only one problem: Both Snyderman and her crewmember were under mandatory quarantine for 21 days. That quarantine was a result of their journey to Liberia to cover the Ebola outbreak, a journey during which cameraman Ashoka Mukpo contracted the disease. The authorities made the quarantine mandatory after another of the crewmembers violated a voluntary quarantine last week.

It's one thing for Liberian citizen Thomas Eric Duncan to carry around an Ebola-ridden woman, get on an airplane to Dallas, walk into a hospital with symptoms, and then walk out again. Such behavior can be attributed, at least in part, to ignorance. It's another thing entirely for a highly educated medical professional to endanger those around her for some miso.

But that's the world of the media, where the proper response to the possibility of contracting Ebola is, "Don't you know who I am?" Double standards abound here; media members lather Americans into a frenzy over the threat of a disease that has, to date, claimed a grand total of one life in the United States. Then they go out for lunch in public after being told that they could be carrying the virus.

The Snyderman story is truly part of a broader egocentrism in the media. The media didn't give one whit about the Internal Revenue

Service targeting conservative non-profit applicants -- but they went absolutely batty over the Department of Justice targeting reporters. The media don't seem to care very much about demands for transparency from the Obama administration by the American public -- but they're fighting mad about the Obama administration's refusal to let them photograph him golfing. After all, it's one thing for normal Americans to get stiffed, and quite another for our betters to feel the effects of government's heavy hand.

The gap between the media elite and the general population has a deleterious impact on America's political future. Media members seem to have no problem with incompetent government overreach so long as they prosper, which is why so few media members worry over Democratic proposals to limit First Amendment press freedoms to government-designated "journalists."

The American people suffer thanks to this elitism. The days of the adversarial media are ending -- most investigative journalism now falls to the blogosphere or the foreign press. The corrupt relationship between media and government means that Americans don't find out about overreach and incompetence until far too late for them to do anything about it.

And so the gap grows. No wonder Snyderman went for soup while under quarantine. After all, it's not like all those other customers work for NBC, or anything.

Why Republicans Don't Get It

October 22, 2014

The Republican Party simply doesn't get it.

A new poll this week shows 2012 presidential nominee and 2008 primary candidate Mitt Romney leading the field of potential 2016 Republican candidates. According to ABC News/Washington Post, 21 percent of Republican voters would vote for Romney in the primaries; Jeb Bush and Mike Huckabee tie at 10 percent, followed by Rand Paul, Chris Christie and Paul Ryan. Altogether, some 44 percent of Republican primary voters want an "establishment" candidate -- by which we mean a candidate for whom social issues are secondary, immigration reform is primary and economics dominates.

The establishment donors on the coasts see this poll and believe that a consolidated funding effort mobilized behind the Chosen One (Romney, Bush, Christie or Ryan) could avoid a messy primary and keep the powder dry for a 2016 showdown with Hillary Clinton.

The conservative base knows this, and they groan.

That's because the conservative base understands that what motivates them is not the marginal tax rate -- nobody in the country knows, offhand, his or her effective tax rate -- but values. And none of the top priorities for Republican donors match the fire-in-the-belly issues that motivate the folks who knock on doors, phone bank and provide the under-$50 donations that could power a Republican to victory.

The divide between the establishment and the base represents a divide between the wallet and the working man, the penthouse and the pews, the Ivy Leagues and the homeschools. Which is why Republican leadership quietly assures its top donors that should

Republicans win the Senate, their first legislative push will encompass corporate tax reform and immigration reform. They will not push primarily for border security, or for protection of religious freedom, or for repeal of Common Core. They will not use their opportunity to govern as an opportunity to draw contrast between conservatism and leftism. Instead, they will seek "common ground" in a vain attempt to show the American people that efficiency deserves re-election.

And the American people will go to sleep, conservatives will vomit in their mouths, and leftists will demonize Republicans all the same.

Conservatives understand that politics simply reflect underlying values. That's why they are passionate. They don't vote their pocketbooks. They vote their guts, and their guts tell them that leftism is immoral on the most basic level.

Republicans, on the other hand, believe that politics are just business by other means. That means that Republicans think Americans, left and right, share the same underlying values. That's a lie, and it's a self-defeating lie at that.

Until Republicans begin to appreciate the moral conflict between right and left, they will dishearten the right and provide easy targets for the left. The nominee won't matter; elections won't matter. And the alienation of the American conservative will deepen and broaden, until, one day, it bursts forth with a renewed fire that consumes the Republican Party whole.

Turn Down for What?

October 29, 2014

On the way to the airport the other day, my Uber driver, an elderly Russian chap, turned on a Top 40 radio station. Not being one to complain, I actually sat and listened to the lyrics. The song blasting through the speakers of the late-model Honda Civic was titled "Habits." The singer, a young, presumably wealthy Swede named Tove Lo (actual name: Tove Nilsson), warbles about her need to visit sex clubs, do drugs, "binge on all my Twinkies, throw up in the tub." She laments that she "drank up all my money."

Why? Well, she explains, "You're gone and I gotta stay high all the time."

The next song featured a rapper named Lil Jon screaming loudly at the listener that it is "Fire up that loud, another round of shots. ... TURN DOWN FOR WHAT!" Translation: We're drunk and crazed, and we won't stop being drunk and crazed. The music video, as described by creator Daniel Kwan explores, "this other universe where dudes are so pumped up on their own d***s -- and they're so into their testosterone -- that the way that the show that is by breaking s*** with their d***s." The video, which shows a young man crashing through ceilings and into furniture as his erect penis swivels wildly in his pants, currently has nearly 130 million views on YouTube.

No wonder Tove Lo needs to stay high all the time.

The end of Western civilization, it turns out, comes with both a bang and a whimper. The bang: endless sex, animalistic, primal, without strings. As Adam Levine whines, "Baby, I'm preying on you tonight, hunt you down, eat you alive, just like animals, animals, like animals." In 1971, according to the National Survey of Young

Women, 30.4 percent of young women aged 15-19 living in metropolitan areas reported having premarital sex. By 1979, that number was 49.8 percent. Today, 62 percent of young women overall have had premarital sex according to the Centers for Disease Control. In 1950, men's median age of first marriage stood at 22.8; today, it stands at 28.2. More people having sex younger, and without commitment is not a recipe for societal happiness.

Thus the whimper. In a culture in which emotional connections are degraded to the level of bovine rutting, is it any wonder that 9.2 percent of Americans -- some 23.9 million people -- have used an illicit drug in the past month, and that nearly a quarter of those aged 18-20 have done so? Or that nearly a third of men over the age of 12 and 16 percent of women have participated in binge drinking in the last month?

From what are these people running? Drugs and alcohol are an escape -- but we are the most prosperous society on the planet. We are wealthier and healthier than any nation in history. So why the angst?

That question sticks in the craw of the materialists of the secular left, who insist that endless supplies of Soma and government-sponsored sex, complete with Malthusian belt -- to borrow terms from Huxley -- should bring happiness. Obviously, it doesn't. America's suicide rate recently hit a 25-year high. Suicide has surged among the middle-aged, those aged 35-64, jumping 30 percent from 1999 to 2010.

Turn down for what? For survival. Or we could just keep going to sex clubs, throwing up in the bathtub and drinking up all our money. After all, isn't that what freedom from consequences -- our God-given pursuit of happiness, according to the left -- is all about?

Lessons for the GOP for 2016

November 5, 2014

On Tuesday, Republicans won a historic electoral victory, sweeping away a Democratic Senate, replacing Democratic governors in blue states like Massachusetts, Maryland and Illinois, and reversing Democratic state legislatures in Nevada, Colorado, Minnesota, New Mexico, Maine, West Virginia and New Hampshire. Republicans now control more state legislatures than they have at any point since the 1920s, and a bigger House majority than they have since 1928.

The celebratory mood for Republicans pervaded the country -- a feeling of hope, lost since President Obama revealed himself to be just as radical as the right suspected, has returned. That hope isn't vain -- when a landslide of such proportion takes place, there is something to it. The question is whether Republicans can capitalize on their newfound opportunity and finally make a strong move toward winning the White House.

Therein lies the problem. Midterm elections have historically been poor predictors of presidential elections. That's because the crowd that turns out for midterms does not mirror the crowd that turns out for presidential elections -- those who turn out for midterms are more highly motivated and generally better informed. In 2010, for example, approximately 84 million Americans voted for in local Congressional race. In 2012, 108 million Americans voted in the same races. Republicans won about 45 million votes in the Congressional races in 2010, with Democrats coming in far behind at 39 million. In 2012, each party earned about 54 million votes. Of the additional 24 million voters who showed up to vote in Congressional races in 2012, 62.5 percent went for Democrats.

That means that Republicans must not sit on their laurels.

For many in the commentariat, that means that Republicans must push forward a compromising, bipartisan agenda. That seems to be the general opinion of those on the political left, who despise Republicans and who, as the evening of Nov. 4 progressed, strongly resembled Arnold Toht at the end of "Raiders of the Lost Ark," their faces falling with each result.

The truth is precisely the reverse. Republicans cannot be seen as the Party of No, as the GOP's enemies would have it -- but they do have an obligation to turn President Obama into the President of No. That means pushing easily comprehended, single-issue bills, short and clear and popular. If President Obama wants to veto those bills, that becomes his problem. But Republicans should not stop passing legislation between 2014 and 2016.

Meanwhile, Republicans must work to exploit holes in the Democratic base. In 2012, President Obama appealed heavily to minority groups for strong turnout; Hillary Clinton does not have the same minority appeal. That means she will focus strongly on winning single women, and driving them to the polls in large numbers. Republicans should therefore push national security issues, family freedom issues -- and they have just the right faces to do that in Senator Joni Ernst, R-Iowa and Mia Love, R-Utah, among others.

Conservatives can see a ray of sunshine at last. Now they must work to ensure that the ray of sunshine doesn't turn into another faded opportunity.

America's Education Crisis

November 12, 2014

An educational crisis has struck Minneapolis' public schools: Black students have a tenfold higher chance of suspension or expulsion than white students. And superintendent Bernadeia Johnson wants to "disrupt that in any way that I can."

Her solution: refusing to suspend black and Hispanic students. "The only way I can think [to solve the disparity] is to take those suspensions back to the individuals and try and probe and ask questions," Johnson explained. Johnson will work with the Department of Education, which originally brought the disparity to light. Now, Johnson will have to review every potential suspension of a non-white, non-Asian student. "Changing the trajectory for our students of color is a moral and ethical imperative, and our actions must be drastically different to achieve our goal of closing the achievement gap by 2020," Johnson stated.

Black and Hispanic students in Minneapolis represent 60.3 percent of the student body. Just 15 percent of teachers are non-white. This has led to pressure to oust some white teachers in favor of minority teachers. But Minnesota has some of the highest-performing students in the nation: Overall, 70 percent of fourth-graders read at or above grade level, as opposed to 34 percent of students nationally; for eighth-graders, 82 percent of students score above grade level, as opposed to 43 percent nationally. The big problem: Black and Hispanic students score extraordinarily low when compared to white students. Is that because the teachers somehow teach better to white and Asian students? Or is the problem with the students?

The students in Minnesota are not an exception. Male black, Hispanic and Native-American students in every state in America lead male students of other ethnicities in suspensions. That's not due to some inherent disadvantage attached to race, of course. It's because black, Hispanic and Native-American children are disproportionately likely to live with single mothers. And children living with single mothers misbehave more often than those living with fathers. A study from Great Britain of 14,000 children showed that children were twice as likely to manifest behavioral problems by the age of 7 than those raised by their natural parents. Those numbers continue to diverge as children grow older.

But instead of dealing with the obvious problem, the government insists that the problem, somehow, lies in the strictness of the Minneapolis public schools. That's inane. School discipline in Asia far outstrips discipline in the United States. Unsurprisingly, school performance in Asia far outstrips school performance in the United States.

The left in America believes that overlooking actual solutions in favor of happy talk about institutional racism helps minority students. It achieves precisely the opposite, making light of misbehavior and destroying the chances for better education for those who seek to gain it.

The achievement gap will never be closed, so long as school districts across the country punish good students, reward bad ones and let political correctness trump educational necessity.

The Ferguson Days of Rage

November 19, 2014

This week, America held its collective breath as it waited on the grand jury indictment verdict for Officer Darren Wilson. Wilson, you'll recall, had the misfortune to run into 6'5", 289-lb. Michael Brown, an 18-year-old black man who had just finished strong-arm robbing a convenience store. Wilson pulled Brown over as he and his accomplice walked in the middle of the street; all available evidence shows that Brown then pushed himself through the driver's side window, punched Wilson, went for his gun, was shot in the hand, ran, turned around, charged Wilson, and was shot to death.

But that doesn't matter. And it has never mattered. Because facts do not matter to those attempting to rectify what they perceive as an unjust universe. For those utopian visionaries -- and, yes, violent thugs who rob stores are minions of the utopian visionaries -- individuals do not exist. Individuals are merely stand-ins for groups. Wilson was a white cop; therefore, he was the Racist White Establishment. Brown was a black teenager; therefore, he was the Innocent Black Victim. The parts have already been written; Wilson was merely unlucky enough to land the starring role.

And so we expect riots no matter what the outcome of the indictment. Should Wilson escape indictment due to complete lack of evidence, the utopians and their rioting henchmen will attribute that acquittal to the Racist White Establishment. Should he be indicted, the utopians and their rioting henchmen will cite Wilson as merely the latest example of the Racist White Establishment. No matter the antecedent, the consequence has been determined in advance: rage, riots, recriminations.

If all of this sounds familiar, that's because it is. Alongside the anti-Racist White Establishment protesters taking to the streets in Ferguson in recent weeks, anti-Israel and pro-ISIS protesters have appeared. All utopian visionaries fighting the status quo -- self-perceived victims -- love their Days of Rage. And these Ragers don't require evidence to incite their emotions. Evidence regarding individuals is for the reasonable; false stories of victims and villains are the fodder for Ragers.

Whether we're watching thousands of Muslims across the world protest and riot over cartoons of Mohammed, or whether we're watching hundreds of people in Ferguson riot over a media-manufactured story about a racial killing, Days of Rage provide the outlet for delusional anger. Radical Muslims need an external enemy to justify their own brutality; protesters in Ferguson need an external enemy to justify their own failure to make good in the freest country in the history of humanity.

Every society has its Ragers. The West's suicidal impulse to humor those Ragers, however, spells the end of the West. When facts become secondary to emotion, truth dies. And a society that doesn't value truth cannot survive. Calling out the National Guard in Ferguson while lending a sympathetic ear to the Ragers does little good, long-term. It merely staves off the inevitable surrender of the reasonable to the Ragers.

Feelingstown, Missouri

November 26, 2014

On Monday night, St. Louis County Prosecuting Attorney Robert McCulloch announced that Officer Darren Wilson, who is white, would not be indicted in the shooting death of black 18-year-old Michael Brown. McCulloch explained the falsehoods permeating the original media accounts of the shooting; he explained that Brown had, by all available physical and credible witness evidence, charged Wilson after attempting to take his gun from him in Wilson's vehicle.

And none of it mattered. The riots went forward as planned; the media steadfastly distributed its prewritten narrative of evil racist white cop murdering innocent young black man. President Obama stepped to the microphones to denounce American racism. He did not recapitulate the evidence; he did not condemn rioters and pledge that law enforcement would crack down on them. Instead, he said that protesters and rioters -- all of them ignoring the fact that a white police officer had not murdered an innocent black man in cold blood -- were justified in their rage.

Indeed, the president said, they had feelings. And those feelings were legitimate, all evidence to the contrary. "There are Americans who agree with it, and there are Americans who are deeply disappointed, even angry. It's an understandable reaction," Obama said. What made disappointment and anger over an evidence-based verdict "understandable"? Obama explained: "There are still problems and communities of color aren't just making these problems up. Separating that from this particular decision, there are issues in which the law too often feels as if it is being applied in a discriminatory fashion."

The key word: feels. Obama did not cite a single instance of the law being applied in a discriminatory fashion -- because in Ferguson it was not. Instead, he made a general statement, of the sort leftists often make, that broad feelings of discontent must be inherently legitimate -- because, after all, if people feel, those feelings must have a basis.

Now, there are certainly individual instances of racism by law enforcement in American society. All such instances should be investigated and prosecuted. But to suggest, as President Obama and the media do, that such instances provide the basis for a justifiable and generalized feeling of discontent is to declare the war on racist activity unwinnable. We cannot fight a shadow-enemy. We can never overcome feelings on a public policy level.

That is why President Obama and the left love discussing feelings. Talking about feelings avoids more difficult conversations about prosecuting individual cases or fighting crime. Feelingstalk means evidence becomes irrelevant because we need no evidence for our feelings -- they are legitimized by virtue of their very being. Self-definition becomes societal definition: if I feel there's a social problem, there's a social problem. In fact, in Feelingstown, facts become insults: If facts debunk feelings, it is the facts that must lose.

Truth is the first casualty of the feelings society; morality is the second.

Civilization is the third. If feelings require no justification in order to receive the presidential seal of approval, we have moved beyond rational political debate. If those feelings require social change, problems become inherently unsolvable.

And so, on to the next Ferguson. Feelings required. No evidence necessary.

The Real Racist Conspiracy In Ferguson

December 3, 2014

After a grand jury in St. Louis, Missouri, voted against the indictment of Officer Darren Wilson in the killing of 18-year-old black man Michael Brown, President Obama gave a short address to the nation. In it, he said he understood why some would feel disappointed at the verdict -- an odd statement, given that all available evidence showed that Brown had robbed a convenience store, attacked Wilson in his vehicle, attempted to grab his gun and charged Wilson before Wilson shot him.

Then Obama dropped a doozy: "We need to recognize that this is not just an issue in Ferguson, this is an issue for America ... there are problems and communities of color aren't just making these problems up."

Obama did not specify what problems he wanted to discuss. Nor did he explain why Ferguson's issues were America's. But the largest lie was the notion that "communities of color" don't make problems up.

Because in Ferguson, that's precisely what a community of color did.

In the immediate aftermath of the Brown shooting, grand jury documents show, witness intimidation and lying became the order of the day. Witness after witness told police that local thugs were intimidating those who had seen the events. One witness told police, according to the St. Louis Police Investigative Report, that threats "had been made to the residents of Canfield Green Apartment Complex." This witness said that "notes had been posted on various apartment buildings threatening people not to talk to the police, and gunshots were still being fired every night."

The witness wasn't alone. Other witnesses stated that supposed witnesses were lying to the media about events, that others who had seen the events were "embellishing their stories" in order to convict Wilson. One witness stated, "You have to understand the mentality of some of these young guys they have nothing to do. When they can latch on the something they embellish it because they want something to do."

Some 16 witnesses testified that Brown's hands were up when he was shot, which was factually false according to the autopsy. Another 12 witnesses said that Wilson shot Brown from behind -- again, false according to the autopsy. One witness testified that Wilson used both a Taser and a gun -- false. Another said that Brown had kneeled before Wilson shot him. When confronted with the fact that the physical evidence made such an account impossible, the witness acknowledged he hadn't seen the event, and then asked if he could leave the grand jury because he was "uncomfortable."

In 1964, Kitty Genovese was stabbed to death outside her apartment complex in New York. The entire nation gasped in horror when it learned that supposed witnesses had not called the police.

Fifty years later, the nation completely ignores the fact that an entire community apparently lied, facilitated lying or intimidated witnesses in order to put an innocent man behind bars, because he happened to be white. At least Kitty Genovese's neighbors didn't actually murder her. Members of the Ferguson community tried to murder Darren Wilson by putting him on death row. Meanwhile, President Obama and those in the media who played up the original narrative cheered them on.

To The Left, Lying About Rape
Is Just Dandy

December 10, 2014

This week, Rolling Stone printed an editor's note retracting one of the most highly praised pieces of investigative journalism in its history. That piece, written by Sabrina Rubin Erdely, alleged that several members of the University of Virginia fraternity Phi Kappa Psi, had raped a 19-year-old student named Jackie, including with foreign objects, as she lay on a floor covered with broken glass. The article resulted in the university suspending the fraternity's activities, and national outrage over the so-called "rape culture" on campus.

That rape culture supposedly leads to one in five women being sexually assaulted on campus -- a faulty statistic from a poll that didn't even ask women if they were raped or sexually assaulted, and instead defined sex while inebriated at any level as rape. With regard to reported rape, the federal government reports a rate of just 1.3 per 1,000 Americans. That is, of course, far too high. But it is not a rape culture by any plausible definition.

Nonetheless, the narrative of women as victims of brutish male society must be forwarded at all costs, for political purposes. If Americans are brutish sexists waiting to rape unsuspecting women, bigger government becomes a necessity. That's why President Obama has cited that one-in-five statistic, and suggested that America experiences "quiet tolerance of sexual assault."

In order to forward that narrative, all rape stories are treated as fact sans investigation of any kind. And so Jackie's story of gang rape received plaudits across the media landscape.

Then it fell apart.

The Washington Post quickly debunked the story. According to the Post, the fraternity says there was no event the night Jackie was allegedly raped, Jackie's friends "have not been able to verify key points in recent days," and one of the men named in Jackie's report stated that "he never met Jackie in person and never took her out on a date."

As the Rolling Stone report collapsed, members of the left jumped to defend Jackie. Sally Kohn of CNN.com tweeted that people should stop questioning Jackie's story: "While aspects of UVA rape story now in question, still unsettles me that pouncing by skeptics mirrored sort of doubt rape victims often face." Feminist Melissa McEwan wrote, "If Jackie's story is partially or wholly untrue, it doesn't validate the reasons for disbelieving her."

Under this logic, Atticus Finch was the villain in "To Kill a Mockingbird." After all, how dare he question the rape allegations of a victimized woman and defend Tom Robinson?

But for the left, it's narrative first, facts second.

The same holds true regarding allegations made by HBO star Lena Dunham, who wrote of her own alleged rape at the hands of an Oberlin "college Republican" named Barry. When it turned out that Barry, a readily identifiable person from Dunham's days at Oberlin, did not rape her, the media largely went silent; Dunham still has not spoken on the issue.

Narrative first. Facts second.

Here is the reality: All decent human beings believe that rape is evil. They also believe that false allegations of rape are wrong. These two positions are not mutually exclusive. They complement one another. False rape allegations do actual rape victims a tremendous disservice: to lump in false accusations of rape with true accusations of rape makes people more skeptical of rape victims generally, a horrible result. Rape should be taken seriously; rape accusations should be taken seriously. That means taking factual questions seriously, not merely throwing the word "rape" around casually, without evidence, and without regard for truth.

The Suicidal Hashtags of the West

December 17, 2014

On Monday, Australian police stormed the Lindt Chocolate Cafe in Sydney, where an Islamist terrorist named Man Haron Monis had taken dozens of hostages and held them for 17 hours. Three people were killed, including Monis, and several others were wounded. Monis, an Iranian immigrant, had a long criminal record, including 40 charges for indecent and sexual assault, as well as an outstanding charge for accessory to murder in the killing of his ex-wife. Before his death, Monis requested an ISIS flag, and forced hostages to hold up the so-called Shahada flag, which proclaims in Arabic, "There Is No God But Allah, and Muhammad Is His Messenger."

In response to this Islamist terror attack on a civilian hub in the center of their city, Australians all over the country took action: They tweeted with the hashtag #illridewithyou. This hashtag came from the mind of one Rachel Jacobs, who witnessed a Muslim woman removing her hijab on the local train after the news of the hostage situation broke. Jacobs tweeted, "I ran after her at the train station. I said 'put it back on. I'll walk with u'. She started to cry and hugged me for about a minute -- then walked off alone." Soon, the hashtag had been launched, and quickly trended globally.

Australia's race discrimination commissioner, Tim Soutphommasane, added, "Let's not allow fear, hatred and division to triumph."

Yes, Australia has a race commissioner, but nobody who thinks it's a bad idea to let Islamist fanatics immigrate, or to keep those same Islamist fanatics in jail after they're charged in the stabbing of their ex-wives.

Priorities!

Never mind that nobody had said a word to the woman in the hijab -- pre-emptive anti-Islamophobia was the first response to an Islamist taking Western hostages in a Western capital.

Across the globe, in the United States, two dueling hashtags debated the relative guilt of American law enforcement. After New York City man Eric Garner resisted arrest, and then died thanks to his pre-existing health conditions after being taken down by police, the hashtag #ICantBreathe went viral. That hashtag fought for prominence with one dedicated to Michael Brown, the 18-year-old black man who was shot to death after attempting to take a gun from a police officer and charging the police officer: #HandsUpDontShoot. Never mind that the first hashtag was taken wildly out of context -- Garner was not choked to death -- and that the second was completely fictitious -- autopsy showed Brown did not have his hands up when he was shot.

These hashtags aren't just the work of lazy activists with nothing better to do. They're signifiers of a suicidal west that believes it bears bloodguilt. No real allegations of Islamophobia or racism are necessary -- those can be assumed. We immediately go into preliminary disassociation mode, attempting to demonstrate to our friends and neighbors that while our civilization may be Islamophobic and racist, we are not. After all, we even tweeted using the day's popular hashtag!

Here's the problem: Islamists don't care about hashtags when they can take hostages and earn the sympathetic hashtags of others. Those who resist law enforcement or attack police officers outright are happy to do so when they become causes celebre, no matter what they do wrong.

The West has its evils. There are instances of racism and Islamophobia. Nobody with a brain would deny that. But to slander the West with a sort of communal guilt for an Original Sin, even as the West is under fire from those who would seek to destroy its civilizational foundations, is nothing less than barbaric.

Jeb Bush Vs. Ted Cruz

December 24, 2014

Last week, former Florida Governor Jeb Bush announced his intention to "actively explore" a run for president. That announcement spurred spasms of joy in some segments of the Republican Party who have been itching for an effective counter to the enthusiasm of the grassroots right. Those Republicans -- largely coastal donors who scorn social conservatives as rubes, and shun the supposed fiscal extremism of the tea party -- have been searching for a candidate who will buck the base on immigration, who doesn't mind hand-in-glove corporatism, and who, most of all, feels the same way they do about the grassroots.

And Jeb Bush promises to fulfill all these criteria. He says he feels "a little out of step with my party" on immigration and recently said that illegal immigration wasn't a "felony" but an "act of love"; his support for Common Core has more than a whiff of cronyism to it; just weeks ago, he told The Wall Street Journal that he would be willing to "lose the primary to win the general without violating [his] principles."

This is the dirty secret of the modern Republican Party: For all the talk about grassroots exasperation with the Republican elites, it is the Republican elites who despise the grassroots. Republican elites do not believe in the dismantling of the welfare state; they believe in its maintenance. They do not believe in the unsophisticated free marketeering of the tea party; they believe in a strong government hand on the economic tiller, so long as that hand is benevolent toward their friends. They do not believe in small government; they believe in large government that serves their ends. If given the choice, a few would even select Hillary Clinton as president over Texas Senator Ted Cruz.

They stake their claim to leadership of the Republican Party on the nonsensical notion that they have a record of victory. Pointing to the dramatic implosions of candidates like Delaware's Christine O'Donnell, who primaried Mike Castle only to be blown out by Chris Coons in her Senatorial race, and Sharron Angle, who lost to Senate Majority Leader Harry Reid, establishment Republicans state that they -- and only they -- know how to win elections. They abide by "The Price Is Right" strategy for electoral victory: campaign just to the right of the Democratic candidate in the hopes that you will win everyone to that candidate's right. The magical middle, in this view, is where victory lies.

And so, in 2008, in an election in which Americans resonated to the theme of war weariness, Republicans establishment geniuses touted a Senator most famous for his foreign policy interventionism. In 2012, coming off an election in which Republicans won a stunning victory thanks to popular hatred of Obamacare, Republicans ran the only man in America outside of Barack Obama to implement Obamacare. Grassroots conservatives reluctantly went along with these nominees after failing to unify around an alternative.

Now, in 2016, when Americans have reacted with outrage to President Obama's executive amnesty, and when Hillary Clinton is likely to be the Democratic nominee, establishment Republicans want to run a man whose most famous position is warmth for illegal immigration and is famously chummy with the Clintons (he gave Hillary an award in 2013 for public service).

Why nominate this man? The most common explanation: His widely perceived alternative, grassroots favorite, Ted Cruz, cannot win. Cruz, establishment Republicans say, polarizes instead of unifying; he alienates rather than attracting. But that notion springs, once again, from "The Price Is Right" strategy: If the middle voter is your target, Cruz isn't your man. But the middle voter was Mitt Romney's target in 2012, and he got him -- Romney won independents 50-45, but lost the election by five million votes. The middle voter was John McCain's target, too -- so much so that

McCain considered naming Democratic Senator Joe Lieberman as his running mate. He lost decisively, too.

Will Ted Cruz lose more decisively than either of his predecessors? That's a possibility. But margin of loss is significantly less important than the direction of the political narrative. Party insiders see the 1964 nomination of right-wing Barry Goldwater as a massive defeat. Those outside the party infrastructure see it for what it was: a ground shift in Republican politics that led to the rise of Ronald Reagan. Better to nominate someone who will change the conversation and lose than someone who will reinforce that the parties stand for the same tired politics of failure.

Or, perhaps, Cruz doesn't lose at all. Perhaps it turns out that voters are driven by vision and passion rather than bromides from the Yorks and Lancasters of American politics. Perhaps Ted Cruz, or someone like him, actually animates people rather than treating them like widgets to be manipulated by those born to the purple. Perhaps politics isn't "The Price Is Right."

Return of the 1960s

December 31, 2014

In 2007, then-Senator Barack Obama signified that he represented a sea-change in the nature of American politics. Obama proclaimed that as a member of the younger generation -- born in 1961, at the tail end of the baby boom -- he no longer wanted to participate in the stale and tired politics of the 1960s. Instead, he wanted to thrust America forward into a "different kind of politics," one beyond the "psychodrama of the baby-boom generation -- a tale rooted in old grudges and revenge plots hatched on a handful of college campuses long ago -- played out on the national stage."

Like most of what President Obama said, this turned out to be a lie. President Obama isn't merely a reflection of 1960s politics. He represents a return to those ugly politics: the nastiness of anti-cop sentiment, the divisiveness of generalized anti-Western foreign policy, the idiocy of a war between the sexes and against the exclusivity of the traditional family structure. President Obama isn't representative of a new breed. He is the child of the 1960s politics he once claimed to abhor.

Those politics, at least, had the excuse of an uglier America -- one fresh with the wounds of Jim Crow, the sins of sexism, the controversy of Vietnam. Today's 1960s reruns seem wildly out of context. But that's the point: For the radicals of the 1960s, just as for the establishment Obamaites of today, context simply does not matter. When you are attempting to craft utopia, context is irrelevant -- and human beings become either tools or obstacles toward the creation of that utopia. The vision never changes. Only the calendar does.

And so we're watching racial tensions on a scale unseen since the 1970s play out across America -- with the support of the political establishment. The images of police officers turning their backs on New York Mayor Bill De Blasio mirror the images of officers booing New York Mayor John Lindsay in 1972 at the funeral of Officer Rocco Laurie. The images of rioters burning down Ferguson mirror the images of rioters burning down Detroit in 1967. Never mind that America of 2014 is not the America of 1967 or 1972 -- if Obama and his allies have to recreate that chaotic era to forward their own political ends, they will.

We're watching the foreign policy of the hard-left McGovernites re-establish itself, this time from the Oval Office. The images of Senator Dianne Feinstein, D-Calif., railing against the CIA on the floor of the Senate over the CIA's use of enhanced interrogation techniques mirror the images of Senator Mark Hatfield, R-Ore., railing against the American military in the aftermath of the Winter Soldier hearings of 1971. The images of the Yazidis starving on mountaintops in Iraq mirror the images of Vietnamese rushing onto boats to escape the horrors of the communists in the aftermath of the Vietnam War.

We're watching the divisive domestic politics of the social radicals reassert themselves. The images of failed Texas gubernatorial candidate Wendy Davis standing in pink sneakers to list the glories of late-term abortion mirror the images of Gloria Steinem blathering about "reproductive freedom" in 1971. The images of Nancy Pelosi touting freedom from "job lock" thanks to Obamacare mirror the images of President Johnson effectively doing the same thanks to the war on poverty.

President Obama and his ilk quest for a return to hopier, changier times -- times like the 1960s. And so they will take us all back to the future. Sadly, our future will then be no more than a reversion to insanity of our past.

Book Two

Evil In America

Self-Love vs. Self-Betterment

January 7, 2015

On Dec. 31, as 2014 began to fade into the past, New York Times columnist Charles Blow tweeted out some deep thoughts from his new book, "Fire In My Bones." "Daring to step into oneself is the bravest, strangest, most natural, most terrifying thing a person can do," Blow wrote regarding his acknowledgement of his own bisexuality, "because when you cease to wrap yourself in artifice you are naked, and when you are naked you are vulnerable. But vulnerability is the leading edge of truth. Being willing to sacrifice a false life is the only way to live a true one." He then added, "It takes more courage to be yourself than it does to do almost anything else. Being yourself, your whole self, without compromise or apology, is a revolutionary act!"

This line of thought doesn't originate with Blow, of course. Jean-Jacques Rousseau spoke similarly; his concept of amour de soi suggested that self-love—that is, love for oneself without reference to outside sources—was the highest form of happiness, and that only amour de soi could drive good action.

This is nonsense; it always was nonsense; it always will be nonsense. No doubt self-destructive tendencies can harm both the individual and society more broadly. But conversely, self-love as the highest form of bravery undermines the notion of objective good and self-sacrifice in pursuit of that objective good. If being yourself is the highest aspiration for mankind, then anyone who stands between you and your own self-regard becomes an enemy. Society must be shifted on its ear to accommodate your perception of yourself.

And so we enter the backwards world in which individual self-perception trumps objective reality. To pick a fringe example, if a fully biological man perceives himself to be a woman, all of society must hereby acknowledge him as a woman, a nonsensical proposition. Logically speaking, a man cannot declare himself a woman without a point of internal reference; it makes no more sense to do this than to declare oneself a purple-headed space alien, given that human beings have no idea what it like to be a purple-headed space alien without being one. All of society is expected to flout reality in order to preserve the self-love of the mentally ill.

More problematic, all of society is expected to adjust to the expected returns self-love brings. If we all believe ourselves geniuses, we expect to be compensated as such. If society fails to comprehend our genius, that is society's fault. To borrow from Jim Croce, we all end up with the steadily depressing, low down, mind messing, working at the car wash blues. That is, until we call on government to recognize that we are each an undiscovered Howard Hughes.

Being comfortable with oneself is not bravery. If it means ignoring the call of a higher purpose, it is cowardice. There are millions of American students who are comfortable with their level of educational and intellectual achievement. That's why they're falling behind their compatriots in other industrialized countries. There are millions of Americans perfectly comfortable with abandoning their children, or murdering their unborn children. That does not make their action right, or public policy designed to stop such action wrong.

Self-betterment used to be the motto of Western civilization. That's because Western civilization used to be based on the premise that man is more than animal. But in freeing man from the shackles of humanity, we have achieved just what Rousseau sought. And so we may yet live like animals again, perhaps happy in the bravery of our amour de soi, but somewhat less happy in the failure of humanity's truly noble aspirations.

Charlie Hebdo Lost

January 14, 2015

The West has the capacity to win a war on radical Islam. But it won't.

It won't because the West is too busy soul-searching to defend its core values. Western leaders mouth slogans about #JeSuisCharlie in the aftermath of the murder of 12 at the Charlie Hebdo headquarters, but they don't mean it; they suggest that the world stands united against radical Islamic terror even as they ignore the bullet-ridden bodies of four at a kosher supermarket in Paris.

The proof: Look at the list of those who attended Sunday's unity march in Paris.

The usual suspects showed up, except for President Obama, who was presumably too busy golfing or watching football. So, too, did several leaders explicitly connected with radical Islam and terrorism.

Palestinian Authority President Mahmoud Abbas, showed up to tell the French people, "Human life is sacred and God has created us all." But that's not what he tells his constituents. Last week, Al-Asima, a publication distributed by the Palestinian Authority, celebrated the murderers of five people at a synagogue in Jerusalem. Abbas routinely meets with terrorists who are released from prison after murdering Jews. As Hamas rained rockets down on Israel, Abbas justified it, telling the United Nations that Palestinians had the "legitimate right to resist this colonial, racist Israeli occupation."

But those are just dead Jews, so welcome to France!

Then there's Turkish Prime Minister Ahmet Davutoglu, who represents a regime that has provided material support to Hamas, including the infamous terror flotilla. Turkey's leader, Recep Tayyip Erdogan, says that the very term "moderate Islam" is "very ugly, it is offensive and an insult to our religion. There is no moderate or immoderate Islam. Islam is Islam and that's it." Turkey's refusal to fight ISIS has led to the rise of that terror group as well.

Sheikh Abdullah bin Zayed al-Nahyan of the United Arab Emirates came to Paris as well. Harvard University rejected Al-Nahyan's $2.5 million donation in 2004 after it emerged that al-Nahyan was associated with a think tank that pushed anti-American and anti-Semitic diatribes.

All three of these regimes, by the way, believe that blasphemy against Mohammed should be criminalized. Allowing them to march in honor of Charlie Hebdo demonstrates the moral idiocy of the West.

But the media hailed the march, nonetheless, as a ground shift in world relations. After all, so many leaders had linked arms in a pro forma tribute to free speech, it just had to mean something.

Except that it doesn't. It doesn't mean a damn thing. It means only that the West is too stupid or empty-hearted to stand up for its principles; we will welcome anyone to our club, even those who want to join the club only to burn it down.

That, in a nutshell, is the problem with the West's policy with regard to radical Islam. When I asked Islamic imam Anjem Choudary—a man who has essentially defended the Charlie Hebdo terrorists—why the West should allow him to live in Britain while attempting to tear down all of its values, he simply stated that he was born in England. He then added, "You can change your laws," and threatened that if no laws were changed to ban material like that of Charlie Hebdo, there would certainly be a "bloodbath."

And the West agrees. Anyone can join our free speech marches, our freedom of religion candlelight vigils—even people who would blow up both of them at the first available opportunity.

The Last Taboo

January 21, 2015

What happens when we run out of taboos?

The question arises thanks to a column in Salon.com from one Jenny Kutner, an assistant editor "focusing on sex, gender and feminism." This particular column focuses on an 18-year-old woman who is currently dating. That wouldn't be odd, except that she is dating her biological father. Apparently, this woman's father left her family when she was 4; when he came back into her life, she was 16. "It was so weird and confusing," she said. "I was seeing my dad for the first time in forever but it was also like, He's so good looking!"

Days later, they had sex. "We discussed whether it was wrong and then we kissed," the woman said. "And then we made out, and then we made love for the first time. That was when I lost my virginity."

Kutner, naturally, describes the activity as merely a manifestation of Genetic Sexual Attraction. She adds, "As sensational as the whole interview might seem (and, admittedly, as it is), it actually forces one to do some rigorous double-checking of one's own beliefs."

Why, exactly, would one double check one's own beliefs when faced with the reality of incest? Any normal society would immediately question the evil father, who abandoned his child, only to come back into her life and take advantage of her sexually. Any normal society would recognize the evil of a father having sex with his genetic offspring. Any normal society would place the onus on those arguing for incest to explain why society is bettered by normalization of incest, rather than placing the onus on the traditionally moral to explain why incest should remain taboo.

But we are not a normal society any longer. We are a society of love.

Love, we now believe, conquers all—including basic standards of morality. As Attorney General Eric Holder said this week in explaining why the Supreme Court should strike down traditional marriage laws, "It is time for our nation to take another critical step forward to ensure the fundamental equality of all Americans—no matter who they are, where they come from, or whom they love." Who are we to judge those who love one another? So long as they can always abort their damaged offspring; so long as the couple believes itself to be operating under standards of consent; so long as an incestuous relationship doesn't affect you directly, who are you to judge?

The normalization of incest does not spring from the normalization of homosexuality, of course. Both the normalization of incest and the normalization of homosexuality spring from the destruction of objective standards of morality in favor of validation of subjective feelings. Society is bettered by heterosexual marriage because man and woman can exclusively create and best raise children. The same is not true of any other form of relationship. But that doesn't matter, because radical relativism is our new standard.

And so we search for new taboos to break. Undoubtedly, the next standard will be normalization of younger and younger teens having sex with older partners. After that, we will see polygamy.

Eventually, the only true taboo left will be responsibility. But that's a taboo no one will be willing to violate, given the social stigma attached. Better to live free, basking in the glow of transgressive bravery. After all, if you're truly brave, you fight the system. And when there is no system, you fight the meaninglessness. And you lose.

Will Republicans Go the Way of the Whigs?

January 28, 2015

In 1856, the Whig Party ran former president Millard Fillmore for president of the United States. Fillmore had last run in 1852; he'd been denied the nomination as the party fell apart over the issue of slavery. In an attempt to bring the party back together that year, the party nominated General Winfield Scott, who promptly imploded in the general election against Democrat Franklin Pierce. "We are slain!" shouted Representative Lewis D. Campbell of Ohio. "The party is dead, dead, dead!" Free Soiler Charles Sumner wrote, "Now is the time for a new organization. Out of this chaos the party of freedom must arise."

Most of the Whig leaders thought this talk overwrought. They insisted that the party would live on. Senator William Seward of New York said, "No new party will arise, nor will any old one fall." Seward thought that if the party elided the slavery issue, it could hold together. But by the same token, without the slavery issue, there was truly no difference between the two parties. As future president Rutherford B. Hayes wrote, "The real grounds of difference upon important political questions no longer correspond with party lines. The progressive Whig is nearer in sentiment to the radical Democrat than the radical Democrat is to the 'fogy' of his own party; vice versa." The party had become a party of convenience rather than principle.

Between 1852 and 1856, as author William E. Gienapp discusses, the break came: Southern Whigs joined the pro-slavery Democrats, while northern Whigs joined the newly formed anti-slavery Republicans. In 1856, the Whig candidate won just one state, while the Republican candidate, John C. Fremont, carried 11 states. James Buchanan carried 19 states. By 1860, the Whigs no longer existed. Abraham Lincoln won the presidency with less than 40 percent of the vote.

This is what happens to parties that lose their reason for being: They disintegrate. The modern Republican Party may be in serious danger of falling into that trap. That's not because of the Republican constituency, which reflects, as it has since the 1980s, the three-pronged approach of fiscal conservatism, foreign policy hawkishness and social traditionalism. It's because the Republican political class seem to reject those unifying factors as divisive.

How else to explain the GOP House's decision last week, in the aftermath of a massive electoral sweep, to table a piece of legislation banning abortion after the 20th week of pregnancy? This is an issue upon which most Americans are united—the vast majority of Americans find late-term abortion morally abhorrent. And yet Representative Renee Ellmers, R-N.C., removed her name from the bill, stating, "We got into trouble last year" over issues like abortion. If Republicans won't stand together on such a basic moral issue, over what issues *will* they unite?

Certainly not illegal immigration, where Republicans divide from their base, pushing a softer approach to President Obama's executive amnesty. Certainly not foreign policy, where President Obama's devastation of the military has been met with Republican resistance but not Republican intransigence. Certainly not Obamacare, where Speaker of the House Boehner recently provided full funding for the last year.

The Republican higher-ups assure us, as Whig leaders did in 1852, that if Republicans nominate someone with name recognition, an old warhorse perhaps, the party can unify once again. Jeb Bush or Mitt Romney fill in for Winfield Scott. But just as Whigs were only able to win two presidential elections over the course of 23 years, both times with military heroes at the head, Republicans have won just one popular presidential election in the last 27 years, that time with a commander in chief incumbent during wartime.

Perhaps the Republican Party isn't dead. But Republican leaders would be wise to take a lesson from the Whigs if they hope to avoid their fate.

Anti-Vaccine Fanatics Kill

February 4, 2015

This week, controversy broke out over whether state governments have the power to require parents to have their children vaccinated. New Jersey Governor Chris Christie, no stranger to compelling his citizens to stay off the roads during blizzards, announced that he had some sympathy for the anti-vaccination position: "I also understand that parents need to have some measure of choice in things as well. So that's the balance the government has to decide." Kentucky Senator Rand Paul doubled down on Christie's remarks, stating, "I have heard of many tragic cases of walking, talking, normal children who wound up with profound mental orders after vaccines. ...The state doesn't own your children."

Christie and Paul aren't the only politicians sympathizing with anti-vaccination fanatics; in 2008, then-Senator Barack Obama repeated widely debunked claims of links between autism and vaccination. Skepticism of vaccination crosses party lines, unfortunately—although the most organized anti-vaccination resistance comes from the New Agey left in places like Santa Monica and Marin County, who worry more about infinitesimal amounts of formaldehyde in vaccines than about death by polio.

Unsurprisingly, older Americans believe that children should be vaccinated against diseases like measles, mumps and whopping cough, by a 73 percent to 21 percent margin. Americans 18-29, by contrast, believe by a 43 percent to 42 percent plurality that government should not mandate such vaccinations.

That's because young people don't remember a time when such diseases claimed lives. They don't remember a time when the vast majority of Americans weren't vaccinated. Older people do. Many of them lost loved ones to polio and measles and mumps and rubella. In 1952, over 3,000 Americans died of polio and well over 21,000 were left with mild or severe paralysis. Thanks to Dr. Jonas Salk's vaccine, there have been zero cases of natural polio in the United States since 1979.

The same is true of measles. According to Dr. Mark Papania of the Centers for Disease Control and Prevention, more than 90 percent of Americans suffered from the measles by age 15 before widespread vaccination beginning in 1962. From 1956 to 1960, he reports, "an average of 542,000 cases were reported annually." That included 450 deaths per year, as well as 150,000 cases of respiratory complications and 4,000 cases of consequent encephalitis per year, many of which resulted in later death. Then mandatory vaccination kicked in. Until a major upswing in 2014, we averaged less than 100 cases of measles per year in the United States since 2000.

The point of mandatory vaccinations is not merely to protect those who are vaccinated. When it comes to measles, mumps and rubella, for example, children cannot be vaccinated until 1 year of age. The only way to prevent them from getting diseases is to ensure that those who surround them do not have those diseases. The same is true for children with diseases like leukemia, as well as pregnant women. Herd immunity is designed to protect third parties.

But Americans have short memories and enormous confidence in junk science. Parents will ignore vaccinations but ensure that their kids are stocked up with the latest homeopathic remedies, Kabbalah bracelets and crystals. St. John's wort, red string and crystals all existed before 1962. They didn't stop the measles. Vaccination did.

That doesn't mean that all vaccinations should be compulsory, of course. There are certain diseases that can only be transmitted by behavior, like HPV. There are others that are too varied for effective herd vaccination, like the flu shot. But when it comes to measles and mumps and rubella and polio, your right to be free of vaccination—and your right to be a dope with the health of your child because you believe Jenny McCarthy's idiocy—ends where my child's right to live begins.

Shut Up, Because the Crusades

February 11, 2015

This week, President Obama spoke at the National Prayer Breakfast, where he proceeded to inform an audience of Christians that they ought not judge radical Muslims currently engaged in beheading journalists, defenestrating gays, crucifying children, and engaging in mass rape of women. Why, pray tell, should Christians remain silent? Because, Obama informed them with Ivy League pride, "Unless we get on our high horse and think that this is unique to some other place, remember that during the Crusades and Inquisition, people committed terrible deeds in the name of Christ. In our home country, slavery and Jim Crow all too often was justified in the name of Christ. So it is not unique to one group or one religion."

At some point in our collective history, our ancestors engaged in tribal warfare and cannibalized their fallen enemies. So shut up about the Nazis, you hypocrites.

Forget Obama's historical ignorance, if you can, for just a moment. Forget that the Crusades, for all their brutality and horror, were a response to Islamic aggression; forget that the Inquisition was an attempt to systematize legal punishment for anti-Christian activity rather than leaving it to the heated mob; forget that all abolitionist leaders were devout Christians; forget that hundreds of thousands of Christians marched to their deaths during the Civil War singing the words "as He died to make men holy, so we die to make men free"; forget that the chief leaders of the civil rights movement were Christian leaders like Reverend Martin Luther King Jr.

Focus instead on the fact that President Obama felt the necessity to defend radical Islam at all. Why defend radical Islam? What is the point?

Obama defends radical Islam because he does not think in terms of ideology, but in terms of power dynamics. If radical Muslims commit terror, it is because they feel helpless and hopeless. If they feel helpless and hopeless, it is because Westerners made them feel that way. If Westerners made them feel that way, it is because Western ideology must be exploitative and evil.

In other words, Obama cites the Crusades as justification for shutting Christians up because the Crusades caused all of this. If Christians had just kept their pieholes shut several thousand years ago, none of this would have happened. Obama's ignorant and bigoted gloss on Christian history isn't a throwaway line: it's the centerpiece of his philosophy. Radical Islam isn't the problem because Christianity is. And we know that Christianity is the problem because radical Islam is violent. In this skewed version of reality, modern Christianity's fantastic record is a direct outgrowth of its disreputable past.

Obama extends this bizarre philosophy to every part of life. Those who murder Jews in Israel aren't motivated by radical Islam: They were exploited by those evil, non-murdering Jews. Those who riot in Ferguson aren't motivated by a corrupt ideology of victimhood: They were exploited long ago by those who cower in their stores, trying to prevent the looting. Those who sire children they abandon, drop out of school and refuse to hold down jobs aren't predictable refuse of a broken philosophy: They are victims of those who get married, stay in school and hold down jobs. Success is the ultimate indicator that your philosophy is evil. Failure is the ultimate indicator that you are a victim, regardless of your ideology.

Obama's philosophy is the philosophy of failure. No wonder radical Islam holds a cherished place in his heart, while Judeo-Christian religion find itself in his doghouse.

Is Israel the Problem, or Are Jews the Problem?

February 18, 2015

In the aftermath of the killing of a man at a Copenhagen synagogue by a member of the Religion of Peace, Israeli Prime Minister Benjamin Netanyahu said, "This wave of attacks is expected to continue. Jews deserve security in every country, but we say to our Jewish brothers and sisters, Israel is your home." Russian emigre Natan Sharansky echoed Netanyahu's call, stating, "There is no future for Jews in western Europe."

In response, European leaders shouted down Netanyahu. "We know there are doubts, questions across the community," said French President Francois Hollande, who was elected with in excess of 93 percent of the Muslim vote. "I will not just let what was said in Israel pass, leading people to believe that Jews no longer have a place in Europe and France, in particular." The same week, Jewish tombstones were spray-painted by the hundreds in eastern France.

But undoubtedly, European anti-Semites will now claim that Netanyahu's comments simply demonstrate *why* Europe must force out its Jews: because Israel is just so awful. That, at least, is what a German court in the city of Wuppertal concluded after convicting two German Palestinians of setting fire to a synagogue. The Wuppertal court stated that the men were simply attempting to bring "attention to the Gaza conflict." In other words, Jews are fair game because of Israel.

But it's precisely the reverse that is true: Israel is fair game because it is Jewish. This is the dirty little secret of anti-Israel policy: It is almost entirely anti-Semitic policy. That is why Muslims attack Jewish synagogues in Paris during the Gaza war: because

Israel is a stand-in for the Jews, not the other way around. Were Israel a Muslim country, the rest of the world would see it as a beacon of light and hope for the future of an entire religion. Because it is Jewish, Muslims target it for destruction, and the rest of the world tut-tuts Israel's nasty habit of attempting to survive. The extra-American world hates Israel because it is Jewish. It does not hate Jews because of Israel. Israel is merely a convenient excuse.

Ironically, radical Muslims, in targeting Jews throughout the world, reinforce the necessity of a state of Israel. Their argument seems to be that Israel is an unnecessary Jewish nationalist cancer; to prove that argument, they suggest killing Jews all over the planet, leaving no place safe for Jews except for Israel.

And so Jews go to Israel by the droves. European governments can rip Netanyahu all they want for his supposedly brusque dismissal of European tolerance, but that supposed tolerance means less and less when Swedish Jews abandon entire cities as the authorities make way for radical Muslims. European governments can condemn the Gaza war, but Jews see that war for what it was: an exercise in Jewish self-preservation, with the Europeans once again attempting to prevent such self-preservation.

Unlike the Europeans, Americans continue to side with Israel because America is founded on Judeo-Christian principles. America embraces Judaism, and so it embraces Israel, not the other way around. The formula is simple: Love Jews; love Israel. Hate Jews; hate Israel. Opposing Israeli action may not be anti-Semitism, but it sure does have a funny habit of backing the agenda of anti-Semites.

Why Rudy and Walker Were Right

February 25, 2015

This week, the media broke news that former New York Mayor Rudy Giuliani said, at an event attended by prospective Republican presidential candidate Wisconsin Governor Scott Walker, that he does not believe President Barack Obama "loves America." This isn't news. Barack Obama doesn't love free enterprise, believes founding philosophy was fatally flawed and sees the American people as rubes with antiquated religious and racist tendencies. Sure, we can all agree that Obama likely loves America's scenery; perhaps he loves America, but doesn't like her very much. But that's not what Giuliani was talking about, and everyone knows it.

But in any case, Giuliani wasn't the media's true target. The true target was Walker.

Using Giuliani's comments as a springboard, media members went hunting for a faux pas from Walker. They asked him whether he thinks Obama loves America; Walker responded, quite rightly, "You should ask the president what he thinks about America. I've never asked him so I don't know." They asked him whether he believed Obama was a Christian; Walker answered, "I don't know. ... You've asked me to make statements about people that I haven't had a conversation with about that."

For the media, this represented a "gotcha" moment. Anyone who doubts President Obama's love of country must be pilloried as cruel and inhumane. Anyone who doubts the religious sincerity of a man who invoked Christianity to support lies about his support for traditional marriage, a man who recently compared Christian history with the acts of ISIS, must be publicly scourged.

Naturally, many Republicans have eagerly jumped on the bandwagon. George F. Will said that all Republicans should say that Obama is a patriot (a strategy that worked brilliantly for John McCain in 2008). Matt Lewis of The Daily Beast wrote that no candidate should question anyone's patriotism or stated faith. The premise seems to be that failing to demonstrate such goodwill touches off media conflagrations that damage conservatives overall. This misses the point.

Democrats have for years been questioning the decency of Republicans as human beings. During the Obamacare rollout, President Obama accused Republicans of wanting to deprive people of healthcare; he openly accused President George W. Bush of being "unpatriotic" for raising the national debt. House Minority Leader Nancy Pelosi said that Republicans are "indifferent" to hungry and poor children. Anyone who opposes any aspect of President Obama's agenda has been deemed a racist.

The point here is not the media's double standard, which is egregious but unchangeable. The point is that this perception of Republicans has pervaded the public arena. Republicans' fundamental burden is not explaining to the American people that Democrats are great people, but wrong on policy. Their great burden is overcoming the generalized perception that they are money-grubbing Snidely Whiplashes bent on strapping widows and orphans to the train tracks.

You cannot overcome that perception by ardently pleading that the very folks who call you racist, sexist, homophobic bigots are well-intentioned but incompetent. If someone calls you a racist, and you respond by stating that they are a reasonable human being with policy differences, you grant their premise: A reasonable person has called you a racist, which means it is reasonable to call you racist. You lose.

And Republicans have been losing, at least in large part, because they grant the fundamental premise of the left: Democrats are well-meaning, even when they are wrong, and Republicans have evil intentions, even when they are right. That is a recipe for disaster in a country where intentions matter more than actions.

The Hillary Cover-Up and the End of Democracy

March 4, 2015

On Monday, The New York Times reported that former Secretary of State Hillary Clinton never—not once—used her official State Department email address for her official communications. Instead, she utilized a private email account, effectively protecting her emails from public scrutiny. The Washington Post then broke the news that Hillary had registered her email address the same day her confirmation hearings for secretary of state began. In other words, Hillary knew she would be secretary of state conducting official business, and coincidentally opened a private email account at the same time to guard her from Freedom of Information Act requests.

Sure, Hillary Clinton has a nasty history with crucial documents going missing—she is the only first lady in American history fingerprinted by the FBI, and the FBI found missing documents with her fingerprints on them in the White House personal quarters. But the media SuperFriends quickly activated to protect Hillary. Glenn Thrush of Politico tweeted that Hillary must have relied on incompetent staffers and lawyers. Ron Fournier of National Journal tut-tutted that this made her "no better" than Republicans. Of course, the media also ignored Saudi Arabia, the United Arab Emirates, Qatar and Oman handing millions to the Clinton charity just before Hillary's big run.

Clinton is hardly the first Obama administration official to utilize a private email account to shield herself. Lisa Jackson of the Environmental Protection Agency used a private email address under the name "Richard Windsor" to conduct official business. According to Vice News' Jason Leopold, the Department of Defense told him that they would not release any emails from former Defense Secretary Chuck Hagel, since "SecDef does not maintain an official email account." Other Obama administration officials using unofficial email accounts include former Health and Human Services Secretary Kathleen Sebelius and Donald Berwick, the former head of the Centers for Medicare and Medicaid Services.

Welcome to the most transparent administration in American history, where the Federal Communications Commission can regulate the internet and keep those regulations secret before a vote, where top government officials can deliberately hide their emails from the public, but where your health records, income and emails are all government business.

The public and private spheres have now been completely reversed. The federal government can punish its own employees for enforcing federal immigration law; if you oppose this, you are a racist, but if you hire an illegal immigrant, you will be fined or imprisoned. The feds can monitor your electronic metadata, but they can hide their own correspondence from records requests. After all, they are our betters, and we must kneel before Zod.

What possible violations of the Constitutional system will Americans actually fight? The list of possibilities grows short. Reports emerged this week suggesting that President Obama will consider banning bullets by executive order, effectively castrating the Second Amendment by fiat. Shrug. The Obama White House announced this week that Obama was "very interested" in unilaterally raising taxes. Shrug.

Democracies die not with a whimper or a bang but with a shrug. When we don't care enough about the system to stop its breakdown—when we're happy with our dictators so long as we agree with them—the constitutional order collapses. But so what? By electing Hillary Clinton the presidency, we'll strike a blow against non-existent generalized sexism in American society. And that's far more important than having an answerable, accountable government.

Is Being Gay a Choice?

March 10, 2015

Last week, Dr. Ben Carson stepped onto a political mine—really, jumped onto it with both feet—when he answered a question from CNN's Chris Cuomo about the nature of homosexuality. "You think being gay is a choice?" Cuomo asked Carson, after Carson rightly stated that being black and being gay are two very different phenomena. "Absolutely," replied Carson. He then went on to explain, "A lot of people who go into prison straight go into prison straight—and when they come out, they're gay."

Carson's unstated line of reasoning is perfectly logical. When Cuomo asked Carson whether he thinks "being gay is a choice," Carson interpreted that question to mean: "Is homosexual behavior a choice." To that, the answer is obviously yes, since *all* non-reflexive behavior is essentially a choice. Cuomo, however, took his question to mean: "Is homosexual inclination a choice." To that, the answer is obviously no—it is either a byproduct of biology or environment. Feelings, in other words, are not choices; it is possible that some feelings can be shaped by behavior, but as a general rule, feelings are not chosen. Behaviors, however, are chosen. Thus, being black—a non-behavioral characteristic—is not like being gay or being straight, in the sense that one cannot choose not to be black, while one chooses one's own sexual behavior.

The divide between Carson's understanding of "being gay" and Cuomo's understanding of the same term demonstrates the rhetorical slight-of-hand that has marked the gay rights movement. By conflating behavior with feeling, and calling it all "orientation," homosexual advocates have conflated biology with choice, and called it all biology.

And even they know that such conflation is a lie.

Take, for example, supposed gay spokesperson Dan Savage. He understands that homosexual behavior is a choice. He compared being gay to being religious: "Faith—religious belief—is not an immutable characteristic." He also compared being gay to "military service and marital status." This is logically correct. But Savage refused to acknowledge the implications of this line of thought, because doing so would force him to recognize that society often discriminates between those behaviors it finds productive and those it finds unproductive in terms of the law (military service, for example, is a protected class because we all benefit from the military service of others; being a member of Code Pink is not protected, because we do not all benefit from someone's membership in Code Pink). Instead, Savage fell back on his trademark vulgarity, telling Dr. Carson to "suck my d---." "If being gay is a choice, prove it," wrote Savage. "Choose it. Choose to be gay yourself."

That is an insipid argument; were the shoe on the other foot, Savage would have to demonstrate that being gay is involuntary by engaging in sexual behavior with every male he meets. Given his prior solicitation of Rick Santorum, Mike Huckabee, and Herman Cain, that may well be his desire, but it's a rotten argument overall.

But arguments no longer matter. Logic no longer matters. Feelings matter. We intuitively understand that behavior defines us rather than feeling; no one would label a vegetarian a person who deplores meat-eating but chows down on steak every night. But when it comes to sexual behavior, we look to get ourselves off the hook: All sexual behavior is involuntary, so how can we be expected to make decisions about it? Hence the left's absurd lie during the Clinton era that everyone lies about sex; hence the asinine notion that chastity until marriage is an impossibility; hence the morally blind belief that societal pressure for sexual morality is discriminatory in the same sense that racism is discriminatory.

The result: No honest discussion can be had about the extent of human choice, the limits of human choice, and our own preferences among the choices human beings make. We are mere animals, forced by our firing neurons to act on each and every impulse. We have no choice. And those who say we do ought to perform oral sex on us.

The Charmless Hillary Juggernaut

March 18, 2015

Hillary Clinton is not a pleasant human being, by all available evidence. She does not convince; she browbeats. She does not discuss; she lectures. Her laugh issues mechanically from her mouth, resonating with a close-but-not-quite verisimilitude that occupies the space known as the uncanny valley. If anyone were to kidnap Hillary Clinton and replace her with a robot of Hillary Clinton, it would take a short circuit for America to realize it. Her campaign slogan should be: "Remarkably Lifelike!"

All of which makes her undeclared candidacy so much more awkward than that of others. Nobody quite knows why Hillary is running, other than that she feels she is owed the presidency based on her rough life growing up rich in Chicago, attending Wellesley and Yale Law before settling down as first lady of Arkansas and then first lady of the United States and then senator and secretary of state. Even Hillary doesn't seem to know. The runup to her campaign has been a prolonged shrug.

Which is why she is now trotting out the children.

First, Hillary's Stand With Hillary super PAC attempted to manufacture a grassroots feel for Hillary's campaign, issuing a faux country song titled "Stand With Hillary," and bearing these incredible lyrics: "Now it's 2016, and this time I'm a thinkin' guys, put your boots on and let's smash this ceiling." The song adds, "I've been thinking about one great lady, like the women in my life. She's a mother, a daughter, and through it all, she's a loving wife." A loving wife might be a bit of a stretch. But then again, so is a country song with men crushing the glass ceiling on behalf of an Ivy League elitist.

That song, naturally, flopped.

And the Hillary machine sprang back into action. A second pro-Hillary super PAC titled BillForFirstLady2016.com released an ad produced by Luke Montgomery, the same filmmaker who created a video featuring young girls dropping the f-bomb regarding supposed pay inequality. This ad features young girls wearing flag spandex and running down the street, urging Hillary to run (get it? Get it? GET IT?).

These girls then speak into camera and tick off five supposed reasons why people should vote for Hillary: to inspire young girls to overcome serious challenges like growing up female in the most female-friendly society in human history; to fight for pay equality by electing a woman who pays her female staffers significantly less than male staffers ("in the USA, having a vajayjay shouldn't mean less pay!" shouts one overproduced, irritating tot); to preserve abortion, which prepubescent girls desperately need; to show the world that female equality is a value, which we will presumably show by electing a woman who takes money from the world's most anti-female regimes; and finally, Bill Clinton will be first lady and "rock the dress."

The ad concludes with a man wearing a Bill Clinton mask, red heels, and a red dress. This, presumably, marks the first time that Bill Clinton has been in a dress that is his own.

If this feels strained, that's because it is. It is condescending, ridiculous, and—naturally—childish. But the charmless juggernaut rolls on, driven by puerile worship, empty bromides and a heaping helping of entitlement.

The Secret Life of Barack Obama

March 25, 2015

There is a unicorn lair in North Korea. We know this because the Dear Leader of North Korea, Kim Jung Un, tells us so. According to the official Korean Central News Agency, archaeologists have "recently reconfirmed" the existence of the unicorn lair dating back to the Koryo Kingdom (918-1392).

President Obama has his own unicorn lair. It is the world as it exists inside his head, Walter Mitty-style. In no way does this world resemble reality; it is a bizarre fantasyland of Obama's own construction, in which he is all-powerful, all-knowing and always right. It is a world in which his foreign policy predictions come true, in which his policies are successful, in which the flaming world he has helped create sparkles rather than burns.

In President Obama's world, Iran is not a threat, but an ally. Iran, in this world, is not an Islamic dictatorship, but a rational actor simply demanding the global respect to which it is entitled. The Ayatollah Khamenei's public statements of "Death to America" constitute a rhetorical love tap, designed for a "domestic political audience"—presumably an audience to whom the ayatollahs must answer, despite the lack of real elections in Iran for well over three decades. Iran's repeated statements that it intends to wipe Israel from the map simply show that Iran requires more concessions, not less. Iran's open suggestion that snap nuclear inspections be ruled out of negotiations show it is untrusting, not untrustworthy. Iran's expansionist policies in Iraq, Syria, Lebanon and Yemen are all growing pains that can be eased by Western kowtowing.

In fact, in President Obama's world, Yemen is a shining example of American foreign policy at work. Just months ago, Obama used

Yemen as his paradigm of functional anti-terrorism; two days ago, Obama's press secretary, Josh Earnest, said that Yemen "did serve as a sort of template for the kind of strategy that we would employ to mitigate the threat from extremists around the world." Earnest claimed that the Obama administration's anti-terror policy in Yemen helped to "stabiliz[e] the country so extremists can't use it to plot against the West." Last month, the American embassy closed in Yemen, with its Marine guard evacuated without its weapons. Last week, the last American forces left the country, which has been plunged into full-scale civil war by the Iranian-backed Houthi militias.

But the real threat to global peace, in President Obama's world, lies with the quarrelsome Jews some 1,200 miles to the northwest. There, the democratic country of Israel has endangered its status as a democracy by failing to negotiate with terrorism-backing Palestinians; there, Prime Minister Benjamin Netanyahu, a troublesome Jew if ever there was one, insists that Iran, not Jews building bathrooms in East Jerusalem, represents a threat to global order. If only the United States could achieve some daylight between itself and the Jewish state, all would be well—even though Jordan, Saudi Arabia and Egypt have never drawn closer to Netanyahu, knowing that Netanyahu is a far better guarantor of their security against an Iranian bomb than Barack Obama.

Delusional dictatorship is a danger to regional peace. But delusional American leadership is a threat to global peace. Nonetheless, things are going swimmingly in Barack Obama's head. Iran is a regional ally, Yemen is a model of peace and security, and Israel is an incipient enemy. The unicorns still roam free, even if free people live in danger of chains.

The Fascist Left and Same-Sex Marriage

April 1, 2015

Last week, Indiana Gov. Mike Pence signed a law with the same name as one signed on the federal level by President Bill Clinton in 1993, which was co-sponsored by Sen. Chuck Schumer, D-N.Y., the presumptive next Senate minority leader. Naturally, Pence found himself on the wrong end of a partisan barrage from ABC News' George Stephanopoulos for signing that law the following Sunday. It sure is nice to be a Democrat.

What exactly does the law state? The Religious Freedom Restoration Act in Indiana states that "a governmental entity may not substantially burden a person's exercise of religion, even if the burden results from a rule of general applicability." That rule does not apply only if the government's action "is in furtherance of a compelling government interest" and is also "the least restrictive means of furthering that compelling government interest." If government does act against someone in violation of that person's religious principles, he or she can assert that violation "as a claim or defense in a judicial or administrative proceeding."

The law does not specifically single out same-sex marriage as an activity against which a religious person may discriminate, but it certainly holds out that possibility. Of course, that possibility is already inherent in a little concept we in the United States used to call freedom—freedom to choose how to conduct one's business and freedom to practice one's religion in one's practice of business.

Under a philosophy of freedom, the market solves the general problem of private discrimination, because if one person decides to discriminate against Jews or blacks or gays, he or she loses money and is put out of business for his or her trouble. Nobody has the right, under a philosophy of freedom, to invoke the power of the government's gun in order to force someone to provide a good or service.

That system is a heck of a lot safer for minorities than a system by which government regulates the proper conduct of voluntary activities. Black Americans should know that, given that Jim Crow was not merely a system of voluntary discrimination but a government-enforced set of regulations designed to ban voluntary transactions involving blacks. Gays, too, should understand that freedom is far preferable to government-enforced societal standards governing consenting transactions, given that government used to be utilized to discriminate openly against homosexual behavior.

But the left has rewritten the concept of freedom to mean "whatever the government allows you to do," and leftists now insist that government cannot allow discrimination—unless, of course, the government is itself enforcing discrimination against religious Christians who don't want to violate their belief in traditional marriage.

Same-sex marriage, it turns out, was never designed to grant legal benefits to same-sex couples. That could have been done under a regime of civil unions. Same-sex marriage was always designed to allow the government to have the power to cram down punishment on anyone who disobeys the government's vision of the public good. One need not be an advocate of discrimination against gays to believe that government does not have the ability to enforce the prevailing social standards of the time in violation of individual rights. There are many situations in which advocates of freedom dislike particular exercises of that freedom but understand that government attacks on individual rights are far more threatening to the public good.

You do not have a right to my services; I have a right to provide my services to whomever I choose. If you believe that your interpretation of public good enables you to bring a gun to the party, you are a bully and a tyrant. So it is with the modern American left, to whom freedom now means only the freedom to do what it is the left wants you to do at point of gun.

Why the Left Lies

April 8, 2015

"When yet another hand clamped over her mouth, Jackie bit it, and the hand became a fist that punched her in the face. 'Grab its motherf---ing leg,' she heard a voice say. And that's when Jackie knew she was going to be raped."

Thus started a 9,000-word article in Rolling Stone magazine about the supposed rash of campus rapes across America. The writer, Sabrina Erdely, began with the horrifying story of Jackie, a college girl who found herself raped by seven men at the Phi Kappa Psi fraternity house at the University of Virginia while two other men, including her date, "gave instruction and encouragement."

The University of Virginia banned Phi Kappa Psi from campus. People vandalized the frat house, hurling rocks through windows and covering the premises with graffiti. Commentators and politicians all over the nation bloviated gravely about the deep problem of sexual brutality on campus. Those who questioned Jackie's story were accused of not taking rape seriously enough; to demand facts equated to shaming a rape victim.

There was only one problem with Erdely's story: It was false. Jackie had lied. And Rolling Stone had no evidence to back up Jackie's story in the first place. This week, Rolling Stone apologized for the story but did not fire Erdely or any of its editors; Erdely apologized not to the fraternity or its members but to virtually everyone else. She added, "In writing each of these stories I must weigh my compassion against my journalistic duty to find the truth."

Herein lies the problem. Journalism does not require sympathy for human beings. It requires sympathy for readers, who deserve truth. But for the left, truth represents a secondary value. It is far more important to forward a particular political narrative than it is to simply state the facts. And that narrative can only be forwarded if there is controversy over the facts. If, for example, everyone agreed that Jackie had been gang raped, there would be no controversy over sending her rapists to prison or prosecuting all those who looked the other way. But the leftist narrative requires an opposition, a group of evil haters who take rape less than seriously. That is how society can be blamed for the alleged rape of one woman by seven men.

So the left specifically chooses to feature situations in which facts are under dispute. Then leftists claim that no one could reasonably dispute the facts; the only people who would dispute facts about the occurrence of an evil are those who sympathize with the evil. Leftists craft Americans who require evidence into victimizers, simply so they can portray themselves as heroes. If you wanted evidence of racism with regard to the shooting of Michael Brown in Ferguson, Missouri, you were a fan of Bull Connor-style police brutality. If you wanted evidence with regard to Lena Dunham's rape accusations, you stood with rapists. Leftists don't require any evidence; they will take any allegations that support the narratives they desire at face value because that's how seriously they take rape, racism, etc.

The left's mythmaking will continue. And there will never be consequences for that mythmaking because like Sabrina Erdely, their failures spring from caring, no matter who gets hurt.

The Romance of Poverty

April 15, 2015

On Tuesday, CNN ran what should have been a puff piece in its travel section about the wonders of visiting Cuba. The title of the piece spelled out the angle: "Why you should travel to Cuba before it looks like everywhere else." The authors, James Williams and Daisy Carrington, write, "Cuba is not like other places, or rather, not like anywhere that exists today. To some outsiders, it looks firmly stuck in the 1950s. Vintage cars roam the streets, the landscape is absent of strip malls and global chains, and the buildings—though crumbling—hark back to a grander time." The authors conclude, "It is these throwbacks that lend Havana, the country's capital, an undeniable charm. A charm that, some worry, is in peril once the U.S. embargo lifts."

Who are these unnamed sources who worry deeply about the charm of poverty degrading into the soulless maw of capitalist enterprise? The left speaks of poverty with the same fervent attachment with which a lover speaks of his partner's quirks. Poverty is charming. Poverty ennobles. Poverty is Mimi from "La Boheme," Fantine from "Les Miserables," Che Guevara (the icon, not the mass murderer) and Gandhi (the icon, not the shamanistic wife beater). Poverty is artists struggling for their bread while crafting masterpieces.

And poverty is equality. Everyone calls each other comrade while they hoe their gardens for scraps of food. There's a real sense of community when everyone shares a general sense of hopelessness.

Most of all, poverty is wonderful—for other people. It's a great place to visit, but not a place you'd like to live.

But you need others to live there so you can visit.

And so the left romanticizes poverty. Primitive civilizations must be preserved, since they represent a simpler, deeper way of life. The poor rubes who occupy such civilizations must be kept that way for their own good, lest they be transformed into shallow husks of themselves by commercialization. John Smith came to America to rape and pillage for gold; Pocahontas stood for the spirituality of the mountains and the inherent value of the eagles. Only those clinging to the bottom rung of material existence can know the colors of the wind.

Now, it turns out that those experiencing poverty like it a lot less than those who look upon it from above with a wistful eye. Those Cubans who still hope to ride their 1959 Chevrolets to Key Largo don't see their throwback vehicles as a selling point; they'd trade them in a heartbeat for a 2005 Honda Civic and the ability to drive it to an actual job. The Cubans who inhabit those quaint, run-down buildings would likely beg to have Banana Republic buy them out and let them retire elsewhere.

But that would ruin the ambience. And so the left insists that Banana Republic stay out. Because, after all, the left appreciates the authenticity of poverty, even as they artificially create it.

Hillary's Vietnam

April 22, 2015

Headless bodies lie in the sand. Above those corpses stand the black-clad minions of ISIS, outlined against the coastline of Libya. This is the second video in three months depicting Islamic terrorists cutting the heads off of Christian captives.

Bodies float in the Mediterranean Sea, face down. Twelve Christian bodies, thrown from a rubber boat by 15 Muslims. Their launch point: Libya.

Approximately 700 more bodies float face down in the Mediterranean, victims of a smuggling operation gone wrong when their rickety craft sunk as it made its way to Italy. Its source location: Libya.

Four American bodies in Benghazi, Libya.

These are the wages of Hillary Clinton's war.

In June 2006, as then-Senator Hillary Clinton, D-N.Y., prepared a run for president, she stated that President George W. Bush had "rushed to war" in Iraq. A few months later, Hillary spoke of her opposition to Bush's surge in Iraq, stating that it was a "losing strategy." Iraq, a war for which Hillary voted, had been conducted on the back of flawed intelligence estimates and without a clear plan.

Five years later, Secretary of State Clinton rushed to war, allegedly manufacturing evidence to do so, and with no plan whatsoever for victory. According to The Washington Times, Clinton "was the moving force inside the Obama administration to encourage US military intervention to unseat [dictator Moammar Gadhafi] in Libya." Clinton claimed that if the West did not intervene in Libya, Gadhafi would pursue a genocide against his enemies; in March 2011, she imagined a scenario in which

"Benghazi had been overrun, a city of 700,000 people, and tens of thousands of people had been slaughtered, hundreds of thousands had fled. ..." That genocide never materialized, nor did the best intelligence estimates support that argument.

Not only that: Hillary also ignored all available evidence suggesting that the Libyan opposition was honeycombed with terrorists. She ignored Admiral James Stavridis, NATO Supreme Commander for Europe, who admitted "flickers in the intelligence of potential al Qaeda, Hezbollah." Al-Qaida backed the Libyan uprising. There was a reason that neither Hillary nor President Obama risked going to Congress for approval of the Libyan adventure: they would have been rejected.

Nonetheless, in October 2011, Hillary arrived in Tripoli to declare victory, stating that she was "proud to stand here on the soil of a free Libya." When Gadhafi was sodomized with a knife and killed two days later, she laughed uproariously on camera: "We came, we saw, he died!"

Gadhafi wasn't the only person who died. Hillary's war ended with terrorist chaos in Libya: a full-scale terror takeover of regions of the country including Benghazi, the exile of the legitimate government, a massive refugee crisis growing day-by-day amidst the upheaval. That refugee crisis has grown significantly worse since Hillary's war. As Vox.com, a leftist outlet, points out, 1,600 migrants "have drowned in the Mediterranean this year." Why? Again, according to Vox.com, when Moammar Gadhafi "ruled Libya, his government had an agreement with Italy to try to intercept and turn back ships leaving for Europe. ... And in the utter chaos that's engulfed Libya over the past few years, there's no government entity really capable of patrolling the Mediterranean."

Hillary Clinton's foreign policy has promoted chaos around the world. Nowhere is that better illustrated than in her signal foreign policy legacy, the collapsed state of Libya.

Ignoring Personal Responsibility Is a Riot

April 29, 2015

Hours after residents of Baltimore, Maryland, set the city aflame, President Barack Obama took to the Rose Garden to explain in professorial style just why America, under his administration, keeps watching young black men loot buildings and attack police officers. "We have seen too many instances of what appears to be police officers interacting with individuals—primarily African-American, often poor—in ways that have raised troubling questions. And it comes up, it seems like, once a week now, or once every couple weeks," Obama said, proclaiming that police brutality against blacks amounted to a "slow-rolling crisis." He added, "This is not new, and we shouldn't pretend that it's new."

Obama's disgusting implication was, of course, that a massive trend of police violence mirroring the racist police violence of the 1950s has broken out across America. That's false. Your chances in America of being killed by hornet attack are 1 in 56,000; your chances in America of being killed by a police officer if you are a black man are 1 in 60,000. Nonetheless, Obama continued by suggesting that police forces had to "do some soul searching," that "some communities ... have to do some soul searching," and that America as a whole had to do some "soul searching."

Fortunately, President Obama is here to heal souls, as Michelle Obama once assured us. And he chooses to heal souls by suggesting that all the ills of inner city communities crash down on those communities through impersonal forces having nothing to do with individual rotten choices.

"Without making any excuses for criminal activities that take place in these communities," Obama said, preparing to excuse criminal activities in the black community, "what we also know is that if you have impoverished communities that have been stripped away of opportunity, where children are born into abject poverty— they've got parents, often because of substance-abuse problems or incarceration or lack of education themselves—can't do right by their kids, if it's more likely that those kids end up in jail or dead than they go to college, in communities where there are no fathers who can provide guidance to young men, communities where there's no investment, and manufacturing has been stripped away, and drugs have flooded the community ... we're not going to solve the problem [with just police]."

This is cowardice. Impoverished communities like Baltimore are not "stripped away" of opportunity—they strip themselves of opportunity through lack of values. Children are not merely "born into abject poverty"—they have parents who get pregnant while in poverty and outside wedlock. Those fathers are not merely absent because of "substance-abuse problems or incarceration or lack of education"—they are absent because they make terrible decisions to do drugs, commit crimes, drop out of school and abandon their children. Kids do not just "end up in jail or dead" rather than in college—they grow up in an environment where crime is a way of life, and they choose to engage in crime. Baltimore does not simply lack investment because of cruel white businessmen; it lacks investment because no sane business owner would drop millions to place a CVS where the last CVS burned.

To blame a mythical white power structure for personal decisions that destroy lives represents an abdication of personal responsibility. Baltimore has a black mayor, a majority black city council, a black police commissioner. Baltimore hasn't had a Republican in a position of true power since 1967. America is not the problem. Baltimore is not the problem. The people who live in Baltimore and choose to pursue irresponsibility, egged on by big government advocates like President Obama, are the problem.

The New Lynch Mob

May 6, 2015

On Sunday, Democratic Maryland State Senator Catherine Pugh lavished praise on state's attorney Marilyn Mosby, who just days before announced that her office would file a bevy of charges against all six officers involved in the death of 25-year-old Freddie Gray. Gray's death drove protests and riots throughout Baltimore, serving as the spark to ignite local rage, and focusing national attention on the state of inner city black Americans. Pugh said that Mosby "really set the bar for the nation in terms of how these sorts of cases ought to be looked at."

Pugh wasn't Mosby's only conspicuous fan. Rep. Elijah Cummings, D-Md., who has represented the failing city of Baltimore for decades, said, "Her integrity is impeccable without a doubt." The widow of Eric Garner, the New York City man who died after police officers used a submission hold on him, said, "I feel like the same scenario that happened in Baltimore also happened with my husband. I would just like to see something done." Race-baiter and riot-stoker extraordinaire Al Sharpton stated, "We cannot keep playing Russian roulette on whether or not we get a good prosecutor or not." Crowds in Baltimore reportedly celebrated Mosby's indictment of the officers. The Huffington Post called her "objectively badass." Fusion called her "America's favorite prosecutor."

What, exactly, did Mosby do to earn such plaudits? She announced that she would charge the six officers, three of whom were black; she did so without laying out a compelling narrative supporting the charges brought (failing to buckle a seatbelt does not amount to either manslaughter or second-degree murder); she brought the charges while simultaneously pandering to the rioters, stating, "I heard your calls of no justice, no peace. ... To the youth of this city, I will seek justice on your behalf. This is a moment. This is your moment. ... As young people, our time is now."

If that sounds more like a campaign speech than an announcement of charges, that's because it *is* a campaign speech. Mosby was elected in January 2015 as the youngest district attorney in America; she reportedly has aspirations to higher office. Before her election, she publicly questioned the jury verdict in the George Zimmerman case and cast racial aspersions on the prosecutor who refused to file charges against Officer Darren Wilson (even Eric Holder's Department of Justice found Wilson's actions against Michael Brown justifiable). Furthermore, Mosby's husband, Nick Mosby, has excused rioting while serving as a Baltimore city councilman. Mosby's prosecution of the case amounts to a serious conflict of interest.

But even were Mosby not personally compromised by the political issues surrounding the case, mob justice seems to be running amok. When Sharpton, Cummings and the rest demand "justice," they aren't demanding justice: They're demanding the heads of police officers, without supporting evidence. In Ferguson, the narrative of the murder of Michael Brown trumped the facts of the case; Sharpton, Cummings and the rest still cite Brown's death in their litany of instances of police brutality.

Mosby's prosecution, however, elevates the lynch mob to legal status. As Alan Dershowitz put it, "this is a show trial." America has a lot of show trials in store, if the mob is to be placated. Marilyn Mosby doesn't care who burns, so long as social justice and political expediency are served. And the mob doesn't care what burns, so long as they get to hijack the political system to serve their thirst for vengeance.

Shut Pam Geller Up, or We Will All Die

May 13, 2015

Last week, Fox News' Bill O'Reilly announced that Pamela Geller, the woman who sponsored a draw Muhammad event in Texas, threatened America's national security. Geller, said O'Reilly, "spurred a violent attack." He continued, "Insulting the entire Muslim world is stupid. ... It does not advance the cause of liberty or get us any closer to defeating the savage jihad." On the same network, Juan Williams stated that Geller "engaged in gratuitous offensive behavior that led to the deaths of two people." The New York Times editorialized that Geller "achieved her provocative goal" with her "exercise in bigotry and hatred posing as a blow for freedom."

Geller, the narrative goes, should never have encouraged people to draw Muhammad because it was "provocative." To which the answer should be: So what? Women attending school in Afghanistan "provokes" radical Muslims into throwing acid on their faces, but that does not mean that women should not go to school in Afghanistan or be condemned for doing so.

Geller, the narrative goes, made Americans less safe by provoking radical Muslims, as though Muslims have no responsibility to act like decent human beings—as though, faced with the prospect of a cartoon of their prophet, Muslims have no choice but to grab guns and go a-huntin'. But that's nonsense. What *truly* spurs radical Muslims into violence is the well-evidenced belief that if they kill enough Muhammad cartoonists, soon people will stop drawing cartoons of Muhammad.

Geller, the narrative goes, was "Islamophobic" in her call for drawings of Muhammad; unlike Charlie Hebdo, Geller was not an equal opportunity offender of all religions, and therefore showed particular animus toward Islam. But failure to equally attack all religions does not make satire of one religion illegitimate—were that the case, The New York Times would have to answer why drawing Muhammad presents deep problems, but running simultaneous ads for the slanderous "Book of Mormon" musical is hunky-dory.

So, why the assault on Geller? The answer is simple: Too many Westerns have bought into the notion that personal responsibility can be jettisoned in favor of judgments about identity. Geller is the problem, in this view, because she is an upper-class Jewish woman from New York City; her rivals are poor Muslims from Phoenix. They are, by the nature of their identities, members of the victim class. She is, by contrast, a member of the victimizing class. Nothing either party can do can change their status in this equation. Therefore, according to Doonesbury cartoonist Garry Trudeau, even the Muslims who shot up Charlie Hebdo in France were justified: "Ridiculing the non-privileged is almost never funny—it's just mean. ... By attacking a powerless, disenfranchised minority with crude, vulgar drawings closer to graffiti than cartoons, Charlie wandered into the realm of hate speech."

How do proponents of this victim/victimizer identity dichotomy determine who falls into which category? They simply look at the socioeconomic status of those involved and make a determination of who is worse off. Thus, black Baltimore rioters were not people acting without any sense of values, but rather victims provoked by injustice from a non-existent white power structure in Baltimore. Before a conflict has even begun, we know who deserves our sympathy.

That calculus leads to more death, more destruction, more chaos. That death, destruction and chaos cannot be laid at the feet of Pamela Geller, but those who continue to perpetuate a narrative in which people who commit evil acts are victims, and those who are their victims are their provocateurs.

Barack Obama's 'Lottery Winners'

May 20, 2015

Last week, President Obama held a summit on poverty at Georgetown University. There, he explained that unrest in major American cities could be traced not to lack of values, but to simple lack of cash—and that lack of cash, he suggested, could be attributed to simple lack of luck. "The top 25 hedge fund managers made more than all of the kindergarten teachers in the country," Obama stated. "You pretty much have more than you'll ever be able to use or anyone in your family will ever be able to use. There's a fairness issue involved here." He added that we should confiscate wealth from those people and redistribute it to "early childhood education"—one of the greatest government boondoggles of all time—because that's "where the question of compassion and 'I'm my brother's keeper' comes into play. And if we can't ask from society's lottery winners to just make that modest investment, then really this conversation [on poverty] is just for show."

This is evil masquerading as generosity.

First, the simple fact that some people earn lots of money while others earn not as much does not implicate "fairness." Your earnings result from the number and value of voluntary transactions seeking your skills, services or goods. It is not unfair that those who understand how to manage billions of dollars on behalf of those who do not earn more than kindergarten teachers; there are far more people qualified to teach kindergarten than to manage money, which is why kindergarten teachers generally hand over their pension funds to money managers.

Second, Barack Obama's subjective view that some people have too much money reeks of monarchic arrogance. President Obama's net worth currently stands at nearly $7 million. He sends his children to the most toney private school in Washington, D.C. He and his wife enjoy taxpayer-sponsored vacations that would make Middle Eastern potentates blush. They also enjoy the favors of Hollywood celebrities who earn as much as hedge fund managers, but never seem to receive the same "you've got enough" Soviet-style central planning routine from the Obamas.

Third, President Obama should not invoke Biblical phraseology without understanding both plain meaning and context. Obama's own half-brother, George, lived as of 2008 on less than $1 per day. And when it comes to Biblical interpretation, the context for "my brother's keeper" comes from Cain and Able: Cain suggests that he need not watch over his brother shortly after killing him out of jealousy for Able's hard work and better sacrifice. Today's Cain is the modern left, which seeks to slay its brothers for the great crime of working harder and sacrificing more.

Finally, Obama's allusion to rich Americans as "lottery winners" insults the intelligence. Warren Buffett did not play the lottery. Nor did Mark Zuckerberg, Steve Jobs or Bill Gates. They worked hard, produced great products and enriched millions of lives. True lottery winners produce nothing; generally speaking, those who buy lottery tickets are disproportionately poor and spendthrift, and often end up broke again after winning the lottery. The only real lottery winner in this discussion is Obama himself, who has produced nothing and somehow lucked into the most powerful position on the planet.

America does not need wealth redistribution. It needs a values conversion. No poor person has a child out of wedlock thanks to the evils of rich people. No poor person drops out of high school because a rich person forced them to do so. Poverty can sometimes be chalked up to luck on an individual level, but it can't be chalked up to luck on a mass scale. And wealth can't be chalked up to luck, either. To do so is to impoverish our own values at the expense of our future.

Ann Coulter's War

May 27, 2015

This week, iconoclastic master Ann Coulter released her new book, "Adios, America!" The book has already been labeled racist by the mainstream left, which fears her argument, and will undoubtedly be marginalized by the mainstream right, which doesn't want to hear it. Coulter's thesis is simple: Since Senator Teddy Kennedy, D-Mass., rammed through the Immigration and Nationality Act of 1965, America's immigration system has transformed from a device for enriching the nation for both native-born and immigrants into a scheme for importing anti-American voters.

What made America America, Coulter argues, was a particular blend of Protestant religion and European civilization that led to the rise of the greatest nation in human history. What will unmake America, she continues, is a deliberate attempt to poison that blend with a flood of immigrants with wildly different values.

Coulter points out that the real number of immigrants currently residing in America illegally far surpasses the 11 million consistently put forth by politicians and media. That 11 million springs from census data, which is notoriously unreliable, given that immigrants here illegally typically don't spend time answering government surveys. The real number, she argues, is far closer to 30 million. And those 30 million immigrants in America illegally drive down wages, shred social safety nets, drive up the crime rate and congeal the American melting pot into a melange of inferior cultural values competing for local dominance.

"The foreign poor are prime Democratic constituents because they're easily demagogued into tribal voting," Coulter points out.

"Race loyalty trumps the melting pot. ... The American electorate isn't moving left—it's shrinking. Democrats figured out they'd never win with Americans, so they implemented an evil, genius plan to change this country by restocking it with voters more favorably disposed to left-wing policies than Americans ever would be."

And the Democrats have achieved their goals. America is more polarized than at any point since the civil rights era, and not by chance. Americans have been told that they have a responsibility to anyone who wants to enter the country, even as they are lectured that it would be gauche for them to ask just who wants to come in. "At what point will Americans remind their government that it has a responsibility to us, not to every sad person in the world?" Coulter laments.

The answer, if the left has its way: never. Bearing nostrums like "diversity is our strength" and "through no fault of their own," Democrats will browbeat Americans into accepting the demise of American values. The shock isn't that millions of foreigners want to get into the United States—that's always been true. The shock isn't even that Democrats want to open the floodgates to unchecked, unscreened immigration—that's been true for decades, given that the modern American left despises founding philosophy and the capitalist system more generally. The shock is that so many conservatives have capitulated, granted the left's premise in the hopes that America's new immigrants will resemble her old immigrants, even though the America that welcomes them has changed dramatically.

Coulter's argument—that the media and our politicians conspire to keep information from us about the effects of mass immigration from non-Western countries, and that such immigration will destroy the fabric of the country—is virtually unassailable. The only question left: Who will stand up to the tidal wave of political correctness to pursue a reasonable and sane immigration policy, rather than the insane combination of ignorance and bullying that currently dictates who gets to live in and help redefine the greatest country in the history of mankind?

Left Exploits Mental Illness to Push PC Agenda

June 3, 2015

My grandfather was deeply mentally ill. He spent nearly a year in a psychiatric institution after being diagnosed with bipolar disorder; he heard the radio talking to him. He became suicidal. He spent years battling the condition, until he was prescribed lithium. For the next several decades, the medication brought his mental illness under control.

Nothing would have been crueler to my grandfather than had society told him that his delusions were correct—that the radio was, in fact, talking to him; that the curtains were indeed threatening him; that he was normal, and that it was the stereotypes of the world inducing his paranoia.

Yet that is the view of the anti-science left that this week declared former Olympic champion Bruce Jenner a woman. Vanity Fair led the way, featuring Jenner wearing a one-piece corset, Photoshopped and made up beyond nearly all recognition. The 22-page profile of Jenner insists that everyone call him Caitlyn, addresses him as "she," and explains that despite the fact that Jenner has all male genitalia and all male genetics, he is in fact a woman— even though the writer explains his own confusion as to gender pronoun usage.

Jenner freely admits that he had doubts right after having his face surgically altered in a 10-hour procedure, but that a counselor from the Los Angeles Gender Center explained it was just the painkillers talking (it would be illegal in California for a counselor to explain to Jenner that he requires serious mental illness treatment beyond bodily mutilation). Jenner also admits that he is doing a reality television show about his sex change for the money: "I'm not doing it for money. ... If I can make a dollar, I certainly am not stupid. [I have] house payments and all that kind of stuff."

It's cruel to allow a mentally ill person to exploit himself in public, but the political left is happy to do so in order to perpetuate the pseudo-scientific nonsense that a man can magically turn into a woman. Their agenda: If men and women are the same but for hormone therapy, implants and repeated surgical intervention, then all disparities between male and female can be attributed to societal biases. And those societally created "gender constructs" can be corrected only by massive government intervention, including re-education of children. Bruce Jenner is merely a tool in this quest for redefinition of gender.

Thus, the White House hailed Jenner as a hero, with presidential advisor Valerie Jarrett tweeting, "Nice to meet you, @Caitlyn_Jenner. The brave choice to live as your authentic self is a powerful example to so many." Except that Caitlyn certainly isn't Jenner's "authentic self," any more than the "authentic self" of an anorexic requires constant liposuction. Surgery is not the solution to mental illness. The post-surgical suicide rate among transgenders remains 20 times higher than that of the general population.

As Dr. Paul McHugh, former psychiatrist in chief at Johns Hopkins Hospital, wrote last year, "'Sex change' is biologically impossible. People who undergo sex-reassignment surgery do not change from men to women or vice versa. Rather, they become feminized men or masculinized women. Claiming that this is civil-rights matter and encouraging surgical intervention is in reality to collaborate with and promote a mental disorder."

And promoting mental disorders hurts no one more than those who suffer from such disorders. Delusions ought not be supported, let alone celebrated. They ought to be treated.

The Right Caves on Social Issues, Then Loses

June 11, 2015

This week, a Wall Street Journal/NBC News poll showed a significant drop in the number of Americans identifying as conservative, and a significant rise in the number of Americans identifying as liberal. As the Journal described, "For the first time since 2010, conservatives are no longer a plurality: 38 percent identify as moderates, compared with 33 percent who identify as conservative and 26 percent as liberal." The Journal, like Gallup, attributes the drop in conservative identification to increased allegiance to leftist social positions, particularly among young people and women.

Predictably enough, the Republican establishment agrees with this analysis. For years, they have been claiming that the only path to national victory stands in de-emphasizing social issues and emphasizing fiscal ones. After all, as they point out, Gallup shows that conservatives beat leftists on economic issues by a margin of 39 percent to 19 percent. If Republicans simply drop social issues altogether, the logic goes, voters will be able to move into the economic realm, where conservatives dominate.

This analysis is dead wrong. It assumes two facts not in evidence: First, that conservatives can successful drop social issues without destroying their own value system and base; second, that leftists will ever allow a consensus on social issues.

First, Republicans cannot dump the value system that underlies conservative thought. Libertarianism is a fine philosophy of government, but a rotten philosophy of life. Without supportive social institutions to back responsible and moral decisions, free societies invariably crumble into the detritus of their own bad decision-making, and then call for the collective to help. Agreeing to an unwritten social contract of self-sufficiency is all well and good, until someone breaks the pact. And in the absence of religious and moral institutions outside government, somebody always breaks the pact.

Second, leftists will never allow a consensus on social issues. The entire goal of the left, in fact, is to promise consensus, and then move the goalposts. Like Charlie Brown aiming to kick Lucy's football, conservatives constantly trust that they will be able to reach an accommodation with the social left. Meanwhile, the social left constantly destroys another heretofore well-accepted social consensus in the interest of casting conservatives as unfeeling.

To that end, the social left called for feminism, defining the movement as the ability of women to work freely; the right agreed. The left quickly redefined feminism to include abortion, the labeling of marriage as a patriarchal institution, and the destruction of any traditional notion of biological sex; the right disagreed. The left labeled the right anti-feminist.

Similarly, the social left called for deregulation of sexual activity; the right conceded. The left quickly redefined deregulation to include special legal protections for homosexuality, and then moved on to same-sex marriage, and now pushes for legal measures against religious businesses and institutions. When the right disagrees, the left labels the right intolerant and homophobic.

All of this destroys political debate and conversation in order to label the right bigoted and nasty. And the right buys into the asinine idea that should they concede to the latest cause celebre, finally they'll have taken social issues off the table. And so the right goes from loss to loss, constantly bewildered as to why leftists keep winning even though the right keeps moving left on social issues.

The real answer would be to fight. If conservatism rests on certain basic notions of morality, that morality cannot be jettisoned in the quixotic search for electoral majorities. Those electoral majorities will never materialize so long as the right runs from its own values, tacitly conceding to the left the moral high ground.

Yes, Rachel Dolezal Is Black

June 17, 2015

This week, Rachel Dolezal, the former local head of the Spokane NAACP, a lecturer in Africana studies at Eastern Washington University, and a proud black woman, was revealed to be a non-proud white woman. She lied about her personal history: She said her parents whipped her when they lived in South Africa, that she underwent rape and physical abuse, that the KKK targeted her with swastikas and nooses. No evidence exists to support any of this. Her parents point out that Dolezal has no black ancestry, and grew up in a Montana home as the child of two white parents.

Nonetheless, Dolezal insists she is black. "I was drawing self-portraits with the brown crayon instead of the peach crayon, and black curly hair," she said to Today. "It's a little more complex than me identifying as black or answering a question of, are you black or white?"

Just two weeks ago, the world went gaga over Bruce Jenner's transformation into Caitlyn Jenner; the left passionately insisted that Jenner's genetics, hormones and penis did not mean he could not be a woman. The president of the United States felt the need to tweet out his support for Jenner, stating, "It takes courage to share your story." Anyone who abided by the antiquated notion that biological sex exists was treated as a Neanderthal holdover.

Now, however, the left insists that Rachel Dolezal is not black. On June 9, The Daily Beast headlined, "Caitlyn Jenner Is Pissing Off Feminists and Bigots—Good for Her." Three days later, The Daily Beast headlined, "BREAKING: NAACP 'Stands Behind' Fake Black Woman." The left insists on preserving non-biological, illegitimate racial barriers because they exploit those racial barriers for political gain; the left insists on destroying biologically based sexual differences because they wish to overthrow all established sexual mores.

So what distinguishes Jenner from Dolezal? On what basis can we reject Dolezal's blackness, given that the left has now redefined objective reality as self-definition? If you want to be a woman, you are a woman. If you want to be black, why can't you be black?

Nick Gillespie of Reason magazine makes the odd argument that Jenner had transformed into a woman because Jenner sincerely believes that he has transformed into a woman, whereas Dolezal had fraudulently lied about her race for gain. Now that Dolezal has averred her sincerity, presumably she is black.

Or perhaps there is some objective measure of race? But that, too, fails on the merits: Sex is significantly more biological than race, and it is significantly more significant than race. Skin color is surely biological, but the relevance of race is purely sociological, as even those on the left acknowledge. As Ian Haney Lopez of U.C. Berkeley writes, biology "refutes the supposition that racial divisions reflect fundamental genetic differences." Black people have black skin, but how black must your skin be for you to be legitimately black? In the Old South, one drop of black blood made you black, and therefore fit for discrimination. But that was a racist societal distinction, not a biologically based one. As Rachel Dolezal puts it, if you go far back enough, "we're all from the African continent."

Perhaps race is a societal construct and can change, but society must uphold racial differences for some greater goal? But that would be pure racism: The goal of fighting racism would be to alleviate racial distinctions, which have no behavioral basis, despite the musings of the would-be comedians at #AskRachelDolezal.

And so we come to this inescapable conclusion: By the left's standards, Rachel Dolezal is black. She can choose her race, just as Bruce Jenner can choose his sex. And she didn't choose. She always felt that way. After all, no one would choose to be black, just as no one would choose to be gay—blacks are so put upon in American society that no one would fake being black for, say, the benefits of employment or mainstream leftist celebration.

Perhaps we can all learn from Rachel Dolezal: Race doesn't matter. Except that it does for people like Rachel Dolezal, which is why she went black. Rachel Dolezal is a poster child for the deconstructionist, victim-manufacturing left. But now she's learning: Once you go black, the left will make you go back.

Confederate Flag Controversy
a Complete Misdirect

June 24, 2015

Last week, evil racist terrorist Dylann Storm Roof shot nine innocent black members of the Emanuel African Methodist Episcopal Church in Charleston, South Carolina. Before their bodies had cooled, President Obama attempted to blame the shootings on the National Rifle Association and lack of gun control; Hillary Clinton blamed the shootings on white supremacy and Donald Trump-like overheated rhetoric; Bill Maher blamed Fox News, and suggested that Fox News ought to be droned like al-Qaida propagandist Anwar Al-Awlaki.

Despite these divisive tactics, Americans united. There were no racial lines to grief: Thousands of blacks and whites marched in Charleston, packed the devastated church, mourned together.

But the American left could not stand such racial unity—it threatens their cherished belief that America continues to represent racial oppression and white supremacy. And so the media and politicians on the left manufactured a racial controversy over the Confederate flag.

Now, there are plenty of excellent reasons to oppose the placement of the Confederate flag on state grounds: The Union won, as it should have; the Confederate battle flag originally represented a new nation founded on reverence for slavery, a deeply evil institution; the Confederate battle flag was utilized by Southern Democrats as a symbol of resistance to federal desegregation during the Jim Crow era. Blacks in America are absolutely right to feel offended by the flag.

By the same token, there are plenty of decent reasons for the Confederate battle flag to stay on longstanding state monuments: to remind viewers of the fact that evil and good live together in every human heart; to remind viewers of the fact that good people did sacrifice on behalf of their states' sovereignty, not merely to defend slavery (most of those who fought and died for the Confederacy did not hold slaves); as a symbol of Southern military heritage, given that the South has always been overrepresented in terms of its military service in the United States.

My own personal belief is that the flag should not be displayed on state grounds, but is perfectly appropriate for display at war memorials. A country and state willing to remove the Confederate flag do not need to do so; a country and state willing to acknowledge their legacy of slavery and racism need not discard their history or monuments acknowledging that history.

Having a national conversation about what to do with Confederate flags and war memorials raises interesting and vital issues. But that conversation has nothing to do with the shooting of black Americans in South Carolina. The left's implication that those who revere the Confederate flag are all budding Dylann Storm Roofs, or that they sympathize with Dylann Storm Roof, is nasty and unsupported by evidence.

It is, however, politically effective. The left's decision to politicize the South Carolina shootings by immediately swiveling to a longstanding racial controversy demonstrates their sick inability to allow America to move beyond racial divides. Every conservative in America called for Roof to fry. That wasn't enough for the left—the same left that defends rioters in Ferguson, Missouri, and Baltimore and hero-worships Che Guevara and Mumia Abu Jamal. That left generated conflict because without racial conflict, it cannot survive as a viable political movement. And for the left, politics trumps American unity every time.

The Real Goal of the Same-Sex Marriage Movement

July 1, 2015

Late last week, after the Supreme Court of the United States declared without any Constitutional basis that the Constitution mandates same-sex marriages be state legitimized across the nation, a disquieting level of triumphalism broke out from coast to coast. The president shined lights representing the gay pride rainbow flag on the White House—a gross boot-on-the-throat display from an anti-religious leader. Corporations, undoubtedly fearful of the consequences of ending up on the wrong side of the riotous left, began tweeting out rainbow symbols. News outlets similarly embraced the rainbow symbol, as though it were uncontroversial to do so; BuzzFeed, Huffington Post, and Mashable all turned their logos rainbow, with BuzzFeed's Ben Smith explaining, "We firmly believe that for a number of issues, including civil rights, women's rights, anti-racism, and LGBT equality, there are not two sides."

Let's move beyond the romantically idiotic language of Justice Kennedy's decision. The notion that gay rights advocates and their allies, who have spent decades suggesting that the institution of marriage represents patriarchal oppression, love and respect marriage so much that they wish to join in its binds, is inane. And the idea that the gay rights movement desperately seeks the tax assistance available to male-female married couples was made false long ago with the promises of civil unions.

No, the gay rights movement and the broader American left celebrated the same-sex marriage decision in wild fashion because the decision established two fundamental notions: First, that government has replaced God in the moral pantheon of the United

States; second, that the new god-government has the power to root out and destroy any God-based institutions, destroying the social capital and fabric that holds together the nation.

The emotion that greeted Justice Kennedy's decision reeks of religious fervor. In ancient Israel, the Jews cheered ecstatically each Yom Kippur when the High Priest emerged from the Holy of Holies; that signified God's acceptance of the repentance of the people. This weekend's Dionysian displays mirrored that sort of delirious jubilation with Justice Kennedy as a stand-in for God: He declared the fundamental morality of homosexuality, not merely its legality. Kennedy went so far as to declare that the government could confer "dignity" on relationships. Now, the notion that the gay rights movement seeks the "dignity" of marriage is similarly ridiculous—movements that seek "dignity" do not hold parades featuring the Seattle Sisters of Perpetual Indulgence and a bevy of chaps in assless chaps. But they do seek the "dignity" of being told by a higher authority that their actions are right, just and good.

With God safely shunted to the side in favor of Justice Kennedy, the next step in the gay rights movement will be the smashing of idolators—namely, those who cling to their religion and church in spite of Justice Kennedy's New New Testament. Leftists have already moved to ban nonprofit status for religious institutions that refuse to acknowledge same-sex marriages; leftists have already sued into oblivion religious business owners who refuse to participate in same-sex weddings. It will not stop there. Religious schools will be targeted. Then, so will homeschooling programs. The secular religion of the left has been set free to pursue its own crusade against the infidel.

Religious institutions were the key social glue binding Americans together; we trust one another because we share values, beliefs and social institutions with them. With all three of those elements being memory-holed by the government in favor of self-expression, social capital will disintegrate; our trust in each other will fall apart, and government will fill the gap. With this week's judicial tyranny, leftists move one step closer to their ultimate goal, as expressed at the 2012 Democratic National Convention:

"Government is the only thing we all belong to." And that will be an ugly America indeed.

The Most Idiotic Comment in Presidential History

July 8, 2015

On Monday, President Obama spoke about his new strategy to take on the terrorist entity Islamic State in Iraq and Syria. In doing so, he explained that the battle against that terrorist group—a group he had once termed "JV"—would amount to a "generational struggle." Why would defeating a ragtag army of primitives take generations? Because, Obama explained, "This is not simply a military effort. Ideologies are not defeated by guns. They're defeated with better ideas." To cap off this airsickness bag of gobbledygook, Obama then concluded, "We will never be at war with Islam."

So let's get this straight. A group Obama said he would degrade and destroy can only be degraded and destroyed with ideas. Its own ideologies—its animating force, according to Obama—have nothing to do with Islam. The cretinism here resembles a perfect Jenga tower of fatuity: Remove one phrase, and the whole structure tumbles.

Americans should gawk at the sheer wonder of Obama's applesauce here. Obama's bad acid trip bumper sticker foreign policy—"Better Ideas Beat Bad Ideologies" over a Grateful Dead peace symbol—reeks of third grade oral presentations. It takes more than great ideas to beat ideologies—it takes heavy weaponry. The victims of the Holocaust didn't sit around thinking to themselves, "Golly, if only we'd been able to come up with a better idea than Nazism, that Hitler sure would have stopped all this nonsense." America didn't end World War II by dropping informational leaflets. We dropped warning leaflets, and then bombs. Large ones. Atomic ones. No armed ideologues in history have been defeated solely by better ideas—at least not before decades of murder, repression and evil.

So what did Obama actually mean? It simply lacks credibility to read the president's comments at face value: No sentient human being could be this dull. He meant that ideologies aren't defeated by American guns, because American guns are backed by American ideas. And American ideas are by nature bad, evil, racist, xenophobic, homophobic, centophobic, and, presumably, arachnophobic. Sure, American ideas backed with guns won World War II—but hey, pretty much any ideas backed with guns would have defeated Nazism, amirite? (Well, except for the ideas of the British, the French, the Czechs, the Polish...)

When it comes to fighting the ideology of ISIS, however, Obama finds Americanism insufficient, since Americanism *creates* ISIS ideology through Islamophobia. That's why Americans with guns can't defeat ISIS, says Obama: Americans with guns *create* ISIS. Only internationalism can win the day!

So far, that internationalism has been a massive failure. Of course, internationalism is always a massive failure, because it isn't an idea, any more than "diplomacy" is an idea. Both are tools, to be used by those who actually have something to say, something to fight for. But President Obama despises traditional Americans who have something to say or fight for. They are the problem. He is the cure. And he would rather disarm those Americans and their rotten ideas than let them loose with guns against those who slaughter babies.

None of this should be surprising from President Obama. He's been clear about his anti-Americanism since "Dreams From My Father"; in that masterwork of falsely nuanced detritus, Obama lambasted the "powerful" for their "dull complacency and ... steady, unthinking application of force, of ... more sophisticated military hardware."

Give Obama this: He didn't lie to us. 66 million Americans blinded themselves to his ideology, proving conclusively that bad ideologies are not always defeated by better ideas. Sadly, Obama's own rotten-to-the-core ideology continues to win victories, and the world continues to lose because of it.

Why Obama Turned Iran Into a Regional Power

July 15, 2015

On Tuesday, Barack Obama championed his legacy-making agreement with the Iranian mullahs. That agreement provides billions of dollars to the Islamist aggressors hellbent on dominating Iraq, Syria, Lebanon, Afghanistan, Yemen, and any place else they can spread their regime of terror. In exchange, the United States receives a pinkie swear that the Iranians will not develop nuclear weapons for a grand total of 10 years; within five years, we will allow weapons embargoes against the state to end, and within eight years, we will allow missile technology to flow into Iran unimpeded.

This deal, Obama said, is a move in a "different direction."

He is right. It *is* a move in a different direction: America used to care when its enemies created spheres of influence across strategically important swaths of territory. President Obama used to pretend to care. In phraseology that now seems charmingly quaint, Obama stated in his 2010 State of the Union Address, "the international community is more united, and the Islamic Republic of Iran is more isolated. And as Iran's leaders continue to ignore their obligations, there should be no doubt: They, too, will face growing consequences. That is a promise."

Consider that promise broken.

America used to worry about its allies being targeted for destruction. Obama's new deal with Iran contains zero restrictions on their terrorist activity across the Middle East and the world, and relieves sanctions on figures including Qasem Soleimani, head of the Iranian Revolutionary Guard Quds Force, a group responsible for the murder of hundreds of American troops. The deal also enriches Iran massively, and Iran has made clear that it will use those increased resources to help its terrorist allies like Hamas and Hezbollah.

America used to fret about such things as the use of weapons of mass destruction—remember how cute it was when President Obama announced a red line with regard to Syrian dictator Bashar Assad's use of chemical weapons? Now, Assad can rest easy: His sponsor state just received the biggest influx of cash since the Iranian Revolution.

Neville Chamberlain could argue that in appeasing Hitler, he was trying to buy time to rebuild a crippled military in the face of an equally powerful force. Winston Churchill argued that Chamberlain's appeasement at Munich in 1938 sprang from a genuine desire to achieve peace and defend Britain. At least Chamberlain loved his country.

President Obama clearly does not. Unlike Chamberlain, he has purposefully hollowed out America's military, and fully embraces Iran's regional aspirations. Chamberlain didn't want Hitler to take over Europe. Obama wants Iran to take over large sections of the Middle East. Like most Europeans, Obama sees America and Israel as greater threats to world peace than Iran or North Korea. His top priority in the Iran deal was forestalling action by the United States and Israel. He achieved that, at the cost of Saudi Arabia and Egypt seeking nuclear weapons, Hamas reinforcing its position as a terrorist cancer in the Gaza Strip, Hezbollah retrenching as the controlling force in Lebanon, Bashar Assad ensuring his continued leadership, Iraq turning into an Iranian client state, Afghanistan preparing for Iranian-influenced sectarian violence, and Houthi-caused chaos in Yemen, for a start. But at least Israel won't drop a couple of bombs on Iran's nuclear reactors.

In 2007, I wrote of then-Senator Obama, "Iran's leaders must be praying every day that Americans turn to a candidate like Barack Obama." Obama's pro-Iran orientation was no secret then, and it is no secret now. Obama's Arab Spring has turned into his Islamist Summer because Obama wanted an Islamist Summer. No wonder America's enemies cheer the man 66 million Americans elected, even as the rest of the world readies for the inevitable onslaught.

Why People Like Trump

July 22, 2015

Last week, 2016 presidential candidate Donald Trump dropped his second headline-making comment of the race. Responding to statements from Senator John McCain, R-Ariz., in which McCain labeled Trump's supporters on immigration "crazies," Trump shot back that McCain wasn't a war hero, because he had been captured. "I like people who weren't captured," Trump said, paraphrasing a 2008 Chris Rock routine in Michael Scott-like fashion.

Trump's shot was mean, nasty, uncalled for, and idiotic.

The media world immediately declared Trump's campaign over. A few days before the comments, Huffington Post—a publication created by onetime failed California gubernatorial candidate Arianna Huffington—announced that it would feature Trump in its entertainment section rather than its politics section. The Wall Street Journal editorial board opined, "It came slightly ahead of schedule, but Donald Trump's inevitable self-immolation arrived on the weekend when he assailed John McCain's war record. The question now is how long his political and media apologists on the right will keep pretending he's a serious candidate."

Trump's rival candidates leapt on the opportunity to throw dirt on Trump's political grave. Governor Rick Perry, R-Texas, said, "I have no confidence that he could adeptly lead our nation's armed forces. His comments over the weekend should completely and immediately disqualify him from seeking our nation's highest office." Senator Marco Rubio, R-Fla., said, "I do think it's a disqualifier as commander in chief." Both trail Trump substantially in the polls.

Trump will, and ought to, take a serious hit in those polls after his McCain idiocy. But he will not go down this easily. That's because Trump exemplifies two qualities many Republican voters seek: brashness and an unwillingness to back down in the face of critics.

Trump's brashness is both his blessing and his curse—but unlike Spider-Man, Trump seems unable to comprehend that with great power comes great responsibility. He says foolish things, and then refuses to back down from them. But that stubbornness seems to act as a counterweight to his brashness, in an odd way: Conservatives hungry for an unapologetic candidate resonate to Trump, even if he should apologize for his latest tomfoolery. Trump puts himself in a position to draw fire from both the establishment Republicans and the media; when he draws that fire, even for good reason, the base leaps to his defense.

Even better for Trump, his long history of making inane comments means that it will be tough for any one comment to finish him. Like Hillary Clinton on the Democratic side, Trump is so flawed a candidate that it's difficult to tell where the fatal flaw may lie. In such a scenario, flaws become assets. Trump has shifted his positions? Sure, but he's done so constantly—he's a man of the moment, many believe, and thus we can believe whatever nostrum falls from his lips now. Trump has engaged in corrupt dealings? Sure, but he's so rich that he won't need to take payoffs, unlike those he's already paid off. Trump never shuts up? Well, at least he won't shut up when told to by those in power.

Upper echelon Republicans make a mistake in disqualifying Trump. Democrats never do this: Hillary won't call Bernie Sanders unfit for office, or vice versa. Trump will undoubtedly disqualify himself eventually, as well he should. Republicans can either learn from Trump's better qualities while discarding his worse ones, or they can try to destroy Trump as quickly as possible. The first strategy would be useful, the second wildly counterproductive. Unfortunately, as usual, the Republicans seem to be pursuing the worst possible option.

Evil in America

July 29, 2015

This week, the Center for Medical Progress, an anti-abortion group dedicated to unmasking the atrocities committed by taxpayer-funded abortion juggernaut Planned Parenthood, released its latest in a series of undercover videos about the organization. In this video, Dr. Savita Ginde, vice president and medical director of Planned Parenthood of the Rocky Mountains, calmly explains to the undercover reporter that the organs of babies killed in the womb can be sold separately. "I think a per-item thing works a little better," she tells the faux buyer while standing over a tray of kidney and spinal cord from a recently aborted baby.

The tape sounds like something from the laboratory of Dr. Josef Mengele. But to the left, the murder of the unborn is routine. Former secretary of state and 2016 presidential candidate Hillary Clinton defended Planned Parenthood, stating that Planned Parenthood has "provided essential services for women," calling the videos "an attack against a woman's right to choose."

Presumably, she then ran out of other euphemisms for the butchering of the unborn.

Meanwhile, former Arkansas governor and 2016 presidential candidate Mike Huckabee drew heavy media fire slamming President Obama's decision to guarantee both Iran's regional power and nuclear weapons within a decade. Huckabee stated, "This president's foreign policy is the most feckless in American history. It is so naive that he would trust the Iranians. By doing so, he will take the Israelis and march them of the door of the oven."

Huckabee's invocation of the Holocaust to describe Obama's facilitation of a genocidal anti-Semitic regime offended President

Obama significantly more than a similarly timed tweet from Ayatollah Khamenei containing imagery of an Obama silhouette with a gun to its head. Obama whined, "The particular comments of Mr. Huckabee are just part of a general pattern we've seen that would be considered ridiculous if it weren't so sad." Clinton said she was "disappointed and I am really offended personally. ... I find this kind of inflammatory rhetoric totally unacceptable."

She does not, however, find the prospect of a regionally dominant Iran lording over Iraq, Syria, Lebanon and Yemen, and building up terrorist groups like Hamas and Hezbollah, all while the United States provides a shield for Iran's nuclear program. The real problem, she and the left believe, lies in likening Obama's Iran policy to Western malfeasance with regard to Hitler.

The left's willingness to participate in Planned Parenthood's genocide against the unborn and the Iranian government's planned genocide against the Jews speaks to the nature of evil. Americans are fearful of invoking Hitlerian analogies because Hitler is seen, wrongly, as a sort of evil apart from the norms of humankind—he must have known he was evil, an evil of a different sort altogether from daily evil. The same holds true, people typically think, of the Germans complicit in his designs. That's inaccurate. Hitler undoubtedly saw himself as a good man. More importantly, millions of Germans joined in Hitler's evil because it was easier to look the other way than to confront the nature of an evil they had allowed to flourish. It is always easier to shrug through life by relying on euphemisms than to stand up to the daily evil we encounter.

For Planned Parenthood, as for leftists and their head-in-the-sand allies throughout America, babies are less than the sum of their parts. For the Obama administration, as for its allies, threats to Jews can be dismissed as irrational byproducts of religious fanaticism, rather than as core goals of an immensely barbaric regime. All of these accessories to evil convince themselves that euphemistic thinking will bring harmony.

Turning a blind eye to evil, however, doesn't make it disappear. It allows it to grow. And those who allow evil to grow in order to protect their own convenience will be held accountable for the end results of the evil they facilitate.

The Age of the Demagogue

August 5, 2015

Last week, President Obama visited the set of Jon Stewart's "The Daily Show" for the third, and presumably final, time. Obama has set records for the most late-night talk show appearances. He's also appeared alongside YouTube star GloZell Green, in the online series "Between Two Ferns," and Miami radio host DJ Laz, aka "The Pimp with the Limp." Obama has treated the White House like his own personal concert venue, complete with selfie-stick video. After all, as they say, you only live once.

Meanwhile, the same week as Obama's final French-kissing session with palace guard Stewart, Obama vowed to push through his support-free nuclear deal with Iran, utilize the power of the executive to curb carbon emissions from power plants and craft more executive action on immigration.

Buffoonish. Powerful. The two descriptors used to oppose one another in the minds of the American electorate. Now they go together like Oval Office and oral sex.

The modern media age has transformed our presidents into celebrities. When Abraham Lincoln resided at the White House, visitors could literally knock on the door and ask to see him. One European, shocked at such laxity, wrote, "one goes right in as if entering a cafe." Lincoln himself had to walk through crowds of people to get to and from his office. The presidency was the highest civil service office—emphasis on the service.

Today, we expect our presidents to treat themselves like royalty. Americans may decry the expense of the British monarchy, but the Kingdom of Obama costs far more. The president's family has access to the White House movie theater, with a 24-hour-per-day projectionist on call. The Obama dog, Bo, has a handler paid six figures. Overall, according to one estimate, the American royal family costs taxpayers $1.4 billion per year, as opposed to the crowned crew in Buckingham Palace, who cost British taxpayers a mere $60 million each year.

And like the British royals, our American royals are celebrities, treated as such. They hobnob with Hollywood celebrities, and even send their children off to intern with them. They shut down traffic in major American cities merely to appear on the telly. They are stars, not servants.

All of which would be fine, had they ceremonial rather than real power. But the president has unified star power with actual power. Early on in President Obama's term, my father noted that Obama seemed to want to plaster his face everywhere; he theorized that Obama used ubiquity as a tool, making himself part of the background noise of American life. That tactic worked not only in embedding Obama in every aspect of public consciousness, from sports (Obama's picking his NCAA brackets!) to reality television (Obama just congratulated Bruce Jenner on becoming Caitlyn!), but in making him feel indispensible. Obama feels far more like the head of a unitary, dictatorial government than he does like a cog in the machine of checks and balances. He bears more resemblance in the political optics to a Castro than to a Calvin Coolidge. We see him everywhere. And that is how he wants it.

It thus seems somewhat jarring for the media to decry the rise of Donald Trump, a reality television star long in the media eye. Trump, we are assured, is a joke—would we really want a celebrity as president? But Obama represents the apotheosis of celebrity as president. Hillary Clinton, too, is a celebrity attempting the White House—had she never met Bill Clinton, she'd be a screechier Barbara Boxer. There's a reason Senator Chuck Schumer, D-N.Y., doesn't merely spout his gun control views before the media—he trots out his cousin, "Trainwreck" comedienne Amy Schumer, to do so.

Perhaps the British have it right: a ceremonial head of state, and a politician to do a politician's job. Americans apparently can't handle a system in which our ceremonial head of state and our actual head of state are the same person—not without swooning at that person's feet, and offering as much power as humanly possible to boot.

The Extreme Party

August 12, 2015

During last Thursday night's inaugural 2016 Republican presidential debate, Fox News' Megyn Kelly got into a spat with Donald Trump over his history of vulgar comments about women. Trump followed up that tiff by dropping a thinly veiled reference to Kelly's menstruation in the media. Those comments prompted Democratic frontrunner Hillary Clinton to praise Kelly—a woman with whom she would never deign to do an interview—bash Trump, and then lash out at Senator Marco Rubio, R-Fla., whom she perceives as the most serious threat to her presidential aspirations.

"Yes, I know [Trump] makes great TV," said Clinton. "I think the guy went way overboard -- offensive, outrageous, pick your adjective. But what Marco Rubio said has as much of an impact in terms of where the Republican Party is today as anybody else on that stage."

What, pray tell, was Rubio's great sin? He said that he believed the Constitution protects the unborn: "What I have advocated is that we pass law in this country that says all human life at every stage of development is worthy of protection. In fact, I think that law already exists. It is called the Constitution of the United States."

According to Clinton and her allies in the media, this makes Rubio—and any Republican who agrees with him—too extreme for the general public. And it's not just abortion. Polls show that 52 percent of Americans say that the Republican Party is more "extreme" in its positions than the Democratic Party; just 35 percent say the reverse.

But is that true?

On abortion, for example, the Republican Party platform states that the Constitution warrants protections for the unborn; the

Democratic Party position states that taxpayers should foot the bill for the killing of unborn children at every stage of pregnancy, including partial-birth abortion, a gruesome procedure in which children are pulled feet-first out of their mother's wombs, their skulls pried open and brains sucked out. Then the Democrats want to fund Planned Parenthood to carve up those babies for organ sale. Which position is more extreme?

On same-sex marriage, the Republican Party wants to pass a Constitutional amendment to enshrine traditional marriage as the only governmentally rewarded form of marriage; until such time, Republicans acknowledge that same-sex marriage is legally a state's rights issue. The Democratic Party wants to force religious Americans to participate in homosexual weddings without recourse to the Constitution. Which is more extreme?

On health care, Republicans want Americans to be able to choose the healthcare they receive and pay for; Democrats want to force Americans to pay into a system from which they receive less than they would if they expended their dollars privately. Extremism, anyone?

The list goes on and on. Democrats want no major changes to the educational system, except for spending more money on corrupt teachers' unions; they also want to use taxpayer dollars to subsidize students majoring in useless subjects at second-tier colleges. Republicans want to allow Americans to keep more of their own money, and they want American parents to be able to spend that money as they see fit on the education of their children. Democrats want to dramatically increase taxes; Republicans want to decrease them. Democrats want no meaningful enforcement of America's immigration system; supposedly, Republicans want to enforce immigration laws.

Yet the media portray Republicans as the extremists. That rhetorical trick has its desired effect: Republicans are seen as nasty and unpleasant, even while Democrats move so far to the left that an open socialist is now their second leading contender for the presidency. Republicans counter by insisting that they are kind and generous, wonderfully moderate. This strategy is destined to fail. But

Republicans have no idea how to fight extremists, even as the left portrays them consistently as America's most extreme political party.

Straight Outta Solutions

August 19, 2015

Over the weekend, the hagiographic film "Straight Outta Compton" pulled in $60 million at the box office. The film follows the trials and travails—but not the woman-beating, gay-bashing, violence-promoting activities—of NWA, the iconic rage hip-hop group made most famous by their anthem, "F--- Tha Police." The theme of the film, according to reviewers, centers on the evils of the Los Angeles Police Department and white authority. Paul Giamatti, playing Paul Giamatti on steroids, screams at a group of stock-casting cops, "You cannot harass my clients because of what they look like!" He tells the group, "You have a unique voice. The world needs to hear it."

But while the world may hear this whitewashed version of NWA's nastiness—after all, Ice Cube now plays cops on TV rather than cursing them—the movie won't be seen in one place: Compton itself. According to CBS Los Angeles, Compton has no movie theaters. "It's a low income area, it's been heavily dis-invested in," says USC professor of sociology Manual Pastor. "When you live in a community that doesn't have that kind of retail, it's a sign that the community is devalued and people within the community feel devalued."

Compton doesn't lack a theater because of a feeling of victimhood. It lacks a theater because Compton overflows with crime. According to Neighborhood Scout, Compton's violent crime rate is 12.87 per 1,000 residents; chances of being victimized by a crime stand at 1 in 78, as opposed to 1 in 249 across California as a whole. The murder rate is reportedly 37 per 100,000 in Compton; the murder rate in the United States is less than 5 per 100,000.

So much for NWA changing the world.

NWA merely reiterated the anti-police propaganda that has kept inner city communities enmeshed in brutality and poverty for generations. Jill Loevy, reporter for The Los Angeles Times, describes in agonizing detail the lack of law and order in South Central Los Angeles, which covers Compton. She talks about how the police are underfunded in such areas, how witnesses are cowed into silence, how informal mechanisms of authority—gangs—fill the gap. "Residents would still holler 'One time!' at the cops," she writes. "The term derived from the memory of police touring black neighborhoods once a day, making no real effort to address crime. 'One time' was a stock anticop insult, just like 'po-po' and 'blue-eyed devil.' Yet it contained a plaintive note—a paradoxical suggestion that more times might be better."

The 14th Amendment to the Constitution, which contains the critical mandate for "equal protection of the laws," was designed to stop selective prosecution. The Civil Rights Act of 1866, the precursor to the 14th Amendment, explicitly stated that citizens—more specifically, black citizens—had to have "full and equal benefit of all laws and proceedings for the security of persons and property ... and shall be subject to like punishment, pains and penalties, and to none other." Leaving parts of America unpoliced, the Radical Republicans who wrote the 14th Amendment understood, placed them squarely in the lap of chaos.

Today, Compton's murder rate looks more like that of war zones than that of a modern American city. That's because any area in which no one enforces law and property rights devolves into pandemonium. Hollywood can glorify NWA; the Democratic Party can humor the counterproductive, criminal-glorifying Black Lives Matter movement. None of it will solve the underlying problem in heavily black inner city areas. Leaving black Americans at the mercy of lawlessness used to be a mandate of racism; now it's a mandate of political correctness. No matter who pushes that agenda, the outcome is the same: disaster.

Ashley Madison, Josh Duggar and the Nasty Left

August 26, 2015

Last week, internet criminals responsible for hacking the adultery website Ashley Madison released full records of those who registered to use the service. The media began perusing the list—and naturally, the first major name to hit the media was Josh Duggar. The media busted Duggar several months ago, too, when they released information that the former "19 Kids and Counting" reality star had molested children as a teenager.

What makes Duggar's infidelity noteworthy? The fact that he purported to be a religious Christian. In his adulthood, Duggar became executive director of Family Research Council Action, the legislative wing of the traditional family values promoting Family Research Council. He spoke frequently about traditional morality and traditional marriage.

The left media finds Duggar's hypocrisy on sexual morality absolutely delicious. The execrable Dan Savage, supposed anti-bullying icon, said that while he generally opposed "outing" adulterers from Ashley Madison—after all, adultery is a natural part of marriage, according to doorknob-licking Savage -- that standard doesn't apply to advocates of Judeo-Christian morality. Savage wrote, "I feel bad for everyone who has been outed by the Ashley Madison hackers—everyone except Josh Duggar. ... Duggar—demagogue, liar, political operative—was a legitimate target for outing." Why? Because, Savage stated, quoting Evan Hurst of Wonkette, "he tried to hurt lots of people, because of how they have sex, which is why it is 100 percent A-OK to take this information and use it to grind that arrogant, fundamentalist pr---'s nuts into a fine powder so that we may snort it up and trip holy karmic balls." Delightful.

One of the great problems with modern American political and moral discussion lies in our hatred for hypocrisy above all other sins. Adultery, according to Savage and his anti-moral moralists, isn't a sin; rather, preaching against adultery and then failing your own standard is the great sin. But that makes all standards irrelevant. This logic sets up a perverse moral system whereby those without standards freely pursue whatever activities they choose, while those with standards are destroyed for their sins. The result: rational people choose to embrace amorality, secure in the knowledge that without standards, they will never be held to account. Bill Clinton can allegedly rape a woman and sexually harass several others, and he will never feel the wrath of the left: he does not promote sexual decency. But Newt Gingrich will never hear the end of his affair with Callista Bisek because he had the temerity to question Clinton's sexual peccadillos in the Oval Office.

The war on hypocrites isn't a war on sin: it's a war on standards. Josh Duggar may be an evil human being, but his evil springs not from the standards he attempted to preach, but from his failure to meet those standards. The left's backward obsession with Duggar shows *their* true hypocrisy: They violate all of their own standards in order to target someone with a different set of values. They are against outing, unless they want to utilize it to fight their enemies; they are in favor of adultery, unless it's convenient to use adultery as a club against their opponents; they're against sexual judgmentalism, unless they can use sexual judgmentalism to bash those loyal to Judeo-Christian beliefs.

Josh Duggar deserves to pay for his sins, and pay richly. He's vile. But those who fight against basic standards of morality don't have any moral authority to act as the agents of that judgment. For such jackals to play at such judgment smacks of the same hypocrisy they condemn.

No, the Democrats Don't Care About Israel

September 2, 2015

For years, the American Israel Public Affairs Committee has hosted President Obama or a high-ranking representative of his administration at their annual conference in Washington, D.C. No matter how anti-Israel the Obama administration's policies have been, no matter how hostile to Israel the president's rhetoric, AIPAC has offered President Obama or his lackeys a platform from which to tout their supposed pro-Israel credentials. AIPAC has always rationalized such outreach as an attempt to keep the pro-Israel position bipartisan, to cultivate supporters for the Jewish state on both sides of the aisle.

What a waste.

With President Obama's despicable Iran deal set for passage this week, with solely Democrat support, the Democratic Party has called the leftist Jewish community's bluff. Leftist Jews have played a sad game with the Democratic Party: They pretend that Israel's safety and security is their top priority, and then make excuses as the Democratic Party moves more and more boldly to undermine that safety and security—because, in truth, leftist Jews care less about Israel and Judaism than abortion and redistributionism. Former George H.W. Bush advisor James Baker discounted the Jewish vote by saying, "F--- the Jews, they don't vote for us anyway." The Obama administration, with the Iran deal, has adopted a similar view: F--- the Jews, they vote for us anyway.

And there is no question that the Iran deal screws the Jews. Under the best-case scenario, Iran receives $150 billion immediately in unfrozen assets and oil money from the United States and her allies. In return, Iran pinky swears not to develop nuclear weapons. But they don't need nukes with all of the benefits President Obama just gave them. Iran wants nukes in order to use such weapons as a deterrent while pursuing terrorist activity across the world, preventing the rest of the world from leveraging sanctions. But now the rest of the world has accepted Iran's terrorist activities openly. President Obama's deal guarantees regional power to Iran—and then allows them to go nuclear with no consequences 10 years from now.

And that's the best-case scenario. Under the worst-case scenario, Iran grabs its money, funnels it into terrorism throughout the world, continues its takeover of Iraq, Syria, Lebanon and Yemen, and precipitates regional wars with virtually all of its neighbors. Meanwhile, Iran secretly builds a nuclear weapon—and Obama's verification regime does nothing either to verify or hold accountable. The deal contemplates a three-month delay between Iranian objections to inspections and supposed sanctions "snapbacks"—and even a "snapback" would require a new vote from the same countries now lifting sanctions, a dubious proposition at best.

The Democratic Party's latest kabuki theater involves allowing supposed pro-Israel allies like Senator Chuck Schumer, D-N.Y., to vote against the deal, knowing that Obama already has the votes locked up to pass it. Obama acts angry, Schumer gets to look tough, and Israel feels the brunt of President Obama's Jew-hating displeasure all the same. Meanwhile, leftist Jews get to comfort themselves with the idea that Democrats split over the Iran deal— and maybe, just maybe, President Obama has Israel's best interests at heart after all.

He doesn't. Neither do Democrats, or their leftist Jewish allies. President Obama's Iran deal will end in blood. And he won't be the only pathetic character in this drama with bloody hands.

Hillary Searches For a Heart

September 9, 2015

Hillary Clinton has now decided to re-relaunch her flailing campaign. She'll do so by showing "more humor and heart," according to The New York Times. In other news, the Wizard gave Joe Biden a brain and Bernie Sanders courage. The Wizard also apparently gave Biden and Sanders better poll numbers: In the latest Monmouth poll, Clinton still leads at 42 percent, but Biden picks up 22 percent and Sanders 20 percent.

That's trouble in Clintonia.

Clinton's new new new campaign will feature her dazzling wit and oozing charm, say her handlers. She'll be heading to "The Ellen DeGeneres Show," where Ellen will undoubtedly dance awkwardly with the former secretary of state—the most awkward dance since Clinton had to fake loving her husband for the cameras during the Lewinsky scandal. She'll also join Jimmy Fallon for "The Tonight Show," and "plans to talk extensively with several nontraditional outlets." Presumably, she'll head to GloZell's bathtub for a round of Froot Loops and foreign affairs.

It won't work. Clinton is like "Star Wars Episode I: The Phantom Menace": overproduced, heartless and starring a lead incapable of drawing sympathy. Some of her fans believe that if she trots out former President Bill Clinton, that will save the day; the Times reports that "Bill Clinton, who has had virtually no presence on the campaign trail, will begin to travel the country to help with fundraising this fall." It won't help—Bill's spontaneity and glee undermine her in the same way that actual hardwood shames Pergo when the two are placed side by side.

Clinton does have a backup strategy: If Clinton can't overcome her status as the Tin Man, she can always go full witch.

Which is the plan, according to her campaign spokeswoman, Jennifer Palmieri: "The true game changer is when there's a personified opponent." She's hoping for a Republican opponent to emerge so she can pounce. Clinton is far more comfortable smothering her opponents with a pillow than cuddling with babies on the campaign trail. That's why Clinton has now placed heavy focus in her campaign speeches on attacking Donald Trump and the other Republicans: She's struggling to connect with Americans other than in opposition to those on the other side.

But what happens if she's unable to smear the person on the other side? What happens if she has to make an affirmative case for her own candidacy?

Clinton will be faced with that challenge if put up against an authentic, famous political cipher like Donald Trump, who now outpolls her nationally. Trump may be the perfect candidate to take down Clinton in a general election, in fact: He's not as susceptible to personal attacks, since everyone knows and has an opinion about Trump already; he's hard to peg down on policy, and actually agrees with Clinton on matters ranging from taxes to affirmative action; most of all, he seems like an unproduced person, rather than a remarkably lifelike robot capable of occasional homo sapiens-like jargon.

Over time, Clinton will likely grow more desperate—and thus, more unattractive. She's billing herself as Chillary Clinton in an attempt to seem like Cool Grandma to the under-30 crowd, but like an old PC, she glitches and freezes up regularly. Eventually, she'll run out of re-re-relaunches. The only question is whether the Democratic National Committee can wheel her to victory before other candidates catch up with her.

Rich Socialists and the
Bernie Sanders Moment

September 16, 2015

California is the land of hypocrites.

As I pulled into the parking lot adjacent to my radio station in Los Angeles, I noticed a Mercedes R500 sitting next to me. Between the Mercedes symbol and the R500 label sat a big, fat bumper sticker: "BERNIE SANDERS 2016."

The Mercedes R500 retailed at $71,000 back in 2006, when the well-off young gentledriver's parents presumably purchased it. Now, their kid pulls up to the pricey Equinox gym (sticker price: $160 per month) with a bumper sticker touting the virtues of redistribution of wealth.

This is the privileged generation of Americans. They've been able to benefit from the free markets of their parents; they can afford to purchase Fine water to sip while running on the world's highest-end ellipticals, and then clean off beneath the rain shower head before heading out to brunch at Gracias Madre. Then, that night, they head off to the LA Memorial Sports Arena to listen to a 73-year-old socialist babble on about the evils of the system that granted them their wealth.

America has become so wealthy that its citizens now ignore the source of that wealth. "It's not all about the money" is an easy thing for rich people to say. But ask the billions around the globe living in abject poverty whether trashing a system that guarantees tremendous baseline economic opportunity seems like a great idea.

But this is what happens when no one teaches young Americans the morality behind the system that guarantees economic opportunity: young Americans decide that "higher morality" dictates the death of that system. Young Americans don't desire an Xbox and a car—they desperately want a feeling of meaning and belonging, none of which capitalism naturally provides.

Socialism, however, does.

The outcome: California. It isn't just the incoherence of bumper stickers and car brands that makes California the center of American hypocrisy. It's the fact that Californians routinely embrace more regulation and higher taxes in order to feel that quick boost of self-esteem, and then spend effort and time attempting to avoid those rules. Nannies expect to be paid in cash, because all the same people who voted for higher employer taxes refuse to pay those taxes. Young Californians only use free market Uber after endorsing higher minimum wage and more restrictions on transportation. Californians take massive tax deductions, but only after voting to raise their own income taxes.

None of this makes California more livable. Instead, Californians live in a fantasy world of their own making: a socialist utopia with a thriving black market, in which the popularly backed economy fails while individuals strive to avoid it. All of which runs fine, until the day that Bernie Sanders actually closes the loopholes and cracks down on the cheating. Then the Mercedes turns into a Yugo, and the bumper sticker finally lands where it belongs: on a product of socialism rather than free markets.

'Clock Boy' and America's Suicidal PC Tendencies

September 23, 2015

Last week, Muslim 14-year-old Ahmed Mohamed made national news after being detained by police for bringing a deconstructed clock to his Texas school. The clock, to inexpert eyes, looked like a bomb. Ahmed's English teacher thought so and called the police; when they questioned Mohamed, he reportedly stonewalled them. They released him after realizing that the device posed no threat and was not meant as a hoax explosive.

But this being Barack Obama's America, that didn't end the story.

The boy's father, a self-proclaimed anti-Islamophobia activist, decided to make a federal case out of his kid's detainment. He called his son's brief detention in an air conditioned room "torture." He called in the terrorism-linked Council on American Islamic Relations to protest Ahmed's treatment. When he reached the police station, he insisted that the police leave handcuffs on his son so that the boy's sister could take pictures. Then, when Dallas Mavericks owner Mark Cuban called up Ahmed to deliver his sympathies and began asking questions about the situation, Ahmed's sister fed him the answers.

None of those details made the press, however. The media simply played the story as a pure case of Islamophobia, a targeted attack on an innocent young Muslim genius who "invented" a clock. Never mind that Ahmed no more "invented" the clock than my daughter "invented" my keyboard by dismantling it. Never mind that children across America have been suspended or even prosecuted for far less than bringing a device with bomblike appearance to school. Form your fingers into a gun, and go home with the threat of prosecution looming. Chew a pop tart into the shape of a firearm, and you can guarantee it'll go on your permanent record.

But build a device that looks awfully like an IED, and so long as you're Muslim, the world will respond with outrage.

We have now come 180 degrees since Sept. 11. In the aftermath of that attack, we vowed we would not be hit again. To prevent that from happening, we told ourselves that if we saw something, we would say something; we also vowed to put political correctness to the side when it came to protecting safety. Now, we'll say something if we see something, unless that something is a suspicious act with regard to a possible explosive held by a young Muslim male.

When a 16-year-old black girl brought a science experiment to school several years back in Florida, she was arrested; Barack Obama didn't say a word, because she wasn't Muslim. But Ahmed now looks forward to a trip to the White House for breaking down an old clock and then getting testy with the police. This is America, post-frontal lobotomy. While we can all recognize and celebrate that Ahmed won't be going to jail, the treatment of Ahmed's case by the president and the press ensure that next time a young Muslim student brings a suspicious object to school, administrators will ignore it for fear of career-ending consequences.

And next time, that suspicious object may not be a disassembled clock.

The Republican Party's Big Choice

September 30, 2015

On Tuesday, members of the House Oversight Committee grilled Planned Parenthood head Cecile Richards over undercover videos linking high-ranking employees with illegal sale of fetal body parts. Under heavy questioning, Richards admitted to supporting sex-selective abortion, acknowledged that the vast majority of Planned Parenthood's nongovernment revenue springs from abortion, and awkwardly attempted to explain away the organization's alleged willingness to utilize special abortion techniques to preserve "samples" from the killed unborn.

That night, Speaker of the House John Boehner, R-Ohio, announced that he would fully fund Planned Parenthood.

Naturally, conservatives feel that they have been betrayed. Again. Since the 2014 elections, Republicans have done nothing to slow or stop Obama's historically egregious Iran deal, which almost guarantees Iranian regional dominance followed by their eventual development of nuclear weapons; Obama's executive amnesty program, which promises to continue to shape the country in heretofore unforeseen ways; and Obama's support for the nation's leading abortion mill.

On Wednesday, House Minority Whip Steny Hoyer, D-Md., said he looked forward to Boehner's last month in the House, and hoped that Boehner would "work with his Republican colleagues and with his Democratic colleagues to effect some progress on important things that we need to be doing." Hoyer added that Boehner "wants to get some things done that are important for the country to get done so that he doesn't leave that for the next leadership. ... I hope he can."

When conservatives hope the Republican leadership does nothing, and Democrats hope the Republican Speaker goes big, that's an excellent indicator that the Republican Party no longer represents its base. No wonder conservatives rally behind anti-establishment figures ranging from Donald Trump to Carly Fiorina; Texas Senator Ted Cruz draws heavy grassroots support for slicing Planned Parenthood funding out of the latest continuing resolution, even if it means Obama vetoing the CR, thus shutting down the government. Conservatives didn't elect Republicans to build a power base. They elected them to enact conservative policy preferences, no matter the cost.

But Republican Party insiders seem puzzled at the rage of the conservative base over their collective decision not to oppose the most controversial elements of President Obama's agenda. Instead, Republicans insist to their voters that they're doing their best, that without 66 votes in the Senate, they can't override the executive branch, and that they will need just a few more dollars, pretty, pretty please.

This conflict lays bare the conflicting agendas of conservatives and Republican leaders. Republican leaders believe the goal of the Republican Party is to gain and maintain power; conservatives believe the goal of the Republican Party is to represent conservative interests, no matter what comes. The Republican Party has become an excellent vehicle for the former goal, and a smoking garbage heap when it comes to the latter.

Republicans may keep winning, because the only alternative for conservatives is to vote Democrat. For now. But the divergence between the base and the leadership will eventually lead to the GOP's collapse, unless Republican leaders begin to re-orient themselves to a conservative true north.

Barack Obama, Jackass

October 7, 2015

Last week, in the aftermath of the mass shooting at Umpqua Community College in Oregon, President Barack Obama took to the microphones to deride anyone who did not agree with his gun control agenda. Stating that it was only good and right to "politicize" the Oregon shooting, Obama stated, "This is a political choice that we make to allow this to happen every few months in America. We collectively are answerable to those families, who lose their loved ones, because of our inaction." Obama then called for "modest" gun regulations, without specifying the nature of those "modest" gun regulations.

No one "allows" mass shootings to happen other than those who refuse to arm guards or give potential victims the ability to protect themselves. But that didn't stop Obama from using the deaths of innocents as a platform for his childish "DO SOMETHING!!!!!" antics. Obama specifically presented no gun agenda, because none of the regulations he has proposed in the past would have stopped an incident like Umpqua Community College. He implies that he's interested in full-scale gun confiscation, but he's far more interested in demonizing his political opposition, painting all of his opponents are mean-spirited and cruel-hearted.

That's because he's a jackass. Leveling personal accusations without a shred of evidence makes you a jackass, and Obama fits that definition to a T.

Now, he's not unique in this regard. Hillary Clinton recently suggested that Republicans who oppose Planned Parenthood resemble "terrorist groups" and that conservatives who oppose illegal immigration want to use Nazi-like "boxcars" to deport millions. Joe Biden infamously stated in 2012 that Republicans wanted to put black people "back in chains." Because leftist policy prescriptions invariably involve ignoring crucial issues in favor of feel-good incoherence, their main political play is name-calling sans evidence.

But Obama has perfected the craft.

The main problem with this tactic isn't its cynical political use—it's that Obama thinks it actually works. Hence, Obama's jackassery doesn't stop at water's edge. Last week, as Vladimir Putin pressed his advantage in Syria, Obama told the world that Putin presented little threat. Why? Putin went into Syria "out of weakness. ... I didn't see, after he made that speech in the United Nations, suddenly the 60-nation coalition that we have start lining up behind him. Iran and Assad make up Mr. Putin's coalition at the moment. The rest of the world makes up ours."

Faculty lounge insults will not stop Putin in Syria. And Obama's vaunted coalition is illusory: No one will stop Putin or Assad, including Obama. But Obama has become so convinced of the success of the Jackass Strategy that he uses it to no avail on America's opponents. Putin is not running against Obama; he's not Mitt Romney. But Obama acts as though Putin is somehow vulnerable to the same sorts of emotional blackmail as Republican opponents. He isn't.

We should be smart enough not to fall for Obama's jackassery when it comes to domestic politics. But America becomes more vulnerable when the president only knows how to insult, and thinks our foreign enemies give a damn about his sneering blather.

The Anti-Jew Anti-Gun Crusade

October 14, 2015

This week, 2016 Republican presidential contender Dr. Ben Carson bore the brunt of the media's ire for his politically incorrect take on the evils of gun control. "Through a combination of removing guns and disseminating propaganda, the Nazis were able to carry out their evil intentions with relatively little resistance," Carson writes in his new book, "A Perfect Union."

Leftists, including the activists of the Anti-Defamation League, promptly condemned Carson. National Director Jonathan Greenblatt explained, "the notion that Hitler's gun-control policy contributed to the Holocaust is historically inaccurate." Nick Baumann of The Huffington Post wrote, "There was some armed Jewish resistance to the power of the Nazi war machine. But it often ended in death for the Jews involved."

This is the height of idiocy. Pretty much everything ended in death for Jews during World War II in Europe. But what gave them a better shot of survival: having a gun or being completely disarmed?

Historically, enemies of the Jews—or any other subject population, for that matter—have sought to disarm the Jews in order to carry out their designs. This goes all the way back to the Bible, in which the Philistines banned all ironsmiths from the Jews, explicitly stating, "Lest the Jews make them swords or spears." Hitler knew the efficacy of gun control, and effectuated it with regard to Jews throughout his regime: While guns were completely banned in Germany in 1920, the laws were liberalized in 1928 before Hitler cracked down on Jews from 1933 to 1938, when full confiscation of all weapons, including knives, from Jews took place. The penalty for Jewish ownership of weapons: condemnation to a concentration camp for up to 20 years. Jews were warned that "they should interpret the new ordinance and the already existing Weapons Law strictly."

Would Jewish weapons have helped prevent the Holocaust? They certainly would have saved more Jewish lives. Jewish resistance in the death camps of Sobibor and Treblinka shut them down; Jewish resistance in the Warsaw Ghetto led to over a thousand German casualties. Armed resistance is invariably a better method of self-defense against tyranny than nothing.

Meanwhile, in the Holy Land, the British sought to prevent Jewish weapons ownership as well, so as to prevent those uppity Jews from seizing control of pre-independence Israel. Jewish independence fighters, victimized by Arab gangs and British authorities who cast a warm eye on them, began manufacturing bullets underground and transporting them using milk trucks. After World War II, Jews were unlikely to surrender their weapons to supposedly friendly authorities. They didn't. The result: a Jewish State.

Guns matter. Self-defense matters.

The left wants Jews to surrender both.

Today, the world turns a blind eye as Palestinian Arabs stab children in the streets of Jerusalem—and they tell the Israelis not to worry so much about Iranian terror support or the Iranian nuclear program. Jews should simply stop being so militaristic, tell their armed citizens to stop fighting with terrorists armed with blades. Surely, that will end the cycle of violence.

But for centuries, the cycle of violence has not ended with regard to Jews. That's because there is no cycle of violence: It's a consistent pattern of Jew-hatred carried forward to violence. Denigrating Jewish self-defense means more dead Jews. More importantly, it means depriving Jews of their humanity. The first human right is the right to defend your life and your family, even if you can't win. More good people with guns fighting tyranny make the world a better place. That was true in 1944, and it's true today. That rule doesn't change just because the world seems indifferent to Jewish suffering, no matter what the era.

Superman Takes on the Cops, Batman Takes on Gentrification, and Captain America Takes on Border Control

October 21, 2015

One of the most depressing features of modern American life lies in the left's total war on every facet of our shared culture. It isn't enough to produce movies with Steve Carell and Julianne Moore and Ellen Page about lesbian partners seeking legal protection for conveyance of property. Now, even comic books must be hijacked in order to promote leftist messaging.

The latest run of Captain America features the newest Cap, Sam Wilson, taking on the Sons of the Serpent—an evil group of tea party types intent on stopping illegal immigration. The writer, Nick Spencer, is an ardent opponent of Donald Trump, and slathered the comic with his dislike for conservatives: the Sons of the Serpent amass at the border to stop the poor, bewildered immigrants here illegally, whereupon the Sons of the Serpent leader announces, "Attention all trespassers! I am the Supreme Serpent! By invading this sovereign land, you defy the laws of God, Nature and the United States Constitution. Therefore, I hereby apprehend you by the power vested in me by the aforementioned God, Nature, et cetera, et cetera." One of the immigrants cries, "Please, whoever you are—we don't want any trouble—"

But the Supreme Serpent will have none of it: he continues, "Until the mighty wall is built, you come here for employment that is rightfully ours! And if denied it, you seek welfare paid for by our tax dollars!"

Thankfully, Captain America stops by to shut down the Minutemen wannabes, shouting, "If you're done threatening a bunch of unarmed folks, mostly women and children ... I'd pack up the pickup and head home if I were you, gentlemen."

It's not just Captain America now mouthing leftist talking points. Superman, once a friend to the cops, has now become their enemy. In the latest run of Superman Action Comics No. 42, the temporarily powerless Man of Steel ends up on the wrong side of the police—a group of faceless fascists looking to shut down any discussion. That's when Superman arrives to take on the riot squad. That follows on the incredibly overrated Grant Morrison making Superman a black president of the United States back in Action Comics No. 9 in 2012.

And then there's Batman No. 44, in which the Caped Crusader stumbles on the body of a slain black teenager. The teenager was shot by a cop while wearing a hoodie. Writer Scott Snyder said, "Of course you want Batman to beat this officer up, and be like, 'How could you?'"

How did this black teenager end up in a confrontation with the police in the first place? He went to the Penguin for a loan since the evil, evil banks wouldn't give him a loan based on his lack of credit history; he needed a loan to keep his father's corner business going. For some reason, all of this is supposedly Bruce Wayne's fault for gentrifying the area—even though gentrification would make his corner business valuable, and therefore saleable. Writer Brian Azzarello explains, "This thing is such a ripple, the way lives are affected by gentrification. ... And if you have no money, you have no voice."

Culture is one of the few areas of American life that allows us to continue to speak with one another. Left and right may have little in common, but we all like our movies and our television shows and our comic books. But when the left decides to turn comics into yet another outlet for their political propaganda, those cultural ties break, leaving yet another, small gap in our common life—and indoctrinating another generation into leftist nonsense.

No, Hillary Didn't Care About Chris Stevens

October 28, 2015

Last week, the media hailed Hillary Clinton's supposed political triumph at a hearing of the House Select Committee on Benghazi concerning the terrorist attack of Sept. 11, 2012 that ended in the murder of four Americans, including American ambassador to Libya, Christopher Stevens. Clinton appeared calm and collected, even as she lied repeatedly: She said that she believed a YouTube video still bore some responsibility for the terrorist attack, despite the fact that she told the Egyptian prime minister the day after the attack that the video had nothing to do with the attack; she insisted that political hack Sidney Blumenthal didn't act as an advisor, even though he routinely emailed with her about policy; she stated that she'd been transparent about her emails, although that nonsense has been rejected by the State Department.

Most of all, Clinton suggested that Stevens had been responsible for his own murder. She said that he "felt comfortable" on the ground, and that he was merely joking when he emailed about whether the Benghazi compound would be closed. "Chris Stevens had ... a really good sense of humor," Clinton laughed. "And I just see him smiling as he's typing this." Stevens' State Department team in Libya sent requests for additional security 600 times. They were rejected.

After Clinton finished lying, she went home and hung out with her entire team. She partied. "I had my whole team come over to my house and we sat around eating Indian food and drinking wine and beer," Clinton told MSNBC's Rachel Maddow. "That's what we did. It was great. ... They did a terrific job, you know, kind of being there behind me and getting me ready, and then, you know, just talk about what we're going to do next."

As an apparent afterthought, she added to Maddow, "The point is, what are we going to do both honor and the people that we lost, and try to make sure this doesn't happen again."

Chris Stevens was always an afterthought to Clinton, despite her crocodile tears at the hearing, where she complained, "I would imagine I've thought more about what happened than all of you put together. I've lost more sleep than all of you put together." She didn't give Stevens her private email address, though Blumenthal had it. She couldn't remember holding a single conversation with Stevens after he was appointed ambassador to Libya. The night of his death she sent an email with the subject line "Chris Smith," mixing up his name with that of fellow diplomat Sean Smith. She spoke to survivors only days later. The night of the attack, she didn't speak with the Secretary of Defense Leon Panetta or the Chairman of the Joint Chiefs of Staff Martin Dempsey.

Clinton's aggressive case for the invasion of Libya led to the overthrow and killing of dictator Moammar Gadhafi—an event for which Clinton was happy to take credit, laughing, "We came, we saw, he died." She then completely ignored Libya as it turned into a terrorist hellhole, because that inconvenient fact undercut her narrative of strength and purpose. Her State Department refused to grant additional security requests because doing so would have implicitly recognized the failure of her war. Then, after Stevens died, Clinton and her team lied to the American people and the families of the slain, pinning the murders on an unforeseeable YouTube video-driven attack, rather than an utterly foreseeable terrorist attack.

Clinton is a coldly manipulative, deeply ambitious politician willing to say and do anything to achieve power. She was always that person, which is why she lied to Americans from in front of the flag-draped caskets of the murdered men in Benghazi. And she is that person now, too, as she laughs and eats Indian food hours after maintaining her lies once again before the American people.

Republicans vs. The Media

November 4, 2015

For years, I have been begging Republicans to stand up to the mainstream media. The left has dominated the media for as long as I've been alive. Yet Republicans have consistently granted leftists in media the patina of legitimacy: they've appeared on their programs, answered their questions without quibble, and allowed the audience to believe that the questions themselves spring from a place of objectivity rather than a desire to harm Republicans.

The political damage has been near incalculable. In 2012, Clinton and George Stephanopoulos singlehandedly redirected the presidential election narrative by asking Republican frontrunner Mitt Romney about banning contraceptives—a policy that no Republican had advocated at any point during the campaign. A few months later, CNN's in-house Barack Obama serviceperson Candy Crowley won the second presidential debate by wrongly telling Romney that Obama had labeled Benghazi a terrorist attack.

So why haven't Republicans fought back? Because Republicans have had a collective action problem. For each Republican willing to label George Stephanopoulos a political hack, there's a camera-loving John McCain willing to grant Stephanopoulos the premise of neutrality for a bit of airtime. For every Republican willing to ask CNBC moderators about their history of leftist questioning, there's a John Kasich willing to praise the moderators as open-minded and fair.

All this came to an end last week. CNBC, in its gauche attempt to grab ratings, set up a rogue's gallery of leftists, all of whom proceeded to berate, bash, and browbeat the various candidates into looking foolish. That continued until Senator Ted Cruz, R., Texas, put a stop to it: "This is not a cage match ... how about talking about the substantive issues people care about?" Cruz pointed out, correctly, that none of the questioners would be voting in a Republican primary—the implication being that the moderators have priorities other than asking honest questions. That started the pile-on. Senator Marco Rubio, R., Fla., jumped in and called the media Hillary Clinton's Super PAC. Governor Chris Christie, R., N.J., bashed moderator John Harwood for being rude, even by New Jersey standards.

And then the candidates came together and said they would no longer abide by rules set by a ratings-seeking, leftist media, and the ratings-seeking, donation-machine Republican National Committee. Instead, they would approve moderators in advance, and demand that those asking the questions be held up to a standard of decency.

The media, naturally, went nearly insane over this slight. Like pearl-clutching CNBC moderator Carl Quintanilla, who peckishly refused to let Cruz answer his question on Obamacare after Cruz slapped the media, the members of the media insisted that the real offenders were the intransigent Republicans. Then the Democratic National Committee announced that MSNBC host Rachel Maddow would be moderating a live presidential forum, humiliating that argument.

The Republican willingness to partake in its own political demise has undermined conservatism for years. Now the mask is off. Thanks to CNBC for that.

The Leftist Tree Must Be Watered With Blood at Mizzou

November 11, 2015

University of Missouri President Tim Wolfe must wonder what he did wrong.

It all began back in September when the black student government president complained that a racist drove by in a truck and allegedly called him a racial slur. Then, in September, a group of black students said that a drunken white racist shouted a slur at them, too.

Ugly, of course. But in any normal world, without further evidence of the incidents, life would have gone on—occasional ugliness from ugly people is a feature of living on Earth. But that wasn't good enough: somehow, Wolfe had to be held responsible, according to the student body. The election of a black student government president was less representative of the campus climate than a couple of shouted names. Thus, the radical group Concerned Student 1950 shut down the university's homecoming parade, and then surrounded Wolfe's car and tried to force him to get out. When he refused and called the police, they protested him as a racist.

And, like a good little leftist, Wolfe apologized. "I am sorry, and my apology is long overdue," he said. "My behavior seemed like I did not care. That was not my intention."

That did not appease the baying crowd, however.

One graduate student began a hunger strike for no apparent reason. But Wolfe continued to scrape and bow before those who would have his head, saying of the would-be revolutionary, "his voice for social justice is important and powerful. He is being heard and I am listening. I am thankful for the leadership provided by him and the other student leaders in raising awareness of racism, injustice and intolerance."

Still not good enough.

The Concerned Student 1950 group released a demand letter. They wanted Wolfe to show them a handwritten letter—not typed, mind you—admitting his own "white privilege." Such privilege apparently included the distinct honor of being fired for his skin color while being forced to maintain that his position is advantageous due to his skin color.

On Friday night, a group of students accosted him at an event, reading him the riot act about the chimera known as "white privilege." He stated, "Systematic oppression is because you don't believe that you have the equal opportunity for success—" At this point, one of the students began screaming at him, accusing him of blaming black students for their own feelings of alienation. Which, given the evidence, would have been a solid accusation. But Wolfe didn't even make it.

Then, 30 black members of the football team—many of whom were on athletic scholarships provided for them despite academic underachievement—announced they wouldn't play football so long as Wolfe remained. The white coach of the team, who earns $3.1 million from the taxpayer-sponsored university, joined the protest. He was not accused of "white privilege."

Finally, on Monday, Wolfe resigned. He said, "It is clear to all of us that change is needed, and we appreciate the thoughtfulness and passion which have gone into the sharing of concerns." Such thoughtfulness apparently included shouting down members of the media and blocking them from covering protests.

But with Wolfe's career in tatters solely due to his race, President Obama's White House finally stepped in—not to defend a fellow liberal administrator, but to praise the rabblerousing students. White House press secretary Josh Earnest said that this was the sort of activity Obama talked about "in his campaign, that a few people speaking up and speaking out can have a profound impact on the communities where we live and work."

Community organizing on a national scale. President Obama's vision has finally reached fruition. And because the tree of leftism must occasionally be watered with the blood of liberal authority figures, Tim Wolfe is out of a job. But no big deal. Such are the wages of "white privilege."

No, It Is Not Un-American to Prefer Christian Refugees to Muslim Refugees

November 18, 2015

On Friday, Muslim terrorists murdered 129 people in Paris. At least one of the ISIS perpetrators apparently entered Europe as a "refugee" from Syria—he was found with a refugee ID. ISIS has already claimed that they have infiltrated the Syrian refugee population to the tune of thousands of terrorists.

On Monday, President Obama announced that it would be purely un-American for Westerners to ban unvetted Muslim immigrants from the Middle East while allowing Christian targets of genocide to enter the West. He called such an idea "shameful," while passionately calling for Americans to "open our hearts" to more refugees. He praised bordering countries Turkey, Jordan and Lebanon for taking in hundreds of thousands of refugees; Obama said that showed their "belief in a common humanity." He added, "And so we have to, each of us, do our part. And the United States has to step up and do its part. And when I hear folks say that, well, maybe we should just admit the Christians but not the Muslims ...That's not American. That's not who we are."

Every aspect of this little speech is wrong. Turkey, Jordan and Lebanon aren't taking in Muslim refugees out of some great commitment to common humanity. They're doing so because their other choice involves setting up fences and machine guns to stop the waves of refugees crossing their frontiers. And as we know, Muslim countries have a rotten history of absorbing fellow members of their ummah: For 70 years, since the creation of the State of Israel, tens of thousands of Palestinian Arabs have lived in refugee camps located in Muslim lands. By contrast, the State of Israel has taken in every

Jewish refugee seeking asylum, from Russian emigres to Moroccan immigrants, from Ethiopian refugees to Syrian expatriates.

And the West has good reason for skepticism toward Muslim refugees. While Muslim refugees who stay in the Middle East split evenly between males and females, the vast majority of refugees entering Europe are males of fighting age. Muslim immigration has already led to massive increases in crime from France to Sweden, and cultural fragmentation from Great Britain to Austria. Terrorism is only the latest threat—and even that threat is obviously not exaggerated. Vetting refugees from Syria is nearly impossible given its status as a failed state. Vetting Muslim refugees is totally impossible given the fact that radical Muslims can easily masquerade as less-radical Muslims.

So why does President Obama, along with the global left, seek more Muslim immigration? Because President Obama does not believe that Islam, as a religious philosophy, presents any threat to the West. He believes that radical Islam doesn't exist. It's merely the hallmark of global poverty, probably affected negatively by climate change; if the West redistributed its wealth, ceased its "colonial" attitudes toward the Middle East, all would be well. The materialism of Marxism would win the day.

Never mind that this argument is entirely without evidence. Never mind that Muslims from Western nations have left wealth to join the impoverished ISIS fighters. Never mind that Osama Bin Laden himself was a wealthy man who lived in a cave to plan attacks against Westerners. Ideology matters, but to the self-centered Marxists of the global left, only their ideology matters: Everyone else has merely fallen into nasty ideas thanks to lack of resources.

And so we must give them our resources, endanger our own citizens. To do anything else would be un-American, according to the people whose idea of Americanism involves the rejection of the very ideas upon which America was founded.

The Death of Free Speech

November 25, 2015

Four in 10 young Americans have no idea what America is.

That's the takeaway from a new Pew Research poll showing that 40 percent of Americans aged 18-34 say that the government should be able to prevent people from making "statements that are offensive to minority groups." This same group of young people has granted broad awareness to the culture of "microaggression"—unintended slights taken as grave insults by their victims; they've also called for "trigger warnings," alerts that certain communications may dredge up unpleasant past memories or ideas. With such ghoulish cruelties haunting the most privileged generation in human history, naturally we'd want to toss out the bedrock of Western civilization: The right to debate, to express unpopular opinions. We wouldn't want to offend.

Unless, of course, we do.

There are those of us who find guns in our face far more offensive than the occasional taunt. We don't like the notion that your disapproval of an opinion gives you the right to call the men with the guns; we find that perspective tyrannical and threatening. We're not interested in your subjective feelings-world, in which you claim that innocuous statements somehow harm you in material ways. We don't believe that self-appointed victim status grants you the ability to use force. We think you ought to develop a thicker skin—the sort of skin necessary to enjoy freedom. If your political agoraphobia prevents you from engaging in the arguments that characterize free countries, that doesn't mean you should lock us all away in our "safe spaces." Those "safe spaces" are called jail cells, and the only people who want to establish them are jackbooted fascists masquerading as hippy-dippy caring experts.

If all of this seems relatively basic, that's because it is. But because America forgot to teach her children those basics, they will be torn out by the root. The American university system has become Ground Zero for the anti-free speech movement. That's because young people always look for a cause for which to fight, an oppressive force to crush. Young people aren't looking for comfort; as George Orwell wrote in 1940 regarding the appeal of the Nazis, "Nearly all western thought since the last war, certainly all 'progressive' thought, has assumed tacitly that human beings desire nothing beyond ease, security and avoidance of pain. In such a view of life there is no room, for instance, for patriotism and the military virtues. Hitler, because in his own joyless mind he feels it with exceptional strength, knows that human beings don't only want comfort, safety, short working-hours, hygiene, birth-control and, in general, common sense; they also, at least intermittently, want struggle and self-sacrifice, not to mention drums, flags and loyalty-parades."

How can today's young people enjoy such struggle?

Since America is the freest country in the history of humanity, the only oppression to be found is self-oppression—and the only way to free people from that is to shackle everyone else. The old rule of politics stated that your right to wave your fist ends with my nose; the leftist perspective is that your right to wave your fist ends with that waving fist generating feelings of unease. So stop waving it. Anywhere.

The real danger here is that the would-be oppressors will win. They already are on university campuses, where those labeled holders of "white privilege" can now be fired or silenced based on the color of their skin. If Americans don't fight back against the free speech opponents, this battle will get ugly: Once one side utilizes actual aggression, it's only a matter of time until battle truly begins.

President Obama's Imaginary World

December 2, 2015

President Obama lives in a world all his own. It's a world in which he's widely beloved but also misunderstood, a world in which everyone is racist except for those who support him, a world in which his foreign policy has been heroically successful and his domestic policy even more so. President Obama lives in Fantasyland.

In this Fantasyland, it's not enough for President Obama to define the world around him in self-serving fashion. He must define his enemies the same way. To that end, while visiting Paris for the Climate Change Summit that will supposedly usher in an era of global cooperation and environmental utopianism, Obama announced that he had finally found a way to defeat Islamic State. Talking about climate change, Obama said, was an "act of defiance that proves nothing will deter us ... What greater rejection of those who would tear down our world than marshaling our best efforts to save it?"

Not to be Debbie Downer, but nothing in ISIS' plans suggests that they care deeply about preventing a bunch of self-important bureaucrats from meeting in well-stocked, toney hotels to destroy the Western economy on behalf of scientific chimeras. ISIS, in fact, probably adores the notion that the West will take itself down a couple economic pegs in order to redistribute the wealth. Certainly other Islamic terrorists have felt that way. Osama Bin Laden, for example, lamented that the West did not spend more money on climate change relief efforts, and stated according to Al Jazeera, "Speaking about climate change is not a matter of intellectual luxury—the phenomenon is an actual fact. All of the industrialized countries, especially the big ones, bear responsibility for the global warming crisis."

Regardless of ISIS' feelings on global warming, they obviously don't sit around in Raqqa lamenting that their plans have been defeated by those dastardly Westerners and their catered diplomatic lunches. But President Obama says they do. That's because he crafts his own enemies based on who he wishes they were. Obama is thoroughly uncomfortable with the idea that those who wish to fight him are members of radical Islam. He wishes they were right-wing American ideologues. So he simply plays them off as such.

Obama did the same thing with regard to the Iran nuclear deal. While handing Iran $150 billion in funding, opening their economy, and granting them a full nuclear weapons program in a decade, Obama claimed that the real enemies of peace were Republicans siding with Iranian hardliners. Never mind that those hardliners didn't exist. Obama created them magically, and then made them Republicans.

Barack Obama is a leftist hammer in search of a conservative nail. No matter who his enemies *actually* are, he'll characterize them as American conservatives for purposes of whacking them over the head. ISIS may have slaughtered Westerners in Paris thanks to radical Islam, but Obama will never acknowledge that: instead, he'll just claim that they're essentially Ted Cruz in keffiyehs.

This isn't rare. Jackie Kennedy once lamented that her husband had been shot by a "silly little communist" rather than dying for civil rights; her allies quickly turned JFK's assassination into a referendum on American conservatism. Obama's doing the same thing now. He has chosen his enemies, and they don't include ISIS. That means that if ISIS must be his enemy, he will simply wave his Fantasyland wand, and they will be transformed into the Republican enemies he so craves.

The problem is, they won't. They'll just keep killing. Reality remains reality, no matter how much President Obama sprinkles fairy dust and claps his hands.

Should We Religiously Profile?

December 9, 2015

Months ago, a concerned American at a school in Texas spotted a 14-year-old Muslim boy toting around a contraption that looked very much like a bomb. That Texan called the police, who came and detained the boy; after learning that the boy's device was actually a disassembled clock, they released him.

Weeks ago, a concerned American in San Bernardino spotted a "half-dozen Middle Eastern men" in the area of an apartment housing Syed Rizwan Farook and Tashfeen Malik. He didn't know what they were doing there, but they seemed suspicious. He didn't call the cops.

In San Bernardino, of course, that political correctness ended in the death of 14 Americans and the wounding of 21 more. In Texas, that failure to bow to political correctness ended in the attorney general of the United States vowing to track down and investigate the local police department.

Welcome to politically correct America, where you are damned if you do, and damned if you don't.

Political correctness costs lives. It doesn't merely require us to abide by the strictures of an arbitrary linguistic code. It isn't just an irritation. It means that we're all supposed to frontally lobotomize ourselves to basic realities. We're supposed to pretend that there's nothing more suspicious about a half-dozen Middle Eastern males coming and going at odd hours from an apartment with a small child than there would be if a half-dozen white males did the same thing. We're supposed to cave to the fantasy that a religious Muslim reaching out to terrorists over the internet poses no more threat than a Christian visiting a pro-life website. We're supposed to blind ourselves in order to avoid the obvious.

That costs lives.

Now, this doesn't mean that we ought to discriminate against individual Muslims, of course. But it does mean that law enforcement ought to look at indicators of possible terrorist connections, and that one preliminary indicator is religious practice of Islam. That indicator isn't sufficient to determine connection to terrorism—far from it. No single indicator generally is. But behavioral profiling involves investigating a variety of factors. As Daniel Wagner, CEO of Risk Solutions, writes about Israel's profiling techniques, "Departing passengers [at Ben Gurion Airport] are questioned by highly trained security agents before they reach the check-in counter. These interviews could last as little as one minute or as long as an hour, based on such factors as age, race, religion and destination."

Ignoring any of these factors represents incompetence.

But the president wants to use the force of law to enshrine incompetence. He suggests that to assess risk differently based on religious observance is somehow a violation of basic American principles, rather than a time-tested technique of all human relations. We obviously must remain on guard for baseless bias and persecution without evidence. But we can't ignore the realities of risk assessment in the name of cultural sensitivity, either.

That's how we end up with the utter stupidity of an MSNBC host suggesting that media stop showing pictures of the San Bernardino female shooter so as not to link her hijab-clad visage with Islam. That's how we end up with Obama suggesting that our own Islamophobia causes terrorism, rather than radical Islam. Most importantly, that's how we end up with more dead Americans.

Security Dies Where Multiculturalism Thrives

December 16, 2015

While Americans fret over Donald Trump's plans to ban Muslim immigration to the United States temporarily thanks to the government's inability to keep us safe, the government continues to prove its inability to keep us safe. This week, we found out that President Obama's Department of Homeland Security prohibited agents from screening foreign citizens applying for visas to enter the country. According to former acting undersecretary at DHS for intelligence and analysis John Cohen, "During that time period immigration officials were not allowed to use or review social media as part of the screening process. ... The primary concern was that it would be viewed negatively if it was disclosed publicly and there were concerns that it would be embarrassing."

He continued, "It was primarily a question of optics. There were concerns from a privacy and civil liberties perspective that while this was not illegal, that it would be viewed negatively if it was disclosed publicly."

So 14 Americans in San Bernardino died for optics.

While President Obama insists that the government must check the metadata of American citizens to catch terrorists, he insists that his own people stop checking the publicly posted Facebook messages of potential terrorists.

This is the essence of multiculturalism. Multiculturalism suggests that all cultures are equal, that they carry equal values, that they pose equal threats to public safety. Extending that logic, we must treat suspects from all cultures with equal care. But what if not all cultures provide an equal threat? What if the people who engage in some cultures are more likely than others to participate in terrorism? Then, in order to maintain the multicultural fiction, we must bend over backwards not to check out threats from such cultures. Either that, or we must violate everyone's civil rights equally.

The former is happening in the United States; the latter is happening in France, where the government has been knocking down the doors of hundreds of mosques on grounds of "preach[ing] hatred" or using "takfiri speech," according to French imam Hassan El Alaoui. In the United States, we'd see such raids as a violation of the First and Fourth Amendments. In France, they have no such amendments. They do, however, have a multicultural view of the world.

Or at least they did. Across Europe, the reality of multiculturalism is hitting home. German chancellor Angela Merkel, who was recently named Time's Person of the Year for taking in one million Syrian refugees, said, "Multiculturalism leads to parallel societies and therefore remains a 'life lie' ... We want and we will reduce the number of refugees noticeably." She was forced to denounce her own former viewpoint thanks to the fallout from her decisions: Refugee camps have turned into hotbeds of rape and child abuse. Mass Muslim immigration into Europe has heightened such challenges for years, of course, but the left and the press have suppressed such information.

No longer.

This is what happens when the West denies its values. Eventually, reality forces the West to confront the truth: Its own culture is superior to others, and that pretending otherwise creates real danger. But so long as leftists like President Obama remain in denial, that danger will only grow.

Hillary Is the Islamic State's Best Recruitment Tool

December 23, 2015

During the little-watched pre-Christmas Democratic debate, former Secretary of State Hillary Clinton accused Donald Trump of being the Islamic State group's chief recruiter. Relying on her penchant for blaming videos for Islamic evil, she stated that the Islamic State is "showing videos of Donald Trump insulting Islam and Muslims in order to recruit more radical jihadists."

Well, no.

The Islamic State's videos—the ones that actually exist, not the ones Clinton makes up in her fevered imagination during debate pee breaks—show that the group uses three main themes in its recruitment. First, it talks about Islamic prophecy. In a video released Nov. 24, titled "No Respite," the narrator explains, in English, over hypnotic chanting: "This is our (caliphate), in all its glory, remaining and expanding. ... It's a state built on the prophetic methodology, striving to follow the Quran and Sunna. ... We are men honored with Islam who climbed its peaks to perform jihad, answering the call to unite under one flag. This is the source of our glory: our obedience to our Lord. ... We only bow to Allah."

So much for President Barack Obama and Hillary Clinton's jabbering nonsensically about the Islamic State's having nothing to do with Islam.

Second, it talks about its string of victories. The video brags that the group's territory is "already greater than Britain, eight times the size of Belgium and 30 times the size of Qatar." It directly challenges America: "You claim to have the greatest army history has known. You may have the numbers and weapons, but your soldiers lack the will and resolve. Still scarred from their defeats in Afghanistan and Iraq, they return dead or suicidal, with over 6,500 of them killing themselves each year." It claims that America's airstrikes have accomplished nothing and that the United States' $250,000 missiles will never be able to defeat the Islamic State and its 50-cent bullets. It adds that the United States lacks the power to put boots on the ground.

In other words, it mocks the Obama administration's agenda. Without losses in Afghanistan and Iraq—both idiotic and precipitous pullouts by the Obama team—and without the constant drumbeat from the left that military men and women are poor victims of circumstance, the Islamic State wouldn't have this particular talking point.

Finally, the Islamic State talks about the emptiness of the West. The group contrasts its own allegiance to Allah with the West's allegiance to "a secular state—built on man-made laws—whose soldiers fight for the interests of ... legislators, liars, fornicators, corporations and for the freedoms of sodomites." The video flashes pictures of Obama, George W. Bush and Bill Clinton. No Trump.

It concludes: "Bring it on, all of you. Your numbers only increase us in faith, and we're counting your banners, which our prophet said would reach 80 in number, and then the flames of war will finally burn you on the hills of Dabiq. Bring it on, for we echo the mighty call of our prophets. ... Show us no respite. Our ally is the greatest. He is Allah, and all glory belongs to him." The reference to Dabiq is to an apocalyptic site in Syria. According to Islamic teachings, it is supposed to host a battle between the Christians and the Muslims that will usher in Armageddon.

So as it turns out, it isn't Trump whom the Islamic State uses to recruit. It's the American government—in particular the victories handed to the group by the American left. Hillary Clinton is a better recruiting tool for the Islamic State than Donald Trump, hands down.

For Obama, It's Not Delusion, It's Purpose

December 30, 2015

Good news, America: the Obama administration has achieved peace in Syria. That's according to John Kirby, the Assistant Secretary of State for the Bureau of Public Affairs and spokesperson at the US State Department, who issued a blog post filled with five-word summations of 2015. Here's their summation of the Syrian crisis: "Bringing Peace, Security to Syria."

So the hundreds of thousands dead, the millions of refugees, the rise of ISIS, the enshrinement of dictator Bashar Assad—none of it ever happened. According to the State Department, everything's going swimmingly.

More good news: the Obama administration has also defeated terrorism: "Winning Fight Against Violent Extremists." Oddly, more Americans now say that America is losing the war on terrorism than at any time since 9/11; 74 percent of Americans say they are dissatisfied with how the war on terror is progressing.

But the news gets even better: the State Department proclaims that it has achieved Iran's disarmament: "Iran Peaceful Nuclear Program Ensured." Well, there is that whole awkward Iran continuing to develop whatever it wants while funding terrorism across the world with money freed up by the United States and its allies. But really, we've stopped the mullahs dead in their tracks.

There are only two possible rationales for this sort of disconnect with reality: first, the Obama administration knows they're full of it, but they keep on gritting their teeth and pushing the misinformation; second, they seriously believe that they are achieving magnificent results. In other words, they're either cynical or delusional.

My money's on delusional.

Barack Obama is a pseudo-intellectual who believes so deeply in the power of his own ideas that he gets lost in them. It never occurs to him that they could breed violence or evil. They're beautiful. Like Dr. Manhattan in "Watchmen," he'd rather build crystal towers of stunning meticulousness on Mars than anything of value here on Earth—but unlike Dr. Manhattan, he won't leave Earth alone. He'll transplant his notions of reality onto the rest of us.

Thus alleged deserter Bowe Bergdahl becomes a soldier who served honorably; Benghazi becomes a battle over a YouTube video; Israel becomes the aggressor against the peaceful Palestinians; ISIS becomes a jayvee threat; Iran becomes a potential ally. Obama has done the calculations on his chalkboard, and they all add up.

Except that they don't. But that won't stop Obama from pursuing his equations, thinking himself the John Nash who revolutionized game theory when he's actually the John Nash pasting headlines about the communist conspiracy to the walls of his study. It's all still beautiful in his head. It's just delusional.

And that delusion has real world costs. This week, we found out that Obama pressured Secretary of Defense Ash Carter to release more Guantanamo Bay terrorists into foreign hands, and even scolded him personally. Reuters reports, "Since then, the Pentagon has been more cooperative. Administration officials said they expect to begin transferring at least 17 detainees to foreign countries in January." The report said Obama fired Carter's predecessor, Chuck Hagel, for slow-walking Gitmo transfers as well.

That's because the Defense Department still has to operate in the realm of reality, where nearly 30 percent of Gitmo releases have either been confirmed re-entering the fray or are suspected of having done so. Obama doesn't have to worry about such realities. He's busy constructing crystal castles on Mars.

Except Mars is right here, on Earth.

And Obama's still the most powerful man on this planet.

Book Three

The Establishment Is Dead

The Tearful Dictator

January 6, 2016

The tyrant cries.

While announcing his new slate of gun control measures designed to pave the way for a national gun registration regime, President Obama welled up in a press conference on Tuesday. He'd spent nearly half an hour berating Republicans, American voters and the National Rifle Association for their supposed intransigence in failing to embrace his executive actions. Finally, he reached up to his eyes, rubbed at them, and as tears wet his cheeks, he stated, "Every time I think about those kids, it gets me mad. ... We need voters who want safer gun laws, and who are disappointed in leaders who stand in their way, to remember come election time."

The American people, you see, have to change. They have to change because they are uncaring. And we know they are uncaring because the most powerful man on the planet weeps when he thinks of the little children.

But you don't, do you?

We've now reached the apex of the Feelings Age. It no longer matter what good policy looks like. It no longer matters what the Constitution says. All that matters is that our politicians care about people like us. During the 2012 election, Mitt Romney won a wide variety of exit polls regarding policy, from leadership skill to values. But he lost the election because Obama clocked him 81 percent to 18 percent on the crucial issue of "cares about people like me."

And now Obama has come to collect.

But he can't do it without the tears. That's because the tears grant him the patina of vulnerability. No one fears the dictator who shows his human side. We view those who violate our rights as nefarious members of an evil cabal, lurking in the night while cackling. We don't view them as highly attuned, sensitive people -- after all, the logic goes, if they were that sensitive, they'd stop before violating the rights of others.

Which is why crying is such an effective tactic for those who would violate your rights. Crying on behalf of victims puts you on the side of the angels, and your opponents on the side of the demons. And we don't tend to care what happens to demons. We're too busy rooting for the angels.

That's why President Obama followed up his lachrymose performance with a call to action against all of his enemies. It's why he talked at length about shredding the Second Amendment in favor of "other rights," as though my right to own a gun endangers your right to pursuit of life, liberty and happiness. It's why the media immediately leapt to cover Obama's waterworks instead of his policies -- because the story is Obama's emotional heroism and essential decency, not his absolute failure to find any real solution to gun violence.

So look for more Obama emotional blackmail. And look for more stories about Obama's emotional journey from the compliant press, which prints narratives about empathetic heroes -- even if those heroes are busy violating other people's rights at every turn.

The West's Terminal Radical Islam Denial Syndrome

January 13, 2016

Last year, there were 452 suicide terror attacks across the world. Four hundred and fifty of them were committed by Muslims. Last month, Muslims pledging allegiance to ISIS murdered 14 people in San Bernardino, California. Last week, thousands of Muslims around Europe, from Germany to Sweden to Switzerland, sexually assaulted hundreds of young women on New Year's Eve. Just days ago, a Muslim man shot a Philadelphia cop at point-blank range and declared that he did it in the name of Islam.

In response, Hillary Clinton declared, "Muslims are peaceful and tolerant people and have nothing whatsoever to do with Islam." She agreed this week that "white terrorism and extremism" are just as much a threat to Americans as ISIS and radical Islam, and then proceeded to blame "gun violence." The mayor of Cologne, Germany, told young women not to walk within "arm's length" of young Muslim men, and leftist commentators explained that the wave of sexual harassment resulted from some generalized, nonspecific religious patriarchal attitudes. The mayor of Philadelphia said that the attack on the police officer had nothing to do with "being a Muslim or the Islamic faith," and that instead, we ought to focus our attention on the pressing issue of gun violence: "There are just too many guns on the streets, and I think our national government needs to do something about that."

If the West keeps this up, there won't be any West of which to speak.

German chancellor Angela Merkel, who just won the Time magazine person of the year for her courageous decision to subject her citizens to the cultural sophistication of Muslims of non-Westernized Syrian Muslim refugees, is now preparing to allow another wave of such refugees into her country to enjoy New Year's Eve activities. According to Politico, Germany can expect another 1.5 million refugees this year, and according to Germany's minister for international development, "Eight to 10 million are still on their way."

Meanwhile, here at home, President Obama will invite a Syrian Muslim refugee to attend his State of the Union address so that he can browbeat Republicans about their supposed xenophobia with regard to the issue. The Syrian Muslim refugee entered the United States after a bombing killed seven family members; he's now living in Troy, Michigan. Obama wrote him a letter recently: "You're part of what makes America great." No word on whether Obama wrote letters to Palestinian Muslim refugees Omar Faraj Saeed Al Hardan, 24, of Houston, who was arrested last week for attempting to provide material support to ISIS, or Aws Mohammed Younis Al-Jayab, who was charged with making a false statement involving international terrorism, according to CNN.

Presumably, some people who don't make America great include Syrian Christian refugees, who have largely been excluded from the United States by the Obama administration. Simultaneously, ISIS happily continues to exploit the Radical Islam Denial Syndrome of the left; they've been planning a "sophisticated" smuggling operation to move people across the border into Turkey, from where refugees then enter the West.

The West is far too powerful to lose to ISIS or radical Islam -- unless the West decides to pretend that radical Islam doesn't exist. In pathological fashion, that's just what our leaders have apparently decided to do.

Donald Trump and the Cult of Personality

January 20, 2016

"Power," Henry Kissinger once told The New York Times, "is the ultimate aphrodisiac." Kissinger might amend that statement today: Now, fame is power, and thus replaces power as the ultimate aphrodisiac. In fact, fame isn't just an aphrodisiac -- it's the ultimate nepenthe, a drug causing forgetfulness. The more famous our politicians are, the more we neglect their positions and character. No wonder the most admired woman in America is criminal Hillary Clinton, the most admired man is criminal Barack Obama, and the second-most admired man is loudmouth Donald Trump.

We assume that fame inoculates our politicians for the same reason we check Yelp reviews: If there are tons of people who recommend a restaurant, they can't all have been bribed. If tons of people like and support a politician, then, he or she must be worthwhile.

But this logic doesn't always work. If several people stand on a street corner and simultaneously look up in the air for no reason, passersby will begin staring up into the air, looking for the rationale behind the mass gaze. Our human desire for informational shortcuts -- our willingness to take another's word for it -- means that we end up looking like idiots when someone points out there's nothing up there.

Our media-reinforcing cycle of fame is more like a street corner of skyward-looking nincompoops than an aggregation of Yelp reviews. Our elites tell us that we ought to look at a given candidate in a given way; we then react to those elites by following their spotlight. Donald Trump has received nearly half of all media coverage in the Republican race since he announced his campaign. That means that a lot of people are willing to overlook his flubs and his foibles -- he's a known face, and that fame protects him from comments that would hurt any other candidate.

The problem here isn't Trump. It's our entire culture of politics. Barack Obama has made ubiquity an art form -- it's hard to imagine that someone who appears regularly with YouTube stars to talk about tampon taxes could actually be malignant. Joe Biden appears on "Parks and Recreation." Hillary Clinton dances with Ellen and makes awful jokes on "Saturday Night Live." Our politicians know that exposure makes us comfortable with them.

In truth, we should never be comfortable with our politicians. We should never trust them. Star worship of Ronald Reagan on the right leads establishment Republicans to idolize even his worst failures, like amnesty; star worship of Bill Clinton on the left leads Democrats to pooh-pooh his brutal treatment of women, and his wife's enabling of that behavior. Our celebrities have become royals, and our politicians have become celebrities.

That means we crown ourselves a king or queen every four years. And America needs no kings and queens. We need unimportant, decent people who focus on how to make themselves unimportant in our lives.

But that's not what we get. Instead, we get glitz and glamour, fun and frolicking with the people who control our freedoms. That's dangerous. We are dangerous, not Trump or even Obama or Hillary Clinton. Until we check our own impulse to blindly follow our celebrity political class, we shouldn't be surprised when our celebrities become politicians and our politicians become tyrants.

Anti-Establishment Does Not Mean Pro-Conservative

January 27, 2016

Donald Trump will change everything.

This seems to be the consensus among anti-establishment Republicans. According to the latest ABC News/Washington Post poll, Trump leads among anti-establishment primary voters with an actual majority of 51 percent. And a full 51 percent of Republicans think Trump is "the best choice to bring needed change to Washington, perhaps the single most crucial attribute to leaned Republicans."

Trump makes this case, too. He's said that he's the establishment's worst nightmare. He says he's too rich too be bought, too independent to care about what his enemies say, too powerful to be stopped. He'll stand up for the American people by standing against the powers-that-be.

Then he turns around and says he'll make deals. "I think the [establishment is] warming up," Trump said this week. "I want to be honest, I have received so many phone calls from people that you would call establishment, from people -- generally speaking ... conservatives, Republicans -- that want to come onto our team. We are getting calls from everybody that it's actually amazing. I'm actually surprised."

Why? Because, says Trump, unlike his chief rival, Senator Ted Cruz, R-Texas, he'll make deals. He's a deal-maker! "Guys like Ted Cruz will never make a deal because he's a strident guy," Trump said. "That's what the country's about really, isn't it?"

And Trump will make deals. He isn't lying. He's friendly with everybody on the Democratic side of the aisle. Here's Trump on

House Minority Leader Nancy Pelosi, D-Calif.: "I think I'm going to be able to get along with Pelosi -- I've always had a good relationship with Nancy Pelosi." Here's Trump on Senate Minority Leader Harry Reid, D-Nev.: He "always treated me nicely. We need that in Washington." Here's Trump on Senator Chuck Schumer, D-N.Y., godfather of amnesty: "I think I'll be able to get along well with Schumer, Chuck Schumer. I was always very good with Schumer. I was close to Schumer in many ways."

For that matter, here's Trump on Hillary Clinton circa 2012: "Hillary Clinton I think is a terrific woman." Here's Trump on President Obama circa 2009: "I think he's doing a really good job. ... He's really a champion."

It's not that Trump represents the establishment. He's still anti-establishment because he's not taking cues from them. He's running his own campaign, and he's following his own advice. But just because you oppose the establishment doesn't mean that you're a conservative. Trump opposes the establishment because he thinks of himself as a political outsider. The base opposes the establishment because they don't want Republicans in the establishment cutting bad deals with Democrats. Which means that Trump's anti-establishment viewpoint doesn't match up with that of the conservative base.

Trump may change Washington, D.C., but not in a way conservatives will like. He could be a Republican Barack Obama, but he won't be a conservative one. And another egomaniac without Constitutional strictures is the last thing we need.

The Establishment Is Dead

February 3, 2016

In Monday's Iowa caucus, Senator Ted Cruz, R-Texas, the man most hated by the Republican establishment, came from behind to nab front-runner Donald Trump. Senator Marco Rubio, R-Fla., the supposed establishment favorite, came in just a point behind Trump. According to conventional wisdom, this should set up a battle royal among anti-establishment Cruz, anti-establishment Trump and establishment Rubio. If Rubio emerges victorious, the pundits explain, the establishment will have lived to fight another day, and put those rowdy conservative grass-roots anti-establishment types in their place.

This is nonsense.

Cruz is the most conservative person in the Republican race. Trump, up until he became the establishment's baton against Cruz, was a thorn in the side of the establishment. And the new establishment darling, Rubio, is arguably the second-most conservative person in the Republican race (the only other contender is Senator Rand Paul). There's a reason the establishment backed then-Republican Florida Governor Charlie Crist over Rubio in 2010.

In fact, there's only one reason the establishment can tolerate Rubio, who is ardently anti-abortion, thoroughly hawkish, and consistently pro-free markets (outside of his bizarre support for sugar subsidies). They support Rubio because he backed the Gang of Eight amnesty bill in 2013. Rubio has been soft on immigration since his days in the Florida state legislature. He briefly adopted Mitt Romney's self-deportation platform in 2012 before flipping left in 2013; then, after serious blowback, he abandoned that position. That's obviously problematic, and a reason for conservatives to question his credentials on that issue. But leaving amnesty aside, calling Rubio "establishment" does a true disservice to the conservative grassroots who elected him in the first place.

So, what does that mean? It means that in the Iowa caucus, openly anti-establishment candidates -- from Trump to Cruz to Rubio to Ben Carson to Rand Paul -- received 88.9 percent of the vote. Jeb Bush, the original establishment favorite, received just 2.8 percent of the vote. John Kasich clocked in at 1.9 percent. Chris Christie received just 1.8 percent.

The story is no different in New Hampshire. There, establishment candidates amount to just 27.6 percent of the electorate, according to the latest RealClearPolitics polling averages. All the talk of the tea party's death was greatly exaggerated -- the tea party took over the Republican Party. The establishment's newfound enthusiasm for Rubio represents a desperation play, an attempt to latch onto the least worst option they can find. But that doesn't mean that Rubio is establishment.

So, conservatives should cheer the results of the Iowa caucus, regardless of which candidate they supported. That doesn't mean the establishment can't rise from the grave -- they co-opted tea partyer Rubio once, and may be able to do so again. But it does mean that for the moment, default successful national Republicanism is conservative. And that's a big win for the grassroots.

How Attitude Trumped
Conservative Thought

February 10, 2016

On Monday, grassroots Republican favorite Donald Trump repeated the phrase when an audience member called Ted Cruz a "p----." He came to this conclusion after determining that Cruz wasn't sufficiently gung-ho about waterboarding possible terrorists. Asked to define conservatism at the last Republican debate, Trump stated, "I think it's a person who doesn't want to take overly risks. I think that's a good thing."

On Tuesday, establishment Republican favorite columnist David Brooks of The New York Times wrote a column called "I Miss Barack Obama." In it, he pilloried Senators Marco Rubio, R-Fla., and Ted Cruz, R-Texas, and lamented that Obama "radiates an ethos of integrity, humanity, good manners and elegance that I'm beginning to miss." In October, Brooks defined conservatism thusly: "conservatism stands for intellectual humility, a belief in steady, incremental change, a preference for reform rather than revolution, a respect for hierarchy, precedence, balance and order, and a tone of voice that is prudent, measured and responsible."

Neither of these definitions are correct, of course. But the fact that Trump and Brooks largely agree on the definition of conservatism while fighting each other tooth and nail demonstrates why conservatism is losing.

Both Trump and Brooks think that conservatism is mainly an attitude. It's not a set of principles and policies; it's not a philosophy of human freedom and small government. Instead, conservatism is merely an orientation toward change: Trump wants slow change, and so does Brooks.

So where do they disagree? They disagree about whether conservatism is militant attitude in pursuit of slow change (Trump) or whether conservatism is elegance in pursuit of slow change (Brooks). Trump thinks Brooks is a "p----," presumably; Brooks thinks Trump is a vulgarian.

Neither one is actually conservative, and yet they're fighting for the mantle of conservative leadership.

The problem, of course, is that conservatism has very little to do with attitude. Conservatism demands Constitutionalism, and in the aftermath of a century of progressive growth of government -- including growth at the hands of so-called conservatives -- change need not be gradual. The attitude matters less than the goal. We can have hard-charging conservatives like Mark Levin; we can have 10-dollar-word conservatives like many of the writers at National Review. What we can't have is nonconservatives redefining conservatism as an attitude, and then ignoring the underlying philosophy.

Yet that's precisely what we have in this race. The entire Republican race thus far has avoided policy differentiations in favor of critiques of attitudes. Who is more palatable, the shifty-seeming Cruz, or the smooth-talking Rubio? Who is more worthwhile, the brusque Chris Christie or the milquetoast Jeb Bush?

Who cares?

Republicans have spent so long in the wilderness that they've forgotten what animated them in the first place. At some point, Republicans forgot that their job was to determine the best face for a conservative philosophy, and instead substituted the face for the philosophy. The conservatism simply fell away.

In the battle between David Brooks' pseudoconservatism and Donald Trump's pseudoconservatism, there are no winners, but there is one major loser: conservatism itself. Conservatives need to worry less about how they fight -- whether they wear creased pants or hurl nasty insults -- and instead contemplate why they're fighting in the first place.

The Day the Constitution Died

February 17, 2016

On Saturday, Supreme Court Justice Antonin Scalia, the foremost thinker of the originalist and textualist judicial philosophy, died. It threw constitutional loyalists across the nation into mourning -- not just because Scalia was a brilliant expositor of the founding document, a great defender of the constitutional order, but also because with Scalia's death, Democrats are just one vote on the Court from destroying the Constitution wholesale.

Scalia believed that the Constitution ought to be applied as it was written -- it wasn't poetry, to be interpreted by the self-proclaimed moral superiors of the Supreme Court, but a legal document requiring specific legal interpretation. As Scalia said, "The Constitution says what it says, and it doesn't say anything more. ... Under the guise of interpreting the Constitution and under the banner of a living Constitution, judges, especially those on the Supreme Court, now wield an enormous amount of political power, because they don't just apply the rules that have been written, they create new rules."

With Scalia gone, the left will look to create a vast bevy of new rules designed to destroy constitutional freedoms. Scalia represented the fifth vote on gun rights, freedom of speech and freedom of religion; now, expect the Supreme Court to reinterpret the Second Amendment to allow full-scale gun confiscation, reinterpret freedom of speech to allow "hate speech" legislation and crackdowns on corporate political speech and reinterpret freedom of religion to allow a full-scale government cram down of anti-religious policy on religious individuals and institutions.

Even as conservatives lamented Scalia's death, Republicans held a debate on Saturday night. At that debate, Republican front-runner

Donald Trump demonstrated that even among the Republican electorate, a significant percentage of Americans no longer care about Scalia-like Constitutional separation of powers. Trump is a bloviating loudmouth, a bullying spoiled rich kid who has never been told no. And he aims to govern like one. Put aside Trump's channeling of Michael Moore this week (he said that George W. Bush was responsible for 9/11 and lied to get America into the Iraq War). What's truly important is Trump's vision of governance.

For Trump, everything in life is about Trump. He says he likes Russian dictator Vladimir Putin because Putin "called me a genius, I like him so far, I have to tell you." He says he'll fix the economy personally: "I'm going to save Social Security. I'm going to bring jobs back from China. I'm going to bring back jobs from Mexico and from Japan ... Vietnam, that's the new one. ... I'm the only one who is going to save Social Security, believe me." Everything boils down to Trump fixing the world through the power of his persona.

None of which has any relationship to the Constitution. Scalia's death represents one threat to the future of checks and balances and limited government; Trump's rise as the leading candidate for a party that used to avoid strongmen in favor of those principles represents another type of threat. Both are potentially fatal to the future of the American idea.

When Manliness Goes Missing

February 24, 2016

By most available information, Donald Trump will win the Republican nomination. He's not a conservative in any meaningful sense -- he shifts his positions at whim, preaches about the worth of big government and suggests that he will personally "win for America." But after eight years of Barack Obama's passive-aggressive emasculation of Americans, many conservatives have embraced Trump because of his unbridled masculinity. He's Joe Pesci in "Goodfellas": a toxic dude who's fun to watch, but who might occasionally shoot somebody just for the hell of it. On Fifth Avenue, apparently. And receive plaudits from his followers.

This is the natural effect of the unmanning of American politics.

Obama told Americans for years on end that they were racist, sexist, bigoted homophobes who just didn't understand that our brash, confident attitude alienated people all around the world and led to terrorism against us. Hillary Clinton is running for president on the basis of her X chromosomes; America, she says, needs a female president. Bernie Sanders says that our unchecked aggressive instincts have ill-served us; we need a kinder, gentler America.

Meanwhile, the Republicans have self-castrated. Senator Mitch McConnell, R-Ky., spent years telling conservatives that Obama couldn't be stopped, and that attempts to stop him would be uncivil and counterproductive. Former Speaker of the House John Boehner did the same. So, too, has new Speaker of the House Paul Ryan. George W. Bush ran on the basis of "compassionate" conservatism, implying that traditional conservatism was too musky for metrosexual America. Marco Rubio's brand of politics relies on a feelings-first approach; Rubio said last week, "If a significant percentage of the American family believes that they are being treated differently than everyone else, we have a problem. And we have to address it as a society and as a country." This is pure Obama, Republican-style.

Trump, however, doesn't bother with the niceties. He's a big, swinging set of political testicles. He says, just like a good mafia boss would, that he'll take care of all of your problems. He threatens his political opponents -- he tells protesters he wants to see them roughed up, and he tells donors to his opposition that he'll target them. He swears like a sailor in public. He unmans his competition: Jeb! Bush is "low-energy," Ted Cruz a "p----," Ben Carson a "pedophile," Rubio a "lightweight," Carly Fiorina a problem "face." He's gross and chauvinistic: He calls women "pieces of a--" and rips Megyn Kelly for bleeding from her "wherever."

He is, in short, a man in the locker room, in all of his ugly glory. He's toxic masculinity. He's not a gentleman, and he's proud of it. He's here to win, and he'll bully, threaten, and beat you until you submit.

Normally, the masculinity gap in American politics could be filled by an upstanding man -- a man, yes, but one tied to values, a man who uses the aggressive instinct in pursuit of defending the innocent and punishing the guilty. But the feminist movement has made such men obsolete. Men were simply too dangerous; it was safer to emasculate them. Now men are expected to be betas; the only alphas left are toxic alphas willing to break every taboo and violate every standard.

There's still a space for masculinity in American politics. But thanks to the vacuum of decent men, indecent men rise. Men like Donald Trump.

The Leftist Fascists Take Over College Campuses

March 2, 2016

Last Thursday, all hell broke loose at California State University Los Angeles. Hundreds of students gathered to chant slogans, block entrances and exits to the student union auditorium, rough up those who wished to enter, pull the fire alarm, and trap other students inside that auditorium under threat of violence. Police officers stood aside and allowed that mob to violate basic safety protocols, reportedly at the behest of the school administration.

Why?

Because I was coming to speak.

I had been scheduled to speak at Cal State Los Angeles for weeks. Young America's Foundation had organized the Fred R. Allen Lecture Series; CSULA represented the kickoff event. Student activists worked hard to publicize the event. Two separate radical professors at the university objected publicly to it, with one challenging "white supremacist" students to wrestle him, and another asking on Facebook, "I say this event is a problem...What we go'n do y'all?!?!"

Then, the Monday before the big conflagration, the president of the university, William Covino, summarily canceled my speech. "After careful consideration, I have decided that it will be best for our campus community if we reschedule Ben Shapiro's appearance for a later date, so that we can arrange for him to appear as part of a group of speakers with differing viewpoints on diversity. Such an event will better represent our university's dedication to the free exchange of ideas and the value of considering multiple viewpoints," Covino stated in Orwellian fashion.

I told Covino to stick it -- this was viewpoint discrimination, and I would show up anyway.

After days of silence, Covino must have determined that he didn't want to risk the legal consequences of barring me, so just two hours before the event, he backed down, adding, "I strongly disagree with Mr. Shapiro's views."

By the time we reached campus, the near-riot had begun. I had to be ushered through a back door by armed security as well as uniformed police. Helicopters circled the area; news trucks parked along the street. The room in which I was slated to speak was nearly empty, because the student protesters had blocked all the doors and were pushing around anyone who wanted to enter. One reporter was assaulted three times; one of the people who wanted to attend my speech was pushed to the ground and kicked. Police smuggled the students in four at a time through the back door until students blocked that door, too. Halfway through my speech, the fire alarm went off. I spoke through it.

When the speech ended, I asked security if I, along with the other students, could go out to confront the protesters. The campus police told me they couldn't guarantee my safety or that of any of those listening to me if we chose to walk outside. Instead, they'd have to spirit me away through a separate building with a large coterie of armed and uniformed police, stuff me into the back of a van, and then escort me from campus with motorcycles flashing their lights.

This is America in 2016, on a state-funded university campus.

And it shouldn't be surprising.

We have spent two generations turning college campuses from places to learn job skills to places to indoctrinate leftism and inculcate an intolerant view of the world that insists on silencing opposition. We have made campuses a fascist "safe space" on behalf of the left. Anyone who disagrees must be shut down, or threatened or hurt.

It's not just college campuses, either. We've entered an era of politics in which baseless feelings count more than facts, in which political correctness means firing those with different viewpoints, in which government actors insist that they can police negative thoughts. We're on the edge of freedom's end, and many Americans don't even see it.

They would have had they been at CSULA that day. And they will soon enough if they don't stand up for their rights today.

Three Reasons Conservatives Should Fear The Trump Phenomenon

March 9, 2016

Donald Trump's candidacy is scary.

Trump isn't frightening because he's anything special personally. He's just a warmed-over mash-up of Pat Buchanan and Ross Perot, a spoiled brat billionaire eccentric with a history of position flipping and bullying foolishness. He has authoritarian tendencies on a personal level, and no awareness of the Constitution or its importance. In other words, he's Barack Obama if Obama weren't ideologically driven and suddenly experienced a precipitous drop in IQ.

So what's so scary about Trump?

First, the idolatry of a certain segment of his following. Trump has drawn some of the worst elements of American life to his campaign. To be sure, most of his supporters are decent Americans who find his approach to politics a revelation: He's an outsider, someone who will "get things done." Some of his followers identify with his hard-line position on illegal immigration and his dislike of free trade, even though Trump could flip those positions in a heartbeat if he felt the political necessity to do so.

But some of Trump's supporters go beyond that. Some are driven by the pure worship of the strong man. Like Obama's cultish support base, some Trump supporters are willing to follow him anywhere, to justify any misbehavior, to view any opposition to Trump as a sort of irreligious disloyalty. When Trump asked voters to hold up their right arms and pledge their allegiance to him, media mocked him as a Hitlerian figure. He's no Hitler -- he's not nearly as smart, as ideologically consistent, or as dangerous. He's a barroom prince. Instead, we should be concerned with the increasing tendency of Americans, both left and right, to hero-worship politicians to the point of blindness.

Which leads to the second reason Trump should concern conservatives: his appeal to nasty causes. Trump desperately wants popularity. He gauges his success by the size of his crowds, his success in the polls, and the compliments he receives in the press. He'll talk up Russian dictator thug Vladimir Putin so long as Putin calls him "brilliant." And he'll go easy on former KKK leader David Duke if Duke endorses him. Trump's lack of moral principle makes him an easy mark for some of the worst people on the planet. Combine the fact that he is drawn to those who would manipulate him with the fact that he has a worshipful crowd following him, and it's not difficult to see how the Trump movement ends in tragedy.

Finally, conservatives should oppose Trump full-throatedly because he's perverting conservatism. Even as he cultivates idolatry and massages white supremacists and global tyrants, Trump proclaims that he's a conservative. Many of us who have spent a lifetime fighting against the false notion that conservatism is a toxic brew of secret racism and fascism; Trump's rise provides easy fodder for the opposition. And his followers refuse to acknowledge that Trump has little to do with conservatism. Instead, they allow him to use the mantle of Lincoln and Reagan and the founders to shield his own egocentric rise from criticism.

Trump's no conservative -- he's a leftist at heart, a man convinced of his own power, a man willing to abandon all principle to serve himself and his allies. His followers think they're his allies, but that only lasts so long as they follow him. Yes, conservatives should fear Trump's rise. And they should resist it however and wherever possible.

What a Trump Nomination
Means for Conservatives

March 16, 2016

For years, conservatives have told themselves the pretty bedtime story that they represent a silent majority in America -- that most Americans want smaller government, individual rights and personal responsibility. We've suggested that if only we nominated precisely the right guy who says the right words -- some illegally grown Ronald Reagan clone, perhaps -- we'd win.

Donald Trump's impending nomination puts all of that to bed.

There can be no doubt: The Republican Party has successful killed the legacy of Ronald Reagan. By consistently moving to the left in every presidential election, by granting the left its general premise that government is generally a tool for good rather than a risky potential instrument of tyranny and by teaching Americans that the problem isn't government itself, but who runs it, Republicans have ensured that the vast majority of Americans no longer hold to conservative principles.

In fact, a significant swath of Republicans themselves don't believe in conservative principles. Trump, obviously, is no conservative. He's a protectionist on trade -- a position that smacks of populist pandering rather than informed conservative economics. He believes in an authoritarian executive branch designed to make deals that achieve a win for Americans, rather than a heavily circumscribed executive branch with prescribed powers of enforcement. He believes that judges sign bills, that legislators exist merely to bargain with the great man in charge and that the military exists to serve as his personal armed forces.

All of this attracts people.

The angrier Trump gets, the more he talks about how he's going to set things right rather than giving Americans the power to do so themselves, and the more Americans flock to him.

So, let's look at the facts. Today, at low ebb, Trump garners approximately 4 in 10 Republican voters. Let's assume that at least half of those Americans aren't conservative -- a fair guess, given that many have admitted bias in polls in favor of government interventionism in the economy, a sneaking love for government entitlement programs and a strong position against immigration -- not for safety reasons, but to prevent economic competition. Meanwhile, more than 4 in 10 Americans support Democrats outright.

This means that at least 6 in 10 Americans support a big government vision of the world.

Which means conservatives have failed.

In order to rebuild, conservatives must recognize that they think individually; leftists think institutionally. While the left took over the universities -- now bastions of pantywaist fascism hell-bent on destroying free speech -- the right slept. While the left took over the public education system wholesale, the right fled to private schools and homeschooling. While the left utilized popular culture as a weapon, conservatives supposedly withdrew and turned off their televisions.

Withdrawal, it turns out, wasn't the best option.

Fighting back on all fronts is. Republicans need to worry less about the next election and significantly more about building a movement of informed Americans who actually understand American values. That movement must start with outreach to parents, and it must extend to the takeover of local institutions or defunding of government institutions outright. The left has bred a generation of Americans who do not recognize the American ideals of the Founding Fathers. Pretending otherwise means flailing uselessly as demagogues like Trump become faux-conservative standard-bearers.

The Day Freedom Died in Cuba

March 23, 2016

In 1959, Fidel Castro and his communist henchmen put a bullet through the head of freedom. Proclaiming the era of equality, they threw dissidents in jail or shot them, cracked down on free speech, closed their markets and seized private property. Thousands of Cubans fled to the liberty of the United States. Over the decades, hundreds of thousands of Cubans left the island any way they could. Learned men floated battered cars 90 miles toward Florida in the hope that they would reach land; young women smuggled their babies into rickety old boats in the desperate desire to escape perennial servitude.

But the spirit of freedom never died. Freedom can never be crushed, after all, so long as freedom lives elsewhere. And for sixty years, it lived just beyond the horizon. President after president signaled support for the aspirations of the Cuban people for something beyond the petty tyranny of the Castros.

Then along came President Obama.

This week, President Obama visited Cuba. There, he was snubbed on the tarmac by tin-pot dictator Raul Castro; he took a staged photo before a massive building-sized mural of genocidal murderer Che Guevara; he smiled and bowed to Castro when they met. Castro treated Obama to a harangue about America's moral inferiority, blustering, "We defend human rights." He adds, "Actually, we find it inconceivable that a government does not defend and ensure the right to health care, any patient, social security, food provision and development, equal pay and the rights of children." Obama nodded along, and then stated placidly, "I personally would not disagree with that." He then added, idiotically,

"The goal of the human rights dialogue is not for the United States to dictate to Cuba how they should govern themselves, but to make sure that we are having a frank and candid conversation around this issue. And hopefully that we can learn from each other."

The United States does not need to learn from Cuba; Cuba needs to learn from the United States. But in his desire to glorify his own name, in his even deeper desire to level the global economic playing field, and in his *greatest* desire to tear out Americanism at the roots, Obama kowtows to some of the worst people on the planet.

And kowtow he does. After that awkward exchange, Raul Castro grabbed Obama's wrist; Obama went limp, and allowed Castro to raise his hanging hand high in the air. Then, hours later in a press briefing, the State Department did not directly say anything about the crackdown on hundreds of dissidents who were jailed just before his arrival. The Cubans arrested one of the dissidents' leaders scheduled to meet with Obama. Ben Rhodes, Obama's national security advisor, shrugged all of that off, stating that the United States understands that the Cuban government sees these political prisoners as criminals under Cuban law. Obama himself did not directly say whether he would give Castro a list of political prisoners for release.

In other words, Obama went to Cuba with the express purpose of snuffing out the last hope that Americans would be willing to stand with freedom. In the end, he won't succeed. America remains free, and Obama's self-congratulatory virtue signaling on behalf of a terroristic authoritarian nightmare doesn't change that. But Obama's actions in legitimizing one of the worst regimes in modern history will damn at least one more generation to their tender mercies.

How the Clintons Made Donald Trump

March 30, 2016

Donald Trump is a boor. He's a vulgarian, a liar, an ignoramus. He has only the most cursory grasp of policy, a stentorian voice and a great big set of self-assurance. He's winning the Republican nomination.

Why?

It is partly because of the Clintons.

While the media point and laugh at the Trump reality show carnival, they forget that the Clintons originally took us all to the circus. This week, we found out that Hillary Clinton's email scandal now occupies the attention of 147 FBI agents, and that she will be questioned by the FBI. We found out that her pig husband allegedly snorted cocaine off the table of one of his former lovers in 1983, as well as gallivanted around her place wearing her nightie while playing the saxophone. And the indispensable Judicial Watch released information that the Obama administration is withholding draft indictments of Hillary Clinton, including an indictment over the Whitewater case during her husband's first term in office.

Nobody bat an eye.

This is the world to which Americans have become accustomed. We've been immunized to scandal. It's difficult to come up with a scandal that could damage Trump. Caught in bed with two hookers? That's just because he's got such lovely hands. Caught beating a dog with a tire iron? The man has passion. Trump is the apex of black socks politics. As the old children's rhyme goes: "Black socks, they never get dirty,/ the longer you wear them, the blacker they get."

We all embraced black socks politics thanks to the Clintons.

The Clintons dragged the office of the presidency through the muck. Now, they're trying to rehabilitate themselves at the expense of Trump. It won't work. Trump doesn't even pretend to have standards: He cheated on his first wife with his second, his second with his third, and presumably at some point will cheat on his third with his fourth (should he live so long). But nobody cares.

Meanwhile, the National Enquirer runs a sourceless, evidenceless story about Senator Ted Cruz, R-TX, supposedly shtupping a series of women not his wife, and the media go ballistic. That's because it's significantly more dangerous in this political day and age to have standards than to abandon all standards before you get started. Bill Clinton can get away with being human because nobody expects anything else. But so can Hillary Clinton, and so can Trump. Those who aspire to something higher have farther to fall.

And so, we're going to be increasingly treated to a series of candidates from both sides of the aisle with checkered pasts and no principles. After all, principles tie you down, force you to behave and put you in the awkward position of having to act decently. Better to skip the standards and go straight for the scandal. If you have enough of them early on and often enough, your candidacy becomes downright unkillable, like an antibiotic-resistant virus.

Hence Trump. Hence Clinton. Hence prospective presidential candidates Kanye West, Kim Kardashian and Jenna Jameson. Why not? After all, at least they're not hypocrites. They're exactly who they say they are. No scandal can touch them.

Trump Whines and Whines
Until He Loses

April 6, 2016

On Tuesday night, Senator Ted Cruz, R-TX, won a sweeping victory over 2016 Republican presidential front-runner Donald Trump in Wisconsin. Cruz won virtually every demographic, nearly 50 percent of the vote and the vast bulk of the delegates. It's becoming increasingly clear that Trump could fail to reach the necessary 1,237 delegates in order to win the nomination outright on the first ballot at the convention. If so, there's no way he wins the nomination at all.

That's because Trump has made himself radioactive.

If Trump had disappeared from the American political scene after his big win in Arizona, he'd have wrapped up the nomination by now. Instead, he defended his lying campaign manager, Corey Lewandowski, after Lewandowski was charged with battery for allegedly grabbing, yanking and bruising a reporter; tweeted nastily about Heidi Cruz's looks; repeatedly suggested that Cruz had violated federal law without evidence; trotted out surrogates to slander anti-Trump women as Cruz's adulteresses; flipped his abortion position four times in less than three days; found himself on the short end of the interview stick with a Wisconsin radio host; labeled health care, housing and education as key functions of the federal government; accused the Republican National Committee and state delegations of attempting to "steal" the nomination from him by engaging in traditional delegate politics; and stated that he would likely select Supreme Court justices who would investigate Hillary Clinton's email server, for starters.

The more Trump talks, the worse he sounds.

Now, Trump's supporters keep saying he's just learning the ropes. After all, he's never run for political office before, so a few hiccups are to be expected. But Trump continues to demonstrate a complete inability to learn. After losing Wisconsin, did Trump turn down his "Spinal Tap" speakers from volume 11 to 8? Of course not. He turned the volume up to 12 with a campaign statement that bragged that Trump's 13-point blowout at Cruz's hands was actually a big win in which he "withstood the onslaught of the establishment yet again." The statement also stated openly, and without evidence, that Cruz had illegally coordinated with his super PACs, and slammed Cruz as being "worse than a puppet -- he is a Trojan horse, being used by the party bosses attempting to steal the nomination from Mr. Trump."

Trump's campaign is flailing because it's not a campaign; it's a self-produced vanity reality TV special. Trump didn't bother to learn the delegate rules because he couldn't be bothered to do so. He doesn't bother to learn the ins and outs of his own policies because, hey, why bother when people flock to you for shouting slogans about building walls? Last month, he fired his data team manager and elevated the second in command. But the second in command apparently doesn't know politics, or even how to access the data itself.

But don't worry: Trump has a very good brain and hires all the best people.

By the time of the Republican National Convention, Trump will be 70-years-old. Sadly, he has significantly less self-control than my 2-year-old daughter. He's spent his entire life being handed things: money, fame, female companionship. Now he can't understand why he's not being handed the nomination. So, like Veruca Salt in "Willy Wonka and the Chocolate Factory," he'll scream.

It won't work. Trump joked months ago that his strategy was to "keep whining and whining until I win." But now he's beginning to lose. And the whining won't stop anytime soon.

The Suicidal Left Throws Bill Clinton Over

April 13, 2016

This week, the Bernie Sanders revolution finally ate its own. The vultures of the hard left forced former Secretary of State Hillary Clinton to sink her own carnivorous beak into the withered flesh of her titular husband, former President Bill Clinton, denouncing his key legislative achievements and relegating him to the dustbin of history.

The hubbub began after Bill Clinton ran into opposition from Black Lives Matter activists at one of his speeches. He proceeded to shred them -- accurately -- for their inane focus on supposed police brutality and criminal justice bias rather than saving actual black lives: "I don't know how you would characterize the gang leaders who got 13-year-old kids hopped up on crack and sent them out onto the streets to murder other African-American children. Maybe you thought they were good citizens. ... You are defending the people who killed the lives you say matter. Tell the truth. You are defending the people who cause young people to go out and take guns. ... They say the welfare reform bill increased poverty. Then why did we have the largest drop in African-American poverty in history when I was president?"

All of this is true.

But for the left, truth must be discarded in favor of the narrative. And so, Clinton was raked over the coals for gainsaying the mythology of the left: that the criminal justice system penalizes innocent young black men disproportionately, that their sentences are longer than whites', and that police enforcement disproportionately targets young black men.

And Hillary Clinton, in order to stave off the onslaught of a 7,000-year-old socialist loonbag, bravely threw Bill onto a political grenade. "I have been consistently speaking out about what I would do as president," she said after Bill's implosion, "And I think it's important for people to recognize we have work to do, that there were a lot of people very scared and concerned about high crime back in the day. And now we've got to say, OK, we have to deal with the consequences. And one of the consequences is, in my view, (the) overincarceration of people who should not have been in the criminal justice system."

Never mind that Bill's decision to fight criminality resulted, at least in part, in the single greatest prolonged reduction in crime in American history. What's important is that Hillary wants to win the nomination. It doesn't matter how many young black people have to die in order for slightly older black people to vote for her.

And die they will. The murder rate is up dramatically over the past two years in cities ranging from Baltimore to New Orleans, from St. Louis to Chicago to New York. This is what happens when the mythology of police as villains destroys their capacity to act as heroes. The high crime neighborhoods are left to those who commit crime.

But Hillary Clinton doesn't care. Neither does Bernie. All that matters is continuing Democratic victory at the expense of truth and American lives.

Your Daughter Must Pee Next to a Man, and You Will Be Compelled to Agree

April 20, 2016

The rules of bigotry according to the left represent a constantly shifting kaleidoscope of nonsense. This week, we learned that if you don't want your small daughter peeing next to a giant man who thinks he is a woman, you are a bigot; if you are a woman who is uncomfortable with a man who thinks he is a woman whipping out his male genitalia to urinate in front of you, you are a bigot; if you are a religious person who doesn't want to participate in an activity you consider sinful, you are a bigot.

Conversely, if you are a man who thinks he is a woman and you want to force a small girl to pee next to you, you are a freedom fighter; if you are a large man who thinks he is a woman and you want to be one of the girls, right down to hulking into a Macy's ladies room, you are a hero; if you are a gay man and you want to force a religious person to serve you, you are a hero.

If all of this seems odd, that's because it is.

It's obviously logically incoherent, to begin with. The left insists that a man who believes he is a woman must be treated as one, even if his biology dictates that he is a male. However, if a man believes he is a man, he cannot discuss vital issues of national import (like abortion) since he lacks the vital prerequisite: a womb. Men cannot understand women, the logic seems to run, unless they *are* women. But men cannot be women, of course, except in the fevered imaginations of people on the left. Even the left doesn't believe that: Leftists simultaneously want to enshrine unchangeable sexual differences (although, according to them, men and women are inherently and unchangingly different with regard to their abortion perspectives) and deny that these differences exist in the first place. (Caitlyn Jenner's twig and berries are irrelevant to the issue of gender, they say).

"This is nonsense," you say.

"Shut up," they say.

In the end, leftists don't have to be coherent -- they just have to control the government gun.

The baseline definition of freedom in Western Civilization has been this: You do not get to force me to serve you, and you do not get to force me to think the way you want me to think. As follows, you cannot force me to think that you are a woman if you are a biological man. You cannot force me to spend my taxpayer dollars to pretend along with your mental illness. You cannot force me to run my business as you see fit because I have no affirmative duty to you.

But the left doesn't believe in freedom -- except the freedom to destroy the right. Thus, leftists believe that Bruce Springsteen has an absolute right to cancel concerts in North Carolina, but that bakers in North Carolina can't stop baking wedding cakes for same-sex couples. The left believes that the government *must* compel elevated pay rates for women, but government should compel men to be treated as women based on their subjective feelings on the subject.

The kaleidoscope of leftist morality never stops shifting. But in the end, only one moral counts: the left's ultimate insistence on use of government force to compel obedience to their kaleidoscopic morality.

What Is Democratic?

April 27, 2016

Having devoured the meanings of the words "establishment" and "conservative" with some fava beans and a nice chianti, Donald Trump has spent the last several weeks cannibalizing yet another word that used to have meaning: democratic. Trump says that the delegate system is undemocratic; he says that caucuses that do not swing his way are undemocratic; he says that candidates cutting deals with one another to stay in or out of particular states is undemocratic; he says that if he does not win the Republican nomination while carrying a plurality of votes, that's undemocratic, too.

All of this assumes, of course, that Trump is the embodiment of the will of the people. By no other definition of "democratic" are any of his accusations remotely true.

First off, there is nothing undemocratic about delegates. Delegates are merely representatives. Some delegates are chosen by popular vote and are bound to vote in favor of the candidate selected at the primary election; some are not. There's nothing wrong with either system. Arguing against bound delegates is arguing against referenda; arguing against unbound delegates is arguing against basic republicanism.

Second, caucuses *are* democratic. People meet democratically and select delegates to represent them at the caucus. These delegates are selected, presumably, based on the trust of those who vote for them. Trump had no complaints about the caucus system in Nevada. He only hated the system in Colorado, where he lost.

Third, candidates cutting deals with one another other isn't undemocratic, unless it's also undemocratic for Trump to call for candidates to drop out of the race based on lack of success. In either case, candidates make their own decisions about whether to put themselves forward for election. The notion that it is undemocratic for Ohio Governor John Kasich to abandon the Indiana caucus in order to let Texas Senator Ted Cruz stop Trump there, is just as silly as the argument that it is undemocratic for Republicans to refuse President Obama's court nominees an up-or-down vote.

Fourth, plurality does not equal majority. The point of the delegate process is to generate an artificial majority from a plurality. That's what happened in 2008, when Senator John McCain, R-AZ won just 46 percent of the popular vote, but a significant majority of delegates. If Trump can't pull off that feat, that's his own fault. Most Republicans don't want Trump. Most Republicans don't want Cruz or Kasich, either. That inability to choose means that delegates that Republican voters selected will now perform what is, in essence, a run-off election with the remaining candidates.

If we could remake all the rules right now from scratch, I'd propose a system of proportional representation in all primaries: Compress the schedule so it doesn't take months to run through the process. If nobody hits a majority, cut off the bottom candidates, then re-run the election process again. That's just my idea, though -- and there's no reason that my idea ought to trump the ideas of the grass-roots activists of various states.

Trump's redefinition of "undemocratic" is merely ad hoc politicking, as always. No substantive changes would have satisfied Trump. And when it comes to the definition of "undemocratic," threatening riots in Cleveland if you don't get your way tops the list.

The Left's Thought-Fascism
Hits ESPN

May 4, 2016

For baseball fans, the performance of Boston Red Sox pitcher Curt Schilling in the 2004 American League Championships ranks among the most memorable gutsy plotlines of all time.

The Red Sox, fighting a World Series winless streak dating back to 1918, were down three games to none to their archrival, the New York Yankees. The Sox then won two straight games. In the crucial Game Six, Schilling was slated to start, despite a torn tendon sheath in his right ankle that required medical staff to literally suture his tendon to deeper tissue. He proceeded to throw seven innings, giving up just one run, and giving us the immoral image of blood seeping through his sock as he dragged his team to victory.

ESPN created a "30 for 30" documentary on the series titled "Four Days In October." The original documentary ran one hour and five minutes, and included a 17-minute segment focusing on Schilling's heroics.

When ESPN re-aired the documentary this week, however, the 17-minute Schilling segment was simply cut.

Why?

Two weeks ago, Schilling posted on Facebook that men who believe they're women shouldn't use the women's bathroom. He shared a meme with a rather hideous gentleman in a skirt, and a leather top with cutouts for his man boobs and stomach, wearing a blonde wig. The caption: "LET HIM IN! To the restroom with your daughter or else you're a narrow minded, judgmental, unloving, racist bigot who needs to die!" Schilling added: "A man is a man no matter what they call themselves. I don't care what they are, who they sleep with, men's room was designed for the penis, women's not so much. Now you need laws telling us differently? Pathetic."

This logic is, of course, inarguable. But it led ESPN to fire him nonetheless, stating: "ESPN is an inclusive company. Curt Schilling has been advised that his conduct was unacceptable and his employment with ESPN has been terminated."

By inclusive, ESPN does not mean ideologically inclusive. They simply mean that if you do not kowtow to politically correct idiocies about men magically becoming women, you will not be tolerated. ESPN is the same channel that rewarded Caitlyn Jenner, nee Bruce, the Arthur Ashe Courage Award for getting a misguided boob job, facial reconstruction surgeries and hormone treatments that will not solve his underlying mental illness. Pointing out that Caitlyn is still a man, however, will get you fired from that same network.

Not only that, but you will be memory-holed. Any person can be wiped from history with a Hillary Clinton-esque cloth at any time if he or she violates the prevailing leftist orthodoxy. Mike Tyson can still star in multiple "30 for 30" episodes after being convicted of rape. But Schilling must be excised from one of the most crucial sporting series in baseball history because he thinks men with penises are still men.

Every area of American life has now been transformed into an enforcement mechanism for leftist groupthink. Entertainment. Education. Even sports.

Conservatives spend all their time and energy focusing on elections. But the real battles are fought in the cultural space, on supposedly minor issues like the employment of All-Star and borderline-hall-of-famer Curt Schilling. If conservatives fail to realize that, elections are only the beginning of their losing streak.

5 Lessons Trump's Nomination Should Teach Republicans

May 10, 2016

We all got it wrong.

Everybody who wrote Donald Trump off as a political charlatan destined to flame out; everybody who called Trump a clown who would return to his reality show and leave us all alone; everybody who suggested that this circus couldn't -- couldn't! -- continue...we were all wrong. Perhaps we were guilty of believing that Trump's mistakes would break out into the mainstream rather than dying slow deaths on cable television. Perhaps we thought that voters would wake up to Trump's bombastic narcissism and turn away. Perhaps, as statistician Nate Silver put it, we were guilty of not predicting "that the Republican Party would lose its f---ing mind."

Whatever the rationale, Trump is surely a shock to everyone but political commentator Ann Coulter and a few other Trump stalwarts.

Now it's time to take away a few lessons.

First, failure to utilize ideological purity tests leads to the rise of leftist candidates within your own party. The bizarre paradox of Trumpian thinking is that the same people complaining about Republicans caving to President Obama want to nominate a lifelong left-leaning ad hoc politician with no centralizing principle other than his own glorification, a man who brags openly that he will cut deals with Democrats. When conservatives object, these Trump fans point to the GOP nominations of former Gov. Mitt Romney, creator of Obamacare, and Sen. John McCain, creator of campaign finance reform and amnesty. They're being hypocritical. McCain and Romney were, by any measure, more conservative overall than Trump. But the feeling that conservatism doesn't matter any longer is hard to quell when, to so many major Republicans, it simply didn't matter that much in 2008 and 2012.

Second, ignoring social issues means that the only way to appeal to disgruntled blue-collar voters is by moving left on economics. There's been a good deal of loose talk about Trump's appeal with disenchanted white voters who didn't show up for Romney. And Trump does indeed appeal to them with lies about the efficacy of tariffs and taxing the rich, which is straight from the Bernie Sanders playbook. These people used to vote Republican -- before the Republican Party decided to toss social policy out the window to pander to New Yorkers like Trump.

Third, moral narrative is far more important than policy knowledge. Trump knows less about policy than my 4-day-old child, and cares less about the Constitution than my boy. But that doesn't matter because he's fighting the "establishment," by which Trump means everyone who disagrees with him. Because he's conflating his "establishment" with a political establishment that insists on cutting deals with President Obama, Republican voters bought in.

Fourth, when there are no good guys, character doesn't matter. One Indiana voter was asked last week about the fact that Trump lies constantly. She said that all politicians lie, and that at least Trump lies differently than other politicians. That's odd logic, but it's true: When all politicians are automatically deemed liars, Trump's lack of character and credibility fades into the woodwork.

Fifth, lack of institutional trust leads to the rise of protofascists, not to a general allegiance to liberty. We hate the media, but instead of seeking honest members of the media, we revel in people who lie to the media and get away with it -- people like Trump. We hate the corrupt political establishment, but instead of seeking people who will abide by Constitutional limitations and minimize the role of government in our lives, we seek a strong man, a *bad* strong man, to break apart the system.

Trump's rise both reflects and foreshadows an ugly future for the country. I hope I'm as wrong on that prediction as I was about Trump's rise.

The Media Have Destroyed Hillary Clinton

May 18, 2016

On Tuesday, The Hill ran a piece with the hilarious title "Hillary's unlikely ally: The media." The media, of course, have been in Hillary Clinton's camp since the start. The vast majority of media figures are Democrats, and one of them, ABC News' George Stephanopoulos, has written openly of his love for his former boss.

But here's the irony: The media have destroyed Clinton.

They've destroyed her unintentionally, of course. They did so by shielding her from the sort of character attacks Donald Trump has weathered for decades; they did so by pulling the plug on guests who mentioned her husband's history of sexual peccadillos and sexual-assault allegations; they did so by dismissing any critiques of her handling of the Benghazi mess as "sexist"; they did so by talking up Clinton as the inevitable First Female President.

The media had no choice but to do this because Clinton is a terrible candidate. She's off-putting and unlikeable, programmatic and lacking improvisational ability. To protect the ruler, the Roman Praetorian Guard had to form a phalanx. The media did so for Clinton for decades.

All of this left her vulnerable.

As a candidate, Clinton is like the Bubble Boy: She's been placed inside the warm cocoon of an all-embracing leftist establishment, never exposed to the normal viruses of everyday politics. The minute she exits that protective bubble, she's hit with those viruses -- and she has no immune system to help her fight them.

Take, for example, Trump's latest line of attack on Clinton. She trotted out the usual "war on women" routine to attack Trump. His response: "Amazing that Crooked Hillary can do a hit ad on me concerning women when her husband was the WORST abuser of woman in U.S. political history." This is both accurate and on point. In the past, those who have repeated the same talking point on CNN have been cut off, a la Kurt Schlichter. But Trump has around 8.26 million Twitter followers and an unending torrent of media coverage, so Clinton will now have to answer. And her usual answer -- talking down to Americans and tut-tutting away accusations -- won't cut it. Not when she has an attack dog like Trump on her tail.

How about Trump? Trump has been made almost impervious to scandal thanks to media attention. The media have treated Trump as a plane-hopping playboy for years -- a cad and a rogue, a charming billionaire "winner." Trump is like black socks: He never gets dirty, and the longer you wear him, the blacker he gets. It's impossible to identify dirt on a man plastered with mud.

Clinton, by contrast, has been portrayed as pure. She has remained untouched, except by the clutching claws of grimy Republican reptiles. What happens when Trump bulls right through the media ropes and takes the attack directly to Clinton's character?

Nothing good will come for Clinton.

The media subsidized Clinton into a position of power. She's now so vulnerable that a 74-year-old charisma-free socialist nearly took her down. Now she's got a worse virus: a case of the Trumps. Her immune system has been so compromised that she may be politically terminal.

Is Hillary Clinton the Only Innocent Person in a 10-Mile Radius?

May 25, 2016

Hillary Clinton is as pure as the driven snow, at least according to Hillary Clinton.

Clinton will tell you how honest and transparent she is, right after cackling hysterically to stall for time. She will tell you that she always cooperates with law enforcement, that she has attempted to turn over all materials to relevant authorities, that it's just one giant coincidence her friends and family are constantly being swept up in prosecutorial dragnets.

It isn't a coincidence.

Just look at the people with whom Clinton surrounds herself.

Her husband, former President Bill Clinton, is a serial philanderer, a perjurer, a sexual assailant and an accused rapist.

Clinton's former Chief of Staff Cheryl Mills stalked out of an FBI interview after being asked about Clinton's emails. Mills worked as a close assistant to Clinton back during the go-go 1990s. According to Judicial Watch, she helped prevent the Clintons from turning over 1.8 million emails to that organization during litigation. Mills was also placed in charge of document production for the State Department on the Benghazi investigation. According to Gregory Hicks, the second-ranking U.S. diplomat in Libya at the time of the attack, lawyers told him not to talk to Congress.

Clinton's assistant, Huma Abedin, has been dragged into the Clinton email-server scandal. Even after she left Clinton's staff at the State Department, Clinton granted her "special government employee" status even as she took pay from the Clinton Foundation.

Abedin's husband is, of course, former Congressman Anthony "Carlos Danger" Weiner.

Clinton's chief fundraiser for years was former Virginia Governor Terry McAuliffe. He's now under investigation by the FBI and the Department of Justice for fundraising improprieties, including his time at the Clinton Global Initiative. He personally guaranteed the Clintons' loan for their Chappaqua home.

Clinton's foreign-policy guru is Bill Clinton's former aide Sidney Blumenthal, a radical-leftist hatchet man so corrupt that the Obama administration refused to allow Clinton to hire him during her role as secretary of state. Nonetheless, the Clinton Foundation paid him $10,000 per month, even as he sent her memos about foreign policy that included subjects upon which he was doing separate business.

So, is Clinton's association with a number of suspicious characters just a giant coincidence? Or, perhaps, is it a sign that Clinton herself is corrupt and surrounds herself with other corrupt individuals willing to protect her?

It's hard to believe the former, given that Clinton sticks by her corrupt friends for decades. Corruption surrounds her like the cloud of dust that always seems to follow Pig-Pen. That won't change if she's placed in the White House -- it will get worse. Power always makes corruption worse. Clinton should know: She's the only first lady ever fingerprinted by the FBI, and she'll presumably be the first secretary of state interviewed by the FBI. As president, she'd make her husband's deeply corrupt administration pale in comparison.

So no, Clinton can't be trusted. There's a reason polls show that even fewer Americans trust her than the narcissistic pathological liar Donald Trump. All of which means that this election cycle now pits the two most dishonest people in the history of American electoral politics against each other.

Notes From a Neo-Nazi Cuckservative

June 1, 2016

Last week, California State University, Los Angeles held a "healing space" event to provide a safe forum for students and professors to unleash their feelings about my campus speech in February, sponsored by the Young America's Foundation. That speech, you may recall, was originally canceled by university President William Covino. After I decided to go to the campus anyway, hundreds of screaming students blocked doorways, assaulted prospective speechgoers and pulled the fire alarm mid-speech. Professors egged on the protesters; one even threatened student organizers. I was forced to enter through a back door and exit surrounded by a full phalanx of armed and uniformed officers, thanks to the near-riotous conditions outside.

So, naturally, the professors and students who caused the commotion had some hurt feelings.

At their little get-together, Covino announced he "would have never invited anybody like Ben Shapiro" to campus. Covino fretted that "very tragically and unfortunately," somebody like me could show up on campus again. Meanwhile, Professor Melina Abdullah, chair of the university's Pan-African Studies department, said that I had advocated "anti-blackness," and then called me a "neo-Nazi." After realizing that it would be odd to label an Orthodox Jew a "neo-Nazi," she shifted her language slightly, saying, "A neo-KKK member -- let's call him that." She said that students came to her feeling "traumatized" by a speech they probably never heard, feeling "brutalized, physically, emotionally and mentally."

I spent the bulk of my speech talking about how racial diversity was irrelevant -- diversity of viewpoint mattered. This was enough to drive chaos and insanity at the school for months. Apparently, quoting Dr. Martin Luther King Jr. -- which I did during the speech -- makes me a "neo-KKK member."

Meanwhile, David Duke, former Ku Klux Klan grand wizard, has labeled me an enemy of the KKK. I've been hit daily on Twitter by certain alt-right white supremacist Donald Trump supporters labeling me a "cuck" -- a weak-kneed leftist who wants to watch his wife copulate with a black man. Prominent Breitbart News columnist Milo Yiannopoulos tweeted a picture of a black child at me upon my announcement of the birth of my second child. The neo-Nazi Daily Stormer routinely attacks me. Some of Trump's alt-right fans tweeted that I, along with my wife and two children, should be sent to the gas chambers.

This is the toxicity of our extreme politics. The campus left, enthused by Sen. Bernie Sanders and sought by Hillary Clinton, calls anyone who disagrees a "neo-KKK member." The KKK, meanwhile, calls anyone who won't support Donald Trump a "cuck." This is what happens when basic American principles are no longer taught; this is what happens when grievance politics replace the principles of the Declaration of Independence and the Constitution of the United States of America. Speaking in favor of free speech makes you a pariah for those who would control speech in order to build their utopia.

So, what about those of us who despise both the KKK and the Black Lives Matter movement? What about those of us who think that white nationalism is despicable, and that the censorious brutality of the "diversity" clique is gross? We've got a long road ahead of us. We'll have to teach a new generation, from scratch, that freedom and liberty still matter, regardless of race. We'll have to attempt to restore the notion of a social fabric, rather than the tribalism that now dominates the conversation. We'll have to stand tall against authoritarianism from both sides.

The Left's Mobocracy

June 8, 2016

For years, the left has been desperate to paint conservatives as the real danger to civil society. Back in 2009, the U.S. Department of Homeland Security called conservatives a threat to safety. In a report, it stated that those who oppose abortion and illegal immigration represent a serious domestic terror threat. After presumptive Republican presidential nominee Donald Trump reprehensibly justified violence against protesters, the media was awash with fears that conservatives would suddenly lose their minds and begin brandishing pitchforks in search of unlucky transgender individuals.

But, for decades, the only real threat of mob violence has come from the political left.

The left proved this once again this week when rioters in San Jose, California ignored do-nothing police officers and assaulted Trump supporters after his campaign rally. They overran police barriers, punched random rallygoers and egged a woman. They spit on people, burned American flags and generally made a violent nuisance of themselves.

The left reacted by blaming Trump.

First off, let's point out that while Trump has encouraged his own rallygoers to participate in violence against peaceful protesters, there has *never* been a pro-Trump mob or riot. Individuals have engaged in bad behavior, but there has never been any mass activity. The same is not true of the political left, which traffics in mob action, from Ferguson, Missouri, to Baltimore, Maryland, to Seattle, Washington, to Occupy Wall Street.

Why? Because when conservatives act badly, they're condemned by both conservatives and leftists. But when leftists riot, leftists simply blame conservatives for the riots.

That's what happened in San Jose.

San Jose Mayor Sam Liccardo said, "At some point, Donald Trump needs to take responsibility for the irresponsible behavior of his campaign." San Jose police Chief Eddie Garcia praised his officers for failing to intervene, saying, "We are not an 'occupying force' and cannot reflect the chaotic tactics of protesters." The San Jose Police Department added that it did not intervene so as to not "further (incite) the crowd and produce more violent behavior."

Presumptive Democratic presidential nominee Hillary Clinton blamed Trump, too: "He created an environment in which it seemed to be acceptable for someone running for president to be inciting violence, to be encouraging his supporters. Now we're seeing people who are against him responding in kind." The internet blogging service Vox was forced to suspend editor Emmett Rensin after telling people to "start a riot" if Trump sets foot in their town.

Trump may be a gross thug individually, but conservatives are generally uninterested in the sort of thuggish hordes that roam the streets looking for skulls to crack. We don't like those sorts of folks; we find them an affront to law and order and clean living.

The left has no such compunction. And so long as their leading lights continue to justify such lawlessness in the name of stopping the rhetoric of the right, we're doomed to more broken eggs, broken noses and broken politics.

Yes, it Matters to Say 'Radical Islam'

June 15, 2016

President Obama took to the microphones on Tuesday to rant about the great evil facing Western civilization: Donald Trump's insistence that Obama use the phrase "radical Islam" in describing a radical Muslim's killing of 49 Americans at a gay club in Orlando, Florida. Obama's original comment on the attack consisted of some platitudes about gun control and some happy talk about "various extremist information that was disseminated over the internet." You know, like in those rogue "Teenage Mutant Ninja Turtles" chat rooms.

After Trump slapped Obama for failing to use the phrase "radical Islam," Obama, clearly disturbed, lashed out: "That's the key, they tell us. We can't beat ISIL unless we call them 'radical Islamists.' What exactly would using this label accomplish? What exactly would it change? Would it make ISIL less committed to trying to kill Americans? Would it bring in more allies? Is there a military strategy that is served by this? The answer is: none of the above. Calling a threat by a different name does not make it go away. This is a political distraction." He added: "There is no magic to the phrase 'radical Islam.' It's a political talking point; it's not a strategy."

If it's a political distraction, why not just do it?

If it's a talking point that bothers millions of Americans, why not just use it?

If words mean nothing, why not just say them?

Because Obama knows that the words "radical Islam" mean something. And he doesn't like what they mean.

The words "radical Islam" don't mean -- contrary to his straw man -- that all Muslims are terrorists, or that Muslims will run to terrorism out of fear of the very term "radical Islam." As Andrew McCarthy rightly points out on National Review: "our enemies despise us and do not judge themselves by how we talk about them. At best, they are indifferent to our language; otherwise, they are so hostile that they mock our 'progressive' obsession over it."

And the words "radical Islam" are not a substitute for strategy, obviously. Hillary Clinton said "radical Islamism" this week, and then said that she'd essentially maintain Obama's Middle East strategy that led to the rise of ISIS and its regional growth and international spread.

What the words "radical Islam" *do* say is that religious ideology matters -- that certain world problems can't be solved by appeal to transnational redistributionism or deliberate attempts to curb American power in favor of great equality among civilizations. Obama thinks that if he ignores the religious ideology of our enemies, they'll come around so long as we pull back and then offer them material goods. That's why his very own State Department suggested that ISIS be given jobs.

But they won't. That's what the phrase "radical Islam" recognizes: The only way to bring people back from the brink is a religious transformation. And that's a pretty serious problem, since people hold their religious beliefs far more closely than any other belief system. It means that it's not enough for a few fringe Muslims to condemn terrorism. It means true reformation, of the sort proposed by Egyptian leader General Abdel-Fattah el-Sissi, not wishful thinking about the current state of the Muslim world, which is replete with fundamentalism that provides impetus to radical Islamic movements.

And *that's* why Obama won't say the phrase. To say it would be to recognize a problem he wishes didn't exist, a problem that undercuts his entire worldview.

And so more Americans will die. The left will babble on endlessly about Islamophobia and gun control while ignoring the only worthwhile goal in a war on radical Islam: the destruction of radical Islam itself.

The Truth Has Been (Omitted)

June 22, 2016

Barack Obama is a dramatic failure.

His economy has been a slow-motion train wreck. His domestic policy has driven racial antagonism to renewed heights and divided Americans from each other along lines of religion and sexual orientation. On foreign policy he has set the world aflame in the name of pretty, meaningless verbiage and a less hegemonic America.

But there's good news: At least he controls the information flow.

This week, Attorney General Loretta Lynch told Americans to believe her rather than their own lying eyes. First, she openly admitted that the FBI would censor the 911 phone call of the jihadi Omar Mateen who murdered 49 Americans at a gay nightclub in Orlando, Florida. The FBI, she said, would remove explicit references to ISIS, ISIS leader Abu Bakr al-Baghdadi and Islam.

The resulting transcript was a masterpiece of hilarious redaction. Here's just a taste: "In the name of God the Merciful, the beneficial (in Arabic) ... Praise be to God, and prayers as well as peace be upon the prophet of (in Arabic). I let you know, I'm in Orlando and I did the shootings. ... My name is I pledge of allegiance to (omitted). ... I pledge allegiance to (omitted), may God protect him (in Arabic) on behalf (omitted)."

This memory holing would make George Orwell cry. In this iteration, Allah becomes God (See, Islam is just like Judaism and Christianity!), but we can't mention terrorist groups and their leaders. In fact, more than a week after the attack, Lynch told the press she didn't know the jihadi's motivation -- a motivation *clearly stated* in the transcript she released.

Insanity.

But this is not unusual for the Obama administration. We know that in the run-up to the Iran deal the Obama administration simply altered reality to fit its narrative: It had fiction writer and deputy national security advisor Ben Rhodes cook up an account where negotiations with the terror state began only after the accession of "moderate" President Hassan Rouhani. Never mind that Obama and company had been negotiating with the mullahs behind the scenes for years before that. The narrative had to be falsified and upheld. When the State Department was forced to admit those lies in a press conference, the White House conveniently chopped out that section of the taped conference for public release.

We also know that the Obama administration lied openly about Obamacare. It knew from the beginning that you couldn't keep your doctor or your plan. It simply hid that fact for years. We know that the Obama State Department sliced out a section of transcript mentioning radical Islam when French President Francois Hollande visited the United States.

He who controls the information flow controls reality.

And the Obama administration is already rewriting reality for the historians of decades hence. We won't find out where they hid most of the political bodies until too late -- just as we won't find out what Clinton hid in her private server until far too late.

This is why a government must not be trusted with massive power. Politicians have every incentive not just to lie in the present but to lie with an eye toward the future. The more power they have over us, the more power they have over the reality we see -- and the more they think they can get away with manipulating that reality.

When Abortion Fans Let the Truth Slip out

June 29, 2016

On Monday, the Supreme Court issued yet another politically driven leftist decision, this time over the contentious issue of abortion. The court explained that not only did the Constitution of the United States mandate that states not infringe upon the phantom right to abortion but that health regulations on abortion clinics in Texas had to be overturned if they made it less convenient for women to kill their babies at such clinics.

To this decision, "The Daily Show" had but one well-considered response: "Celebrate the #SCOTUS ruling! Go knock someone up in Texas!"

The right reacted without outrage; even the left found the tweet sufficiently indiscreet to merit a bit of tut-tutting.

The left shouldn't have bothered. The left's old abortion position -- "safe, legal and rare" -- never made any logical sense. If abortion kills a human child, then it shouldn't be legal. If abortion kills a nonhuman, it shouldn't be rare. Nobody cares about whether polyp removals are rare. The left fully believes that abortion is merely another form of birth control. I saw this firsthand in 2012 at the Democratic National Convention in Charlotte, North Carolina. Young men walked around wearing buttons reading "I LOVE PRO-CHOICE WOMEN."

Of course they do.

In fact, abortion as birth control is implicit in their new set of revisions to the Democratic Party platform. The latest version of the DNC document calls for revocation of *all* restrictions on abortion at the state and federal levels -- yes, all, including partial-birth abortion, the gruesome procedure in which late-term children are carved up in the womb. They want you to fund abortions, too, both at home and abroad.

That's not "safe, legal and rare." That's "let's kill as many babies as we want."

And Hillary Clinton agrees with all of this. On Monday, she tweeted: "This fight isn't over: The next president has to protect women's health. Women won't be 'punished' for exercising their basic rights." Babies are not a punishment; they're a gift. But Clinton believes babies are only a gift if the mother decides that she wants it. Otherwise the baby is merely a collection of cells.

Defining what constitutes life based on convenience is the height of evil. Slaveholders in the South did precisely that in the antebellum era, arguing that blacks living below the Mason-Dixon Line were property. What business was it of those nosey parkers in Boston, Massachusetts, what a plantation owner in South Carolina thought of his slaves? The Nazis did that to Jews; Jews were subhuman, and therefore unfit for human treatment. The Hutus did it to the Tutsis. ISIS does it to Yazidis. The essence of inhumanity lies in the purposeful dehumanization of other human beings.

That is what the Democratic Party does explicitly. Democrats only get embarrassed when someone on their own side is uncouth enough to admit it publicly.

Hillary Clinton: Too Big to Jail

July 6, 2016

On Monday America celebrated the 240th anniversary of the adoption of the Declaration of Independence, which condemned King George III for "(obstructing) the Administration of Justice." On Tuesday the American left celebrated as the federal government obstructed the administration of justice on behalf of one of its ruling families, the Clintons.

Last week the attorney general of the United States met with former President Bill Clinton, whose wife and foundation were under FBI investigation. They both insisted nothing untoward happened. Days later The New York Times reported that Hillary Clinton might offer Lynch a position in her administration.

Over the holiday weekend the Obama administration announced that President Obama would fly to North Carolina with Clinton aboard Air Force One in order to campaign with her. Americans would, in part, foot the bill for the travel.

On Tuesday FBI Director James Comey called a supposedly impromptu press conference to announce his findings in the investigation of Clinton's private email server. He began by announcing that nobody knew what he was about to say, which seems implausible given that Obama was preparing to go onstage with Clinton at the time. Is it even within the realm of imagination that Obama would stand next to Clinton hours after Comey announced the intent to prosecute her? Of course not.

Then, Comey proceeded to lay out all the reasons why Clinton should have been indicted: She set up multiple private email servers, all of which were vulnerable to hack; she did not set them up in order to use one mobile device, as she has so often stated; she transmitted and received highly classified material; her team deleted emails that could have contained relevant and classified information; she knew that classified information was crossing her server. He concluded that Clinton's team was "extremely careless in their handling of very sensitive, highly classified information."

This was all criminal activity.

But Clinton is a member of the Royal Family. Thus, said Comey, she was innocent. Comey tried to say he wouldn't recommend prosecution because she didn't have the requisite intent, but the law doesn't *require* intent; it requires merely "gross negligence" under 18 U.S.C. 793. In fact, even the level of intent required to charge under statutes like 18 U.S.C. 1924 and 18 U.S.C. 798 was clearly met: the intent to place classified information in a nonapproved, non-classified place.

Nonetheless, Clinton would be allowed to roam free -- and become president. "To be clear," Comey intoned, "this is not to suggest that in similar circumstances, a person who engaged in this activity would face no consequences. To the contrary, those individuals are often subject to security or administrative sanctions. But that is not what we are deciding now."

One rule for the peons, one for the potentates.

This is the Wilsonian legacy, finally achieved after a century of waiting: the Big Man (or Woman), unanswerable to the law, approved by the population without regard to equality under the law. We now elect our dictators. And they are unanswerable to us -- except, presumably, once every four years. The commonfolk, on the other hand, find themselves on the wrong side of the government gun every day.

Tyranny doesn't start with jackboots. It begins with the notion that a different law applies to the powerful than to the powerless. Under Barack Obama tyranny has become a way of life. Ronald Reagan always said that freedom was one generation away from extinction. It looks like we've finally found that generation.

For Obama, Leftist Rhetoric Is Always Innocent and Conservatives Are Always Guilty

July 13, 2016

When it comes to the linkage between violence and rhetoric, I abide by a fairly simple rule: If you're not advocating violence, you're not responsible for violence. That doesn't mean your rhetoric is decent or appropriate; it may be vile, awful and factually incorrect. But it isn't the cause for violence.

President Barack Obama also abides by a simple rule when it comes to linking violence and rhetoric: If he doesn't like the rhetoric, it's responsible for violence. And if there's violence associated with rhetoric he likes, then the violence must have been caused by something else.

This shining double standard was on full display this week after an anti-white racist black man shot 14 police officers in Dallas just hours after Obama appeared on national television explaining that alleged instances of police brutality and racism were "not isolated incidents" but rather "symptomatic of a broader set of racial disparities that exist in our criminal justice system." Obama was happy to label the shootings of Alton Sterling in Louisiana and Philando Castile in Minnesota, without evidence, as part of a broader racist trend in law enforcement across the country.

Then Micah Xavier Johnson opened fire on white police officers -- and anti-police racist radicals attacked officers in Minnesota, Tennessee, Missouri, Georgia and Texas again -- and Obama suddenly got amnesia. Now, it turned out, rhetoric had nothing to do with their actions. In fact, said Obama, he had no idea why Johnson -

- who explicitly said he wanted to murder white cops -- would do such a thing. "I think it's very hard to untangle the motives of this shooter," Obama said while in Poland. "What triggers that, what feeds it, what sets it off -- I'll leave that to psychologists and people who study these kinds of incidents." He did blame one element for the attack, however: lack of gun control. "If you care about the safety of our police officers," he lied, "you can't set aside the gun issue and pretend that that's irrelevant."

Odd how this works. When a white racist shoots up a black church in Charleston, South Carolina, Obama targets America's legacy of racism, and the entire media call for a national fight against Confederate flags; when a nut tries to shoot up a Planned Parenthood building in Colorado, the left emerges to claim that the pro-life movement bears culpability. But when an Orlando jihadi shoots up a gay nightclub, Obama and company declare the motives totally mysterious and then impugn Christian social conservatives and the National Rifle Association.

Here's the truth: Obama's rhetoric isn't responsible for murder, but it's certainly responsible for death. That's because Obama's racist rhetoric has led to the greatest rise in racial polarization since the 1970s. In 2010, just 13 percent of Americans worried about race relations, whereas in April 2016, 35 percent of Americans did. That racial polarization has, in turn, led to distrust of police officers, many of whom respond by pulling out of the communities that need their help most. Crime rates go up, including murder rates. Ironically, Obama's supposed rage at white officers killing blacks leads to more blacks killing blacks in cities no longer policed by whites.

But there's good news: Obama can always blame everyone else. When you're held responsible for your feelings rather than your actions, it's always simple to direct attention toward the evil conservatives who insist that all lives matter rather than care enough about black lives to save them by endorsing the police who work to protect black men and women every day.

When Do Values Trump Democracy?

July 20, 2016

Last Friday, a splinter of the powerful Turkish military attempted a coup against President Recep Tayyip Erdogan, an Islamist with a taste for the authoritarian. Erdogan has spent the past decade purging the military of secularists and integrating his own brand of radical Islam into government; in the process, he's also accrued a $182 million fortune and three palaces, including a $650 million Saddam-esque monstrosity. He's cracked down on journalists, gone soft on the Islamic State group and threatened to get rid of the constitutional court. He is, in short, an aspiring dictator.

The coup, unfortunately, failed.

Or perhaps the coup was a setup. Erdogan has used the failure of the coup as an excuse to completely purge his enemies. He has demanded that the United States hand over a moderate cleric he sees as his enemy; he has detained or suspended 20,000 police, civil service, judiciary and army members; he has called to reinstate the death penalty for those who attempted the coup; 1,500 finance ministry officials were thrown out; and 30 governors were fired, as well.

In response, U.S. Secretary of State John Kerry blustered, "NATO ... has a requirement with respect to democracy." Given that the Obama administration stood by and did nothing after Syrian dictator Bashar Assad used chemical weapons on his own citizens, Erdogan probably laughed out loud at this missive.

So, was the coup moral?

Some on the left say no. A columnist for The Guardian, Owen Jones, tweeted: "You don't have to support Turkey's government. An attack on democracy is an attack on democracy everywhere."

Except, of course, that it isn't. An attempted coup against Adolf Hitler, who became chancellor of Germany legitimately in 1932, or against Benito Mussolini, who became prime minister of Italy through democratic means in 1922, would have been fully justified. Today a coup against the "elected" government in Iran would be similarly decent, as would a coup against the "elected" government in Hamas-controlled Gaza.

For well over a century, the left has mistaken the means of democracy for democratic values. That confusion has converted republics into tyrannies. Just because people elect their dictators doesn't make the dictators legitimate. This is the whole point of the Constitution of the United States. There are certain rights that are inviolable, even by a majority. If a majority voted to enslave a minority, according to Jones' logic, a coup would be illegitimate; after all, that would be overturning the popular will. That, presumably, is why he is a socialist. For him, morality follows the majority.

But morality doesn't follow the majority. Democracy and classical liberalism should go hand in hand, but they don't always; a people trained in classical liberalism will vote for it, but a people trained in tyranny will vote for tyranny. That's what's been happening in Turkey. Increasingly, it's what's happening everywhere.

Values must trump democracy if the two come into conflict. They don't have to. But it's our job to educate our children and, indeed, populations around the world about the meaning of classical liberal values. If we don't, people will choose their own chains. And just because you choose your chains doesn't mean those chains are somehow any less oppressive.

When Americans Want to Elect Mommy or Daddy

July 27, 2016

Americans want to elect Daddy or Mommy.

That's what this election has become. It hasn't been about competing or contrasting visions of government. It hasn't been about rooting out corruption in Washington or bringing change to the system. It certainly hasn't been about principle.

No, this election has become a simple decision: Do you want the thickheaded loudmouth who understands your problems, or do you want the cold and calculating robotic manipulator who doesn't? Do you want the real-life Archie Bunker, or would you prefer Mary Tyler Moore in "Ordinary People"?

That's what the latest polls tell us. They tell us that Americans aren't happy with either of their choices. Fully 45 percent of Democrats wish someone other than Hillary Clinton had won the primary, and the same percentage of Republicans wish someone other than Donald Trump had been nominated. Sixty-eight percent of Americans think Clinton isn't honest or trustworthy; 54 percent think she's running for personal gain rather than the good of the country; 57 percent say Clinton would divide the country as president; and just 38 percent say they'd be proud to have her as president. Trump's numbers are bad, too, but he has a significant advantage on honesty (with 55 percent saying he's dishonest). Forty-seven percent say he's running for personal gain, and 55 percent say he'd divide the country as president.

Trump is now beating Clinton where it counts. People believe that he understands their problems and believe that Clinton doesn't.

Here's the bigger problem, however: Electing politicians who "understand your problems" is a recipe for disaster. Governing properly isn't about identifying with the feelings of constituents; that position logically leads to a politics of individual "problem-solving" focused solely on curing constituents' ills. Governing properly should be about understanding that government's job *isn't* to solve Americans' problems; it's about moving aside obstacles so that Americans can solve their own problems.

No longer.

Bill Clinton is truly the father of the "feel your pain" politics, the notion that politicians ought to be beer buddies, folks who get what we feel and respond to it. This is a successful campaign strategy, but it changes what we're looking for. Now we're looking for candidates who can demonstrate that they get us and candidates who can provide for us. We're looking for President Benjamin Spock.

But government is not our parent. Though comedian Chris Rock may think that Barack Obama is the "dad of the country," he most certainly isn't. And if we think of our presidents that way, we're likely to stop holding them accountable. Even children of abusive parents love their parents. And even when nearly 7 in 10 Americans believe that the country is moving in the wrong direction, 56 percent of Americans think President Obama's doing a terrific job.

This means that our government is no longer accountable to us, even in our own minds. Government just becomes a popularity contest rather than a tool for the protection of rights. And our presidents become our parents; our parents become our dictators; and our dictators become unanswerable. It's comforting to think that politicians care about you, but they're lying. They don't. They care about themselves. And to project daddy and mommy issues onto those we elect is to hand over our God-given rights for the cheap promises of baby kissers.

Trump Simply Can't Stop Himself

August 3, 2016

This week, Donald Trump decided to step on every rake in a 30-mile radius. Fresh off of Hillary Clinton's pathetic display of insanely soporific robotics -- she really is remarkably lifelike for an evil cyborg sent from the future to kill Sarah Connor -- Trump decided to redirect the news cycle. He did so by attacking a Gold Star family who spoke at the Democratic National Convention.

After the Khan family excoriated Trump for his proposed Muslim immigration ban by speaking in emotional terms about their slain son, Capt. Humayun Khan, Trump couldn't stop himself. He fired back. He did so by questioning why the mother, Ghazala Khan, hadn't spoken out, implying strongly that her religion prevented her from doing so. He then said that he has made sacrifices akin to those made by the Khan family.

Forget right or wrong (and this was wrong). This is idiotic.

But Trump can't stop himself. If there's one baseline character trait that makes Trump Trump it's his utter inability to stop himself from hitting back. The Clinton campaign could run a puppy across a Trump stage wearing an "I'm With Her" collar, and Trump would find himself punting it and then telling the media the puppy had it coming.

This, of course, is precisely what animated many conservatives to vote for Trump in the first place. They watched him knock Jeb! Bush through a wall repeatedly and figured that he'd do the same with Clinton -- he'd hit her with the kitchen sink, and then grab the bathroom sink and hit her again.

Unfortunately, Trump's willingness to hit back provides him with an almost infinite number of targets. When you're a presidential candidate, you're on everybody's mind for months at a time. Many of those people will say negative things about you. If you're going to run after every squirrel, you'll find yourself both tired and behind in the race.

But that's Trump.

And his supporters continue to convince themselves that this is smart. For months, now, they've been suggesting that Trump will somehow right the ship, that he's playing 19-dimensional chess. They shout that Trump's opponents should shut up and jump on the Trump Train. And so, Trump keeps being Trump. After all, what incentive does he have to change? He'll always have his base, and it will continue to cheer him along. And because Trump is motivated by praise and criticism, he'll react to it.

Trump's supporters were a cheap date. Unwilling to condemn Trump's morally asinine comments, willing to follow Trump down every rabbit hole, they've actually made Trump a *weaker* candidate. That's why Clinton, the weakest major party candidate of my lifetime, is now destroying Trump in the polls. Somehow, Trump is finding a way to lose to a living embodiment of corruption and nastiness.

Can Trump turn it around? That's unlikely. After all, that would require him to turn his back on the squirrels and focus on his actual opponents. He'd have to stop obsessing about Ted Cruz and worry about Hillary Clinton. He'd have to leave the Khan family alone and focus on President Obama. He'd have to stop being Donald Trump.

And Trump will always be Trump.

No, Barack Obama Isn't a Feminist -- He's a Self-Aggrandizing Tool

August 10, 2016

This week, President Obama penned a ridiculous piece in Glamour magazine. It dripped with self-regard and oozed with moral preening. Barack Obama, said Barack Obama, is a true feminist. This, of course, might not have been obvious from the fact that the Obama White House has paid women 89 cents for every dollar earned by a man, as of July. It might not have been obvious from the Obama administration's belief that even men can be women, so long as they think it so -- and they can invade women's bathrooms, based on that subjective belief.

But Obama, said Obama, is indeed a feminist.

And he is also here to change souls. "The most important change," he lectured, "may be the toughest of all -- and that's changing ourselves."

How should Americans change themselves? Obama explained: "We need to keep changing the attitude that permits the routine harassment of women, whether they're walking down the street or daring to go online. We need to keep changing the attitude that teaches men to feel threatened by the presence and success of women."

This sort of unearned moral righteousness induces nausea. Notice that Obama doesn't offer any solutions to these supposedly widespread problems -- he just throws out the notion that he *understands* women's problems. To borrow some feminist language, that's an extraordinarily patriarchal attitude -- to condescend to tell women that you *understand* their problems and therefore need not present solutions. As the subtext goes, all women really want is someone who can *feel* along with them.

But it's worse than that. According to Obama, "We need to keep changing the attitude that punishes women for their sexuality and rewards men for theirs." But why should anyone be rewarded for their sexuality? Do we reward people for other bodily functions and choices? Do we reward people for their eating habits? How about their bowel movements? The only sort of sexuality that society should celebrate is the kind that takes place responsibly within the bounds of marriage, given that if sexuality produces children, we want children to be born into solid, two-parent families, with their parents present. Society should be -- at best -- neutral about other sorts of sexuality. It seems bizarre that feminism should ask for promiscuity to be treated as virtue for women just because bad people have done so for men.

This stuff isn't feminism. It's just politically correct virtue-signaling.

I fully believe in the basic notion of original feminism: that women should be able to make whatever career choices they want, based on merit. I grew up in a home in which my dad was a stay-at-home dad and my mom ran television and film companies. My wife is a doctor. I'm certainly at home with the kids more than she is, but she took time off for both of our kids. I want my daughter to be able to pursue whatever dream she sees fit.

But I don't believe that America's soul needs changing. That's because I know that Americans agree with me. If they didn't, my mom's career wouldn't have been possible, and neither would my wife's. I don't spend every day worrying about my daughter's possibilities, because in a free country she can go as far as her skills and decisions take her. If she faces obstacles from sexists, I'll be right there calling for action, if she wants my help. But I'm not going to pretend for the sake of political correctness and popularity that sexism is widespread and pervasive. It isn't. America is a glorious place for women, and the only way to make it even better is to target actual sexist activity, to stop slandering men as sexists without evidence and to tell our daughters that there are no glass ceilings, just a world of options waiting for them.

After all, that happens to be the truth.

Trump Isn't an Easy Decision, and Nobody Should Pretend He Is

August 17, 2016

Serious acrimony has now broken out among conservatives regarding whether to vote for Donald Trump.

As I've made clear, as of now I have no intention to vote for Trump. He's personally unpalatable, of course -- a serial adulterer who brags about sleeping with married women and says doesn't repent, an extreme narcissist with delusions of grandeur. He's not conservative. He thinks Planned Parenthood does wonderful work, he has no coherent foreign policy, he wants to leave entitlement programs in place, he supports tariffs and government subsidies, he doesn't care if Republicans lose the Senate and he has nothing to say about religious freedom for business owners, among a myriad of other policy shortcomings. He's volatile and nasty. He has mocked prisoners of war and a disabled journalist, compared his own sacrifices to those of Gold Star families and gone soft on the Ku Klux Klan. He lies constantly, about nearly everything.

Just as importantly, Trump is doing serious brand damage to conservatism. He's poisoning the well with female voters, minorities and young people. Many ardent conservatives have been co-opted into lying for him and perverting their own conservatism in order to stop Hillary Clinton. If Trump wins, he'll turn conservatism into Trumpism; if he loses and conservatives go along for the ride, he'll have sunk conservatism for an entire generation of voters.

Not supporting Trump is a perfectly defensible position, but it's a tough call.

On the other hand, I fully understand and sympathize with the position of those who say they must hold their nose and vote for

Trump in order to stop Clinton. She'll be a full-scale disaster. She'll appoint a fifth Supreme Court justice to gut the First and Second Amendments. She'll cripple our military. She'll cram down tax increases and use the regulatory infrastructure to snap the knees of American industry.

Choosing Trump over Clinton is a perfectly defensible position, but it's a tough call.

Each morning these days, I ask myself the same question: Which is more costly to America, a possible loss of conservatism to Trumpist, nationalist populism and all its attendant lying, which could forever prevent the resurrection of constitutional Republicanism, or another four years of Hillary Clinton's radical destruction, which could deal the deathblow to American freedoms?

This is a serious question, and good people will come down on both sides of it. But acknowledging that the choice isn't easy seems like a stretch for many commentators. Some insist that foregoing the Trump Train makes you a traitor. In order to reach this conclusion, they either ignore Trump's foibles or lie about what a wonderful conservative he is. Some insist that jumping on the Trump Train makes you a traitor. In order to reach this conclusion, they downplay Clinton's evils or exaggerate Trump's riskiness.

It *does* make you a traitor to conservatism to lie for Trump or lie to your audience that he is a serious conservative. Lying isn't just nonconservative. It's plainly immoral. But neither voting for Trump nor refusing to vote for him makes you a traitor.

Nobody knows the answer to the hypothetical I pose to myself each morning, because nobody has a crystal ball. But one thing is certain: If we don't recognize that the choice is tough -- thanks to Trump's utterly incomprehensible foolishness and vitriol and Clinton's radical leftist corruption -- we're not taking the question seriously. More importantly, we're destined to go to war with our own ideological allies after the election is over. And there's no need for that war. Our war should be on behalf of conservatism. Trump has divided conservatives on the proper tactics. But once Nov. 9 hits, we're all on the same page again: We must either stop leftist policies from President Trump or President Clinton. And we'll need to be allies.

The first step should be recognizing the good will of those who fight alongside us, even if we don't make the same risk calculations with regard to a conservative future.

Hillary's Corruption Is Overwhelming

August 24, 2016

After over two decades in the heart of America's spotlight, Hillary Clinton is still an unknown quantity for most Americans. That's thanks to one factor and one factor only: the love and worship of the mainstream media.

Over the weekend, no less than six terrible stories broke that would have crippled anyone else's campaign. First, we learned that Clinton aide and confidante Huma Abedin acted as assistant editor on the radical Journal of Muslim Minority Affairs, where she greenlit pieces that stated that "pushing (mothers) out into the open labor market is a clear demonstration of a lack of respect of womanhood and motherhood," among other things.

Next, we found out that Clinton had blamed former Secretary of State Colin Powell for giving her the idea to set up a private email server at a dinner party, and that Powell not only denied giving her the idea but also denied ever having a dinner conversation with her on the topic. Former Secretary of State Condoleezza Rice, who Clinton claimed was present for the conversation, has also denied the story.

Then we discovered that the Clinton State Department oversaw some $6 billion in mismanagement, fraud and incompetence.

Meanwhile, it was revealed that Clinton's pay-for-play -- Clinton Foundation donations in exchange for access to the State Department -- ran deeper than originally thought.

And we learned that the FBI and Justice Department are investigating the Podesta Group -- co-founded by Clinton campaign chairman John Podesta -- over its ties with former Ukrainian President and Vladimir Putin ally Viktor Yanukovych.

Finally, we found out that the FBI uncovered some 15,000 emails that Clinton failed to disclose to the State Department. Presumably, they do not all concern yoga and Chelsea Clinton's wedding plans.

So, what was the media's response to this tidal wave of incompetence and corruption?

They focused on the Trump campaign's internal mess, naturally. That's what they always do.

And that's why Trump became the Republican nominee.

The media once painted former Gov. Mitt Romney the way they paint Donald Trump, and they excoriated anyone who dared to ask about President Barack Obama's botched Benghazi policy. They scoffed at Romney's suggestion that Obama's Russian policy had emboldened Moscow. They castigated legislators like former Rep. Michele Bachmann for connecting Huma Abedin to Islamic radicalism via the Journal of Muslim Minority Affairs.

By the time Trump came along, the American people had already rejected the media's capacity for truth-telling. So when the media targeted Trump and Trump refused to be cowed by them, many Republicans resonated to Trump's call. They believed that Trump would hit Clinton with all the material the media covered up and ignored.

So far, that hasn't panned out. Trump's been far too distractible to focus on Clinton. But that doesn't mean that he couldn't. If Trump were to target Clinton, he'd be doing the job Americans thought they elected him to do: exposing the empress who's protected by the media Praetorian Guard.

If he doesn't, Clinton will become president, scandals and all. The media are still the gatekeepers, and they still have no intention of allowing Clinton to become the story when Trump's tweets can be.

We Have Nothing Left Holding Us Together

August 31, 2016

On Friday, a South Carolina high school stopped students from bringing American flags to a football game against a heavily Hispanic rival school. Why? The principal was presumably worried that waving the flag might offend the Hispanic students. According to the principal, "This decision would be made anytime that the American flag, or any other symbol, sign, cheer, or action on the part of our fans would potentially compromise the safety of all in attendance at a school event."

This isn't the first such situation. The 9th U.S. Circuit Court of Appeals ruled last year that a public school in California could ban students from wearing a shirt emblazoned with an American flag on Cinco de Mayo thanks to fears over racial conflict at the school. The lawyer for the children complained, "This opens the door for a school to suppress any viewpoints that are opposed by a band of vocal and violent bullies."

Meanwhile, has-been San Francisco 49ers quarterback Colin Kaepernick has been widely praised in the media for refusing to stand for the national anthem during football games. "I am not going to stand up to show pride in a flag for a country that oppresses black people and people of color," explained the man earning an average of $19,000,000 per year for sitting on the bench. He continued: "To me, this is bigger than football and it would be selfish on my part to look the other way. There are bodies in the street and people getting paid leave and getting away with murder."

We're watching the end of America in real time.

That doesn't mean that the country's on the verge of actual implosion. But the idea of America required a common definition of *being* American: a love of country on the basis of its founding philosophy. That has now been undermined by the left.

Love of country doesn't mean that you have to love everything about America, or that you can't criticize America. But loving America means understanding that the country was founded on a unique basis -- a uniquely *good* basis. That's what the flag stands for. Not ethnic superiority or racial solidarity or police brutality but the notion of individual liberty and equal rights before God. But with the destruction of that central principle, the ties that bind us together are fraying. And the left loves that.

In fact, the two defining philosophical iterations of the modern left both make war with the ties that bind us together. In President Obama's landmark second inaugural address, he openly said, "Being true to our founding documents...does not mean we all define liberty in exactly the same way." This is the kind of definition worshipped by Justice Anthony Kennedy, who has singlehandedly redefined the Constitution. He said, "At the heart of liberty is the right to define one's own concept of existence, of meaning, of the universe, and of the mystery of human life."

But this means that liberty has no real definition outside of "stuff I want to do." And we all want to do different stuff, sometimes at the expense of other people's liberty. Subjective definitions of liberty, rather than a common definition, means a conflict of all against all, or at least a conflict of a government controlled by some who are targeting everyone else. It means that our flag is no longer a common symbol for our shared definition of liberty. It's just a rag that means different things to different people based on their subjective experiences and definitions of reality.

And that means we have nothing holding us together.

The only way to restore the ties that bind us is to rededicate ourselves to the notion of liberty for which generations of Americans fought and died. But that won't happen so long as the left insists that their feelings are more important than your rights.

Hillary's Email Scandal Takes Down the FBI

September 7, 2016

For months Americans wondered whether the FBI, led by Director James Comey, would take down the most corrupt woman in the history of American politics, Hillary Clinton.

As it turns out, Hillary Clinton took down the FBI.

According to new documents from the FBI's investigation of Clinton, the agency was fully aware that Clinton lied when she said she set up a private server in order to utilize one Blackberry device -- she used 13 mobile devices and two phone numbers. The FBI knew that Clinton's aides destroyed old Blackberrys by cracking them in half or hitting them with a hammer. The FBI knew full well that Clinton had passed classified information over her private server -- she admitted that she didn't even know how classified information worked, instead stating that she thought the "C" appearing at the top of documents probably had something to do with alphabetizing files. The FBI recognized that Clinton wiped her server after a New York Times article revealed her private sever and email use; that she brought her Blackberry into a secure State Department area; that she never turned over nearly 18,000 work-related emails; that she discussed an undercover asset on the server and put his family in danger; and that she refused to take Blackberrys from the State Department out of fear they could be discoverable under Freedom of Information Act requests.

That's not all.

The FBI also allowed Clinton aide Cheryl Mills to act as Clinton's lawyer during her FBI hearing, even though Mills was a material witness. In doing so, the agency granted Mills legal privilege where none existed. And the FBI didn't bother asking Clinton whether she intended to hide information. Officials gave her the benefit of the doubt every single step of the way.

And then the FBI recommended to the Department of Justice that she not be indicted.

The fix was in.

The press seems sanguine about the possibility of Clinton in the White House. That's bizarre given her corruption. It's even more bizarre when you consider that she has now undermined Americans' trust in the chief domestic intelligence agency in the country, making it a laughingstock and a political Hackey Sack. Director Comey entered this investigation well-liked and well-respected across the political aisle. He will exit having destroyed his reputation for honesty on the shoals of Clinton's lies.

There is no excuse for Clinton escaping charges. Not one. The FBI's own documents prove that she took action that you would only take if you were attempting to obstruct justice, destroy evidence and lie to law enforcement. And yet the FBI, as a wing of the Obama White House, went out of its way to ensure that the Democratic presidential candidate would evade prosecution. That means it lacks basic legitimacy.

It's not the only agency the Obama administration has exposed as a political hammer. It has corrupted the Internal Revenue Service, the Department of Justice, the Environmental Protection Agency, the State Department and the Department of Health and Human Services. The list is nearly endless. No wonder so many Americans seem willing to turn to a man who promises to burn the entire structure down, Donald Trump. There's little worth saving here, unless you're a Democrat hoping to uphold the integrity of institutions dedicated to preserving scandal-ridden Democrats.

Hillary Clinton Sees Her Own Voters
As the 47 Percent

September 14, 2016

How many times must the left tell Americans what it thinks of them before Americans realize a simple fact: Leftist leaders simply don't like half the country? In 2012, the media lost its mind over former Gov. Mitt Romney's statement that 47 percent of Americans "who are dependent upon government, who believe that they are victims, who believe the government has a responsibility to care for them" would vote for President Obama. This apparently demonstrated that Romney hates everyday Americans. Disdains them. Sees them as moochers.

In 2008, then-Sen. Barack Obama claimed that small-town Americans in the Midwest are benighted hicks. "It's not surprising then they get bitter, they cling to guns or religion or antipathy toward people who aren't like them or anti-immigrant sentiment or anti-trade sentiment as a way to explain their frustrations," he said. This received attention from the conservative press, but was downplayed by the mainstream media, or brushed off as accurate.

This weekend, Hillary Clinton echoed Obama. She said: "To just be grossly generalistic, you could put half of Trump's supporters into what I call the basket of deplorables. Right? The racist, sexist, homophobic, xenophobic, Islamophobic -- you name it. And unfortunately there are people like that." The other half of Trump supporters, Clinton said, are little better: "But that other basket of people are people who feel that the government has let them down, the economy has let them down, nobody cares about them, nobody worries about what happens to their lives and their futures, and they're just desperate for change. ... Those are people we have to understand and empathize with as well."

Clinton's language is far more telling than Obama's. Democrats routinely see voters they don't understand as morally deficient. That provides them the comforting illusion that disagreement reflects lack of virtue. And that means that their policies need not succeed -- success or failure is irrelevant to the ethical question of how to vote. Good people will vote for them regardless of track record, while bad people will oppose them.

But Clinton's language goes further. Where Obama simply labels his opponents as bad guys, Clinton suggests that Romney was right: Those who are her potential supporters are pathetic losers waiting for government to save them. They are disappointed with the economy. They think the government must do more. They just need some tender, loving care from Clinton, and then they'll realize that Trump isn't the man for them.

This means that the sneering tone so many people detected in Romney exists among Democrats *for their own constituents*. Clinton doesn't label her potential voters self-sufficient Americans seeking an equal opportunity. No. They're grievance-mongers, ne'er-do-wells and people who believe they are victims, who believe government has an obligation to take care of them. And she thinks she can draw them to the Democratic Party.

So, where are all the good Americans? To Democrats they don't exist. There are just the deplorables and the needies -- and the elites who control them. *That's* the scariest thing about the Clinton vision for America. Nobody deserves freedom because nobody wants freedom. Everyone is either a racist or in need of saving; everyone needs a cure, either of their soul or their material well-being. And Clinton thinks she can provide that cure, by crushing half of Trump's supporters and co-opting the other half.

She's only missing one thing: Most Trump supporters, and most Americans, aren't bitter clingers or victims. They're independent human beings, waiting for a candidate who wants to grant them that independence -- if any elite is willing to stand up for it.

What to Expect in the First Debate

September 20, 2016

Thanks to the nomination of volatile reality television star Donald Trump, the first presidential debate between Trump and the soporific Hillary Clinton is widely expected to draw record numbers. With the polls knotted up and the swing states in heavy contention, conventional wisdom says that the debate will be exciting, a bloodletting between the staid Clinton and the aggressive Trump.

But actually, it could be massively boring.

Right now, Trump's agenda is simple: appear sane. Clinton has been attempting, somewhat successfully, to portray Trump as an escapee from a mental hospital, a madman on the loose, a man who would unleash nuclear war if handed the keys to the nuclear arsenal. In the past few weeks, Trump's campaign manager, Kellyanne Conway, has apparently been able to get Trump under control. Like a pent-up movie monster chained to the wall of a dank dungeon, Trump's aggression waits -- lurks. But it has not reappeared since Trump's infamous attack on the gold star Khan family. Every so often, we've seen flashes of Crazy Trump (Vladimir Putin's a great guy! Do we really know whether Obama was born in the United States?). But he's been sticking to the teleprompter onstage and avoiding press scrums offstage. The man who once criticized Clinton for avoiding a press conference for well over 200 days has now gone over 50 days without a presser. Real Donald Trump is in hiding, @realdonaldtrump has been handed over to a blind trust, and Teleprompter Trump is on the loose.

That means that Clinton's task during the first debate will be to break into the dungeon and free the monster. To that end, The New York Times reports that Clinton has been speaking with psychologists to explore where she can poke Trump, in order to prompt him to turn into the Hulk -- complete with purple pants. According to the Times, "They are undertaking a forensic-style analysis of Mr. Trump's performances in the Republican primary debates, cataloging strengths and weaknesses as well as trigger points that caused him to lash out in less-than-presidential ways."

Trump's task: Avoid those pitfalls, take six Valium, and wake up president.

Meanwhile, Clinton's main goal will be to appear lifelike. With questions swirling around her health and stamina, she'll be expected to flash energy and wit. She'll also be expected to not appear as a complete liar, which is an uphill task -- it's far easier for a seemingly crazy person to appear stable (every Hollywood actor) than for a serial liar to appear honest. She's got an uphill battle, but she'll mostly want to avoid controversy from Trump.

This means that the debate will come to whether Trump can avoid being portrayed as a character from "One Flew Over The Cuckoo's Nest," and whether Clinton can avoid being portrayed as the title player from "Weekend at Bernie's."

Sounds riveting.

This is what happens when the standards for our politicians finally hit rock bottom: We end up with a discussion between a guy who simply needs to act like a normal person and a woman who simply needs to act like a warm body. It would serve Americans right that after selecting candidates for entertainment value they end up with the season finale of "Joe Millionaire."

Excuses for Losing Just Don't Cut It

September 28, 2016

When Mitt Romney lost in 2012, there was very little discussion of blame. Everyone assumed that Romney simply lost because he didn't do a good enough job of convincing voters to punch the ballot for him. He didn't debate Barack Obama properly; he didn't stand up to Candy Crowley; he backed off of the Benghazi issue, or botched it completely; he gratuitously insulted 47 percent of Americans.

Romney lost, Republicans generally believed, because Romney deserved to lose -- even if he deserved to win morally.

That's not so for Donald Trump.

Never has a presidential candidate had so many ready-made excuses for his mess of a campaign. Since the primaries, Trump's defenders have justified his every gaffe by saying, "Well, he's just a businessman!" His anti-conservative heresies have been excused with a wave of the hand and a comment of, "Well, conservatism has never accomplished anything, anyway!" His general ignorance with regard to basic issues has been shrugged away: "He's learning!" His general unpopularity has been attributed not to his own narcissistic nastiness but to an unnamed group of conspirators out to get him. Sometimes, it's the eeeeevil "cuck" Never Trumpers hiding in their holes, waiting to strike him down at any moment. Sometimes, it's the Machiavellian "establishment" seeking to crush this supposed change agent. And sometimes, it's a suspiciously defective earpiece forcing him to go soft on David Duke and the Ku Klux Klan.

Now, after his airplane vomit bag of a debate performance -- a performance in which he spent the first 30 minutes bloodying Hillary Clinton, only to revert to insecure, incoherent defenses of birtherism, his business record and his Iraq war opposition -- Trump has a whole new set of excuses.

First, Trump's defenders attack his microphone. Yes, his microphone. According to Trump, some nefarious conspiracy took place to sabotage his weapon of mass instruction, throwing him off his game. This seems both implausible and irrelevant.

More realistically, Trump's defenders rightly point out that debate moderator Lester Holt hit Trump far harder than he hit Clinton. That's absolutely true. Holt interrupted Trump far more frequently -- although, in Holt's defense, Trump bulldozed both him and Clinton routinely. Holt asked Trump about birtherism and his Iraq war opposition and his IRS records and his mean comments about Clinton's "look," but didn't ask Clinton about the Clinton Foundation or Benghazi. And he asked her zero follow-up questions about her private email server. Holt clearly did Clinton's dirty work.

So what?

Trump has known this entire campaign that the media would target him. He said so before the debate. He had every opportunity to swivel and hit both Clinton and the media, and he failed to do so. That's on him.

This entire campaign is on him. It's nobody's fault but Trump's that he spends the morning after the debate complaining about a Miss Universe contestant gaining too much weight. It's nobody's fault but Trump's that he ignored hitting Clinton over the Clinton Foundation so he could massage his own feelings over his prior business bankruptcies.

Trump is the candidate. It's time for those who defend him to own it.

If they don't, if they keep allowing Trump to get away with excusing all of his failures by blaming somebody else, then they'll be paving the way to his defeat. Losers whine about the playing conditions and the referees. Winners change their game plans. Those who whine for Trump won't be winning for him.

How Donald Trump Became the Issue

October 5, 2016

On Tuesday night, by consensus, Republican vice presidential candidate Mike Pence wiped the floor with Democratic vice presidential candidate Tim Kaine. Kaine appeared nervous, flustered and confused; Pence appeared comfortable and in control. Pence's attacks on Hillary Clinton's corruption and policy evils were well-calibrated and hard-hitting.

There was only one problem: Kaine spent the entire evening hitting Donald Trump, and Pence spent the night attempting to treat Trump as though he was the child on the milk carton. Kaine slammed Trump's imbecilic comments over the course of the campaign, from Mexican judges to Miss Universe; Pence slapped back weakly with Clinton's "deplorables" comment, and then registered for the Federal Witness Protection Program.

No wonder Trump was reportedly fighting mad at his running mate, according to CNN's John King. Pence didn't defend him. He spent the night trying to fight Clinton instead.

And that's a tactic Trump just won't stomach.

Going into the 2012 election, Republicans were looking for a candidate who could do one thing, and one thing well: place a glaring spotlight on Clinton, and leave it there. Clinton is one of the least popular major party candidates in American history. She had trouble escaping a brutal primary season with a near-octogenarian nutcase Vermont senator with no history of accomplishment other than being from the same state that produced Ben and Jerry's ice cream. And she has been facing down a federal investigation for setting up a private server in order to destroy or hide classified information.

So naturally, Republicans nominated the one man capable of drawing headlines to himself: Trump.

And he hasn't failed.

After the Democratic National Convention, he stepped directly into the media-set bear trap of the gold star Khan family. Then, in an attempt to correct course, he rightly went quiet for weeks, sticking to the teleprompter and avoiding the media.

But during the first presidential debate, Trump couldn't stop being Trump. Taunted by Clinton into defending himself over everything from IRS records to his position on the Iraq War to the aforementioned Miss Universe comment, Trump melted down. And he spent the next week melting down, allowing the media to direct all of its fire against him instead of the FBI's rigged investigation of Clinton, the continuing collapse of Clinton's Syria policy and the implosion of Obamacare. He jabbered about her cheating on Bill Clinton. And blabbed about Miss Universe's weight again and again.

Donald Trump made Election 2016 about Donald Trump.

Pence tried his best to put the genie back in the bottle during the vice presidential debate. VP debates simply don't have that kind of weight. But Pence may have given Trump a chance -- one last chance -- to reset.

And so, the question, as always, returns to Trump. Can he control himself? The Trump campaign now says that Trump will hit Clinton over her intimidation of her husband's alleged rape and sexual harassment victims. But can Trump attack in methodical fashion, or will he lose his mind when Clinton jabs him? Can Trump even stand a week of decent coverage of his running mate, whom the media will rightly characterize as a candidate focused on the 2020 or 2024 elections?

The smart money's on Trump failing. But Trump has beaten the house before. The problem is that he'll have to beat the house by folding a bad hand rather than going all in. And that's never been his strength.

The Astounding Hypocrisy of Hollywood, the Media and the Democrats on the Trump Tape

October 12, 2016

This week has been a full-scale disaster for Republican candidate Donald Trump. His poll numbers are dropping toward Australia. His establishment-Republican supporters are panicking. His campaign has swiveled toward slapping defectors rather than drawing new voters.

All of this is because Trump turned out to be a Hollywood media celebrity with Democratic leanings...who ran as a Republican.

How else could we explain the media's sudden obsession with a 2005 tape of Trump riding on an "Access Hollywood" bus? In the tape, Trump jabbers in disgusting fashion about wanting to "f---" a married woman and his tendency to "just start kissing (women)." He said: "It's like a magnet. Just kiss. I don't even wait. And when you're a star, they let you do it. You can do anything. ... Grab them by the p---y. You can do anything."

This is reprehensible. It's repulsive. It's a celebration of sexual abuse. But the left's sudden shock and dismay don't wash.

Trump said all of this on a lot in Hollywood. Here are a couple of other Hollywood names that might jog your memory: Roman Polanski and Woody Allen. Polanski earned a standing ovation at the 2003 Oscars after winning an Academy Award for "The Pianist." He was convicted of raping a 13-year-old girl both vaginally and anally in 1977. The offense happened at Jack Nicholson's home. Woody Allen's ex-wife and children still say that he sexually abused his adopted daughter when she was 7 years old. But he continues to receive plaudits and rave reviews from his friends in Tinseltown.

And the Hollywood casting couch remains alive and well. But Trump said that he engaged in precisely the same behaviors other Hollywood stars often engage in, and the Hollywoodites are up in arms.

Is it possible that's because he's a Republican?

Then there's the media. NBC had access to this tape for 11 years. A producer from "The Apprentice" claims that there are "far worse" tapes of Trump than those released by "Access Hollywood." But Trump somehow maintained a top-rated show on NBC for over a decade despite such activities, and NBC continued to play him up as a wonderful rough-and-tumble business genius. Yet MSNBC and NBC are now ripping Trump up and down for precisely the sort of behavior they overlooked when he was earning them cash.

Is it possible that's because he's a Republican?

Then there are the Democrats. They claim that Trump's comments are disqualifying. Yet they backed President Bill Clinton despite allegations of rape, sexual assault and sexual harassment; and now they back Hillary Clinton despite allegations that she has targeted her husband's victims. They lauded the late Sen. Ted Kennedy as a moral force in the Senate, despite the fact that he drove a car off a bridge with a woman in the back seat and left her to drown. They still worship at the altar of John F. Kennedy Jr., who allegedly sexually harassed interns on a grand scale. But Trump's the end of the world.

Is it possible that's because he's a Republican?

Here's the truth: Trump isn't a Republican in anything other than name. His politics are statist, and he donated more money to Democrats than Republicans between 1980 and 2010. He's a Hollywood insider, a man who appeared at the Emmy Awards alongside Megan Mullally of "Will & Grace." He's a media member, too -- NBC paid him for years. All of these groups knew what Trump was for decades. But they'll punish him because he's a Republican. That's how social standards work for the left: If you have the right politics, you can get away with anything. If you have the wrong ones, it'll ignore its own hypocrisy to nail you to the wall.

The Democratic Normal Shouldn't Be Normal

October 19, 2016

There's no question that this election cycle has seen a bevy of radical media double standards. Donald Trump's sexual harassment and assault accusers have been treated as headline news; allegations about intimidation of sexual harassment and assault victims by Hillary Clinton have been utterly ignored. Trumpian bigotry against a Mexican judge dominated the news cycle for weeks; Clinton-connected bigotry against Catholics went completely unnoticed. We heard for a full week about a Miss Universe contestant Trump allegedly called "Miss Piggy" back in 1997; we've heard very little about Hillary Clinton's perverse dealings with the media and the FBI. We've heard for months about Trump's toxic impact on politics; we've seen precious few headlines about the firebombing of a GOP campaign headquarters in North Carolina or shattered windows at other GOP operations or the repeated violent attempts to disrupt Trump rallies or hurt Trump fans.

Part of this is the allure of novelty: Trump's a new figure in politics, and every bit of information now hitting the newsstands seems fresh. Meanwhile, Clinton's been in politics for decades, which means that every allegation of corruption and nastiness merely reinforces general perceptions about her.

But there's something else afoot here: Most Americans simply expect Democrats to act like Hillary Clinton and get away with it.

Take, for example, the new allegations by James O'Keefe that Clinton-associated parties are involved in promoting voter fraud and violence at Trump rallies. O'Keefe's Project Veritas went undercover with a Democratic operative who openly admitted to encouraging people to rent cars in order to drive to precincts and vote illegally. "You use shells," said the operative. "Use shell companies. Cars come in from one company; the paychecks come from another. There's no bus involved, so you can't prove that it's en masse, so it doesn't tip people off."

The operative also admitted to attempting to provoke violence at Trump events. "You put people in the line, at the front which means that they have to get there at six in the morning because they have to get in front of the rally," he said, "so that when Trump comes down the rope line, they're the ones asking him the question in front of the reporter, because they're pre-placed there." The activist admitted that a 69-year-old woman supposedly beaten up by a Trump supporter was actually working for him. That event generated major national headlines: "Arrest warrant issued in assault of 69-year-old female protester at NC Trump rally," blared The Washington Post at the time; "69-year-old says she was 'cold-cocked' by Trump supporter during protest," said Mediaite; "Video shows aftermath of 69-year-old woman punched at a Trump rally," reported The Los Angeles Times.

None of this seems to rate national attention. Has that 69-year-old woman, Shirley Teter, appeared on national news anytime this week? Apparently not. How about the firebombing of the Trump offices? Nope. And when's the next time Hillary Clinton will be asked about her position on voter ID now that it appears some associated with her campaign have been deliberately flouting voting law?

Some of this is due to the media's leftism. But a good deal of it is due to the fact that corruption regularized over time simply becomes background noise. Nobody expects anything else from Democrats. Americans have accepted the Democratic Party as the party of voter fraud and political violence since the 1960s. They've accepted Hillary Clinton as the candidate of manipulation and corruption since the 1990s. Democratic evils are normal; Republican evils are an ever-present source of news and interest.

That's terrible for the country. All corruption should be shocking. The fact that it isn't helps explain why the 2016 election has become a competition in pursuing new lows: The old lows just don't register anymore.

An Honest Question for All
Voting Americans

October 26, 2016

In 1996, "The Simpsons" did a "Treehouse of Horror" episode featuring Bill Clinton running against Bob Dole. Halfway through the episode, during a presidential debate, Homer Simpson reveals that both candidates are "hideous space reptiles," complete with dripping fangs, tentacles and one eye each: Kodos and Kang. The crowd screams in shock and horror. Then one of the aliens, Kodos, speaks: "It's true; we are aliens. But what are you going to do about it? It's a two-party system. You have to vote for one of us." The crowd mutters in stunned agreement. One fellow speaks up: "Well, I believe I'll vote for a third-party candidate!" "Go ahead," says Kang, "throw your vote away." Both aliens laugh hysterically as the crowd frets.

Welcome to election 2016.

But this election does raise a serious question for people of all political affiliations: Do the political ends justify the means? Is there *anyone* who agrees with you on policy for whom you would not vote?

The myth of the binary vote would force a "no" answer. If you must choose between two candidates, you choose the one who best reflects your policy priorities. But what if the candidate who best reflects your policy priorities is utterly unpalatable as a politician or a human being? What do you do then?

You vote for him or her anyway.

Take, as a hypothetical, a David Duke senatorial candidacy in Louisiana. A vicious racist and anti-Semite, former Ku Klux Klan head Duke is indeed running for Senate, and he's garnering some 5 percent of the vote there; he'll be included in the broadcast debate. Assume, for a moment, that Duke were the prospective 60th vote in the Senate to repeal Obamacare. Would Republicans vote for him?

Most Republicans, asked about voting for David Duke, would likely say no to his candidacy no matter the circumstances. But some wouldn't. They'd simply say that Duke on policy would be better than his Democratic opponent. Why lose a Senate seat to prove a point?

This is precisely the argument now taking place over Donald Trump on the Republican side of the aisle. No, Trump isn't David Duke, of course. But that's not the point: The argument in favor of Trump has had little to do with his qualities, and much to do with his status as the Not Hillary. That's dangerous moral territory, at best. It's basic "ends justify the means" logic. And that logic approves of *any action by a candidate* so long as that candidate votes the right way on an issue about which you care.

Conservatives used to mock such thinking. We used to scoff at Democrats calling Sen. Teddy Kennedy, D-Mass, a man who left a woman to drown in the back of his car, the "lion of the Senate." We used to sneer at the Democratic notion that Bill Clinton could get away with sexual assault so long as he backed abortion-on-demand.

Perhaps years of Democratic rule from the White House has forced Republicans to abandon the notion that character matters in the slightest; perhaps we've just decided to become Democrats of the right. If so, let's be honest about it. But let's also recognize where such voting logic leads: directly to the worst people in positions of the greatest power. Many Trump supporters are fond of saying that they'd back Stalin to stop Hitler. But that's not the question. The real question is whether they'd vote for Hitler to stop the Communist threat in 1933 Germany, or vote for the Communists to stop Hitler. After all, it was a binary choice.

Or perhaps it wasn't. Perhaps more people should have stood up and said "no" to the available choices.

If we all demanded more from our candidates, we'd get better candidates. But the binary election system creates a collective-action problem: If conservatives stand by their guns on character and Democrats don't, Democrats have an inherent political advantage.

Unless, of course, Republicans can start making the case for character, rather than adopting the belief that character simply doesn't matter. Unless Republicans forego Kodos and Kang and demand something better. If they don't, we're doomed to a lifetime of Kodos-vs.-Kang elections, all the while patting ourselves on the back that we're saving the country from the lesser of two evils.

What FBI Director Comey Did Wrong
November 2, 2016

In July, FBI Director James Comey shattered his near-sterling reputation by letting Hillary Clinton off the hook. After delivering a meticulous case against Clinton for setting up a private server and allowing classified information to flow into it illegally, he inexplicably decided not to recommend indictment by the Department of Justice.

This followed hard on President Obama announcing he would begin publicly campaigning for Clinton, Attorney General Loretta Lynch meeting secretly with Bill Clinton at a tarmac in Arizona and the FBI performing a peremptory interview with Hillary Clinton -- after which Clinton attended a late showing of "Hamilton." Minutes before Obama took the stage with Clinton, allowing her to use a lectern with the presidential seal, Comey announced there would be no indictment.

Comey's decision set off jubilation in Democratic circles, and rage in conservative ones. I wrote for National Review, "This sort of open moral debauchery would have made Boss Tweed blush."

Then came last Friday.

Comey announced, in a letter to lawmakers, that new emails had been found on a device in Anthony Weiner's possession -- no, not *that* device -- and that they could shed new light on the Clinton private server investigation. All hell broke loose. Democrats immediately labeled Comey faithless, a political hack manipulated by the Russians. Republicans said that all was forgiven and that Comey had finally correct his original error.

In reality, Comey merely committed the cardinal moral sin: He valued his institution over doing the right thing. He did it in July, and he did it again in October.

In July, Comey decided that he didn't want the FBI dragged into the presidential election. To that end, he stepped beyond the normal powers delegated to the director of the FBI and publicly requested that the DOJ not intervene with Clinton. His goal: to protect the FBI from accusations by the left of politicization. And just to demonstrate how apolitical the FBI supposedly was, Comey listed all the findings of the investigation.

The result: The left was overjoyed, and the right thought the FBI rigged.

Now, Comey wants to ensure that the FBI isn't accused of being a Hillary Clinton tool. He knew as soon as he heard about Weiner's device that he'd eventually have to tell the public about the re-initiation of the Clinton investigation, and he feared that if he waited until after the election he'd expose the FBI to a thousand Hillary-controlled-the-FBI allegations. So he came forward.

The result: The right was overjoyed, and the left thought the FBI rigged.

Whenever someone seeks to protect an institution rather than telling the truth, the institution pays the price. When NFL Commissioner Roger Goodell attempted to soft-pedal the abuse of women in the NFL in order to "protect the shield," he only ended up destroying the brand. When Chief Justice John Roberts voted to uphold Obamacare in the name of protecting the reputation of the Supreme Court, he only ended up destroying that reputation. Comey has destroyed the reputation of the FBI.

The only solution to the complete undermining of institutions lies in the honesty of those who head those institutions. At least Comey came clean this time. For Comey and the FBI, though, it's too little, too late.

Is Race Baiting Finished?

November 9, 2016

Donald Trump won the most shocking election victory in American history on Tuesday evening. He did so in the face of a media calling him racist, labeling his supporters "deplorables" and terming his victory a sign of "whitelash," as Van Jones of CNN put it. He won a higher percentage of blacks and Hispanics than Mitt Romney in 2012; Hillary Clinton drew a far lower turnout among minorities than Barack Obama.

All of this suggests that the left's race card may be dead.

It may be dead because Obama's presidency killed it.

Obama came into office on the wings of high-flown rhetoric about coming together as a nation, healing our centurieslong racial rift. Instead, he delivered a racially polarized presidency, suggesting that American law enforcement was plagued by systemic anti-black bias and that the American justice system sought to crush minorities. The despicable Black Lives Matter movement earned White House invites, and police departments earned Department of Justice consent decrees.

Mitt Romney -- perhaps the most decent man to run for the White House in the last century -- was pilloried by all of these forces as a nefarious agent of bigotry. Vice President Joe Biden said openly that Romney wanted to put black people "back in chains." Obama himself stated that Romney wanted to push America back to the 1950s -- a backhanded reference to segregation.

The media treated any and all opposition to Obama's policies as a form of covert racism; MSNBC trafficked in such nonsense for eight long years. Hosts on CNN held up their hands in the "hands up, don't shoot" posture, even though that posture itself was based on a lie. The media routinely crafted narrative lies about police-involved killings, ranging from Michael Brown to Freddie Gray, and then covered the ensuing riots as "uprisings" and spontaneous outbursts of underprivileged rage against the white superstructure, even in cities with a black majority, like Baltimore, Maryland.

On college campuses, professors preached the lie of "white privilege," the concept that all racial inequalities in American society must be due to a structural imbalance created by whiteness. "Safe spaces," including racially segregated spaces, became common, even as white students were told that to say that the phrase "I'm colorblind" was a "microaggression" requiring a "trigger warning."

By the time Trump came around, the American people were sick and tired of it all. They didn't want to hear about Trump's supposedly Hitlerian tendencies -- the media had already punched itself out with Romney. They didn't want to hear from Clinton and Obama about American "deplorables" -- not after watching American cities burn with Obama's tacit approval. They didn't want to hear from diversity-oriented, six-figure-earning college professors about white privilege. They just wanted a candidate who told them they weren't a bunch of racists, that America was still a good and great place.

So the race card failed.

But it is a mistake to think it's gone forever. The demographics are still shifting. The race card is dead with white voters, but it's still very much alive with minority voters. And Democrats will not run another white person for the presidency again -- not after Clinton's dramatic failure among minorities in the wake of Obama's new minority-heavy electoral coalition. Meanwhile, Trump has an opportunity, as president, to reach out and demonstrate that the race card is a lie and a sham. Here's hoping he does it, rather than hunkering down in a bubble of his own support.

America's Celebrity Class Versus Flyover Country

November 16, 2016

On the Saturday night after Donald Trump's stunning presidential victory over Hillary Clinton, "Saturday Night Live" decided to forego its mandate -- humor -- in favor of a full-on political wake. Kate McKinnon, who has done a creditable job mocking Clinton for most of this election cycle, led off the show with a full rendition of the recently deceased Leonard Cohen's "Hallelujah." There were zero laughs and plenty of delicious, delicious celebrity tears.

McKinnon wasn't the only one crying. Lady Gaga, who introduced Clinton at her last pre-election rally, apparently wept openly backstage as Clinton lost on election night. So did Cher. Katy Perry was so overcome that she skipped singing the national anthem.

Lena Dunham of "Girls" and bragging-about-sexually-abusing-her-sister-in-her-memoir fame penned an open letter: "I touched my face and realized I was crying. 'Can we please go home?' I said to my boyfriend. I could tell he was having trouble breathing, and I could feel my chin breaking into hives. ... At home I got in the shower and began to cry even harder. My boyfriend, who had already wept, watched me as I mumbled incoherently, clutching myself."

To put it mildly, bwahahaha. Or less mildly, BWAHAHAHA.

The left spent its time during this election cycle lecturing Americans from the Hollywood Hills. It didn't work. After years of President Barack Obama traipsing into studios in Los Angeles to read mean tweets, after nearly a decade of listening to the sophomoric unearned moral superiority of actors and actresses who earn millions for reading lines other people write, after watching 9/11 truther rappers go to the White House, Americans said no to celebrity culture.

And they did so by electing a celebrity.

The great irony of Trump's victory is that he was an anti-celebrity celebrity. He had all the perks of celebrity, but he reveled in them. He didn't try to claim that he was a better human being than white middle-class voters in Wisconsin by virtue of living in New York in a penthouse covered in gold leaf. Trump played the everyman on television, and it worked.

Meanwhile, celebrities who didn't grow up in tremendous wealth hobnobbed with the elites. Singers and actresses taped a "Fight Song" rendition for the Democratic National Convention. Dunham appeared onstage at the convention. Beyonce and Jay-Z campaigned for Clinton. So did Bruce Springsteen. And all of them did so for a woman whose closest contact with flyover country came during a highly choreographed stop at Chipotle.

Americans may never get over their obsession with celebrity. But they sure don't want to hear those celebrities talk down to them. Hollywood has disconnected itself from rural America, and rural Americans were more than willing to punish Hollywood for that sin. If Democrats hope to win down the road, they'll have to do better than trotting out the scornful glitterati.

Will Conservatives Stand up to Trump if They Must?

November 23, 2016

Here's an alternate-reality scenario.

It's 2016, and the president-elect of the United States is ready to take office. Her chief advisor pledges a trillion-dollar stimulus package directed at infrastructure. The advisor explains: "It's everything related to jobs. The conservatives are going to go crazy. I'm the guy pushing a trillion-dollar infrastructure plan. ... It's the greatest opportunity to rebuild everything. Shipyards, iron works, get them all jacked up. We're just going to throw it up against the wall and see if it sticks. It will be as exciting as the 1930s. ... We'll govern for 50 years."

Meanwhile, President-elect Hillary Clinton allegedly meets with foreign business interests working to enrich her. She deploys her allies to inform ambassadors that if they patronize the Clinton Foundation, she'd appreciate it. She says that she'll divest herself of all connections to the Clinton Foundation but refuses to hand it off to any third party to handle, insisting instead that Chelsea Clinton run the place. Meanwhile, she brings Clinton into top-level diplomatic meetings without informing the press. When Vice President-elect Tim Kaine is met with protests at a public event, she takes to Twitter to castigate the attendees, demanding an apology. She goes on to criticize talk radio and Fox News for unfairness. "Equal time for us?" she asks.

This is an alternate reality. But each and every statement and event mentioned above has already happened to President-elect Donald Trump.

Trump's top advisor, Stephen Bannon, is pushing economic statism, grinning at the destruction of conservative economists. Trump met off the record with property developers Sagar and Atul Chordia, the builders of the first Trump-brand property in India, as well as developer Kalpesh Mehta, whose firm claims to be the "exclusive India representative of the Trump Organization." He sneaked Ivanka Trump into a meeting with Japanese Prime Minister Shinzo Abe. He tweeted his thoughts on the cast of "Hamilton" and the one-sided comedy of "Saturday Night Live," asking, "Equal time for us?"

The point of this exercise isn't to rip Trump. It's to point out that conservatives who rightly tore Hillary Clinton apart for pay-for-play corruption and hardcore big government leftism shouldn't grant Trump a free hand just because he leads the Republican Party. In fact, that's the biggest mistake Republicans can make.

Trump has already challenged traditional conservative standards. He's made Republicans back off their "character matters" arguments. He's forced Republicans to swallow anti-conservative heresies on economics (free trade is a negative; entitlements should be left alone), social issues (he thinks same-sex marriage should be enshrined by the Supreme Court and praises Planned Parenthood) and foreign policy (his coziness with Russia used to be taboo). Republicans did all of this to stop Hillary Clinton.

But now, Clinton has been dispatched. That means it's time for conservatives to hold Trump accountable. There's no longer any "better than Hillary" excuse making. It's time for Trump to perform.

It's too early to tell whether Trump will become a decent president. But conservatives ought to fight for something better than "not Hillary" -- or else, they can simply acknowledge that they had no real objective standards for those who seek to govern other than political convenience.

Why Does the Left Go Easy on Dictators?

November 30, 2016

When evil Cuban dictator Fidel Castro finally died last Friday, the left seemed deeply ambivalent. President Obama noted "the countless ways in which Fidel Castro altered the course of individual lives, families, and of the Cuban nation," as though Castro had been some sort of high school guidance counselor. Former President Jimmy Carter recalled all the wonderful times he spent by the sea with Castro, the sun gleaming off the waves. He said, "We remember fondly our visits with him in Cuba and his love of his country." Canadian Prime Minister Justin Trudeau -- aka handsome Bernie Sanders -- described Castro as "remarkable ... a larger than life leader who served his people for almost half a century."

Meanwhile, around the world, dictators wept in solidarity with Castro. Palestinian Authority dictator Mahmoud Abbas, who is currently in the 11th year of a four-year term in office, ordered the flags dropped to half-staff around his trashed territory. Russian dictator Vladimir Putin sent a telegram to Cuban President Raul Castro, saying, "Free and independent Cuba, which (Fidel Castro) and his allies built, became an influential member of the international community and became an inspiring example for many countries and nations." Chinese dictator Xi Jinping called Castro "a close comrade and a sincere friend," adding, "His glorious image and great achievements will be recorded in history forever."

What were Castro's great achievements? He presided over the economic destruction of one of the most quickly developing countries in Latin America; he arrested and imprisoned hundreds of thousands of dissidents; he caused the self-imposed exile of millions of Cubans; he watched and participated in the drowning of thousands of Cubans attempting to escape his prison island; he worked with mass murderer Che Guevara to murder political opponents. Castro was, simply put, one of the worst people in a century full of awful human beings.

So why did the left emerge to pay its respects this week?

Because at least Castro sought utopia.

Radical leftism believes that the quest for a utopian world, a world free of unfairness, justifies any cruelty against individuals. Individual rights are obstacles to communal greatness. The bricks of the tower of Babel will be mortared with the blood of those sacrificed on behalf of the vision. That's because the state -- which is really just an extension of "the people," who only exist en masse, never as individuals -- is the source of all rights. No rights can be violated if the state declares them defunct.

That's why the left only pays token homage to those who suffer at the hands of history's greatest monsters -- as Josef Stalin apocryphally put it, you can't make an omelet without breaking eggs. No wonder the left defended Stalin all the way until news broke in 1956 that Soviet leader Nikita Khrushchev had criticized Stalin's purges. Until then, Walter Duranty of The New York Times had whitewashed the murder of millions in the Ukrainian Holodomor -- he declared that he had seen the future, and it worked. And Hollywood even portrayed Stalin's show trials in a positive light in "Mission to Moscow." Today, Hollywood produces fawning biopics like "Che" (directed by Steven Soderbergh) and "The Motorcycle Diaries" (produced by Robert Redford), and The New York Times titled its obituary for Castro, "A Revolutionary Who Defied the U.S. And Held Cuba in His Thrall."

Dictators everywhere are safe so long as leftism reigns. And leftism will continue to reign so long as men dream of a collective heaven on Earth rather than of individual rights protected from such utopian totalitarians.

When Democracy Fails

December 7, 2016

One of the great lies of the 21st century is that republicanism and freedom are inevitable. Actually, representative government and individual liberty are the exception, not the rule, and individual liberty often dissipates in the name of the collective, along with truly representative government. And yet, it's that feeling of inevitability that allows us to attack the basic values that undergird republicanism and freedom. Because we never think that those institutions are under assault, we're unafraid of chipping away at their foundations in the name of partisan politics.

If we chip away enough at those foundations, the superstructure will crumble.

Democracy relies on three factors, as expressed by Harvard University's Yascha Mounk and the University of Melbourne's Roberto Stefan Foa: a belief that democracy is itself important, a belief that nondemocratic forms of government are wrong and a belief that the democratic system is legitimate. If those beliefs erode, so, too, do republicanism and freedom.

The left has been hammering away at those three beliefs for a full century. Leftism is based on the notion that if you give government massive power, it will revenge itself on the bourgeois who have stomped you down. More basically, Marxism is based on the notion that human beings cannot become decent without a new system. That system cannot be removed democratically, since we are all products of the democratic system, and are therefore corrupt.

Leftism, too, has scorned democracy as the only solution. Fascism of the proletariat would be better. In 2010, New York Times columnist Thomas Friedman said: "What if we could just be China for a day? I mean, just, just, just one day. You know, I mean, where we could actually, you know, authorize the right solutions, and I do think there is a sense of that, on, on everything from the economy to environment." That's not rare. The left spent most of the 1930s gazing enviously across the seas toward the fascist left in Italy, Germany and the Soviet Union.

Finally, the left has declared repeatedly that American democracy is illegitimate because it stands in favor of cruel capitalism. It's plutocratic and corrupt, and it must be heavily regulated. Today, the left claims that millions of voters are disenfranchised simply on the basis of race without evidence to support such idiocy.

But here's the problem in 2016: All three of the foundations of democracy are now being undermined by the reactionary right, too. Democracy, say many on the right, is not important so long as it means making America great again -- who cares if Carrier Corp. must be leveraged into keeping jobs at home, so long as the jobs remain at home? Democracy, say many on the right, isn't the only solution -- why not just trust Trump to do what's right? After all, he's certainly popular! And democracy doesn't work anyway, say many on the right -- the people must be lied to in order to get them to vote correctly. And voter fraud is rampant!

So we now have partisan politics that suggest that power is more important than reliable institutions or deeper values. That's a danger point for American politics. Donald Trump may turn out to be a wonderful president; we may yet see a new birth of freedom in America. But so long as partisans on both sides are prepared to blow up democracy in order to save it, we're at risk of an explosion.

'But the Democrats are Hypocrites!'

December 14, 2016

This week, the Washington Post reported that the CIA now believes that Russian-supported hacks of the Democratic National Committee and Hillary Clinton's campaign chair John Podesta were designed to boost Donald Trump's election prospects. The FBI apparently disagrees; it believes that the Russian intervention was designed to undermine faith in the election system generally. But all intelligence agencies agree that there was Russian support for the hacks themselves.

Democrats have fallen all over themselves to claim that this means that Russian President Vladimir Putin shifted the results of the election to Trump. But there's no evidence of that. Clinton was deeply unpopular for the entire election cycle -- a January 2016 YouGov/The Economist poll showed unfavorable ratings at 56 percent; in November, that same poll found her unfavorable ratings to be -- you guessed it -- 56 percent. It wasn't WikiLeaks that destroyed Hillary Clinton. It was Hillary Clinton. Even FBI Director James Comey's announcement that he would be reopening the investigation into Clinton's emails came courtesy of Anthony Weiner's laptop, not WikiLeaks.

Republicans, in response, have noted that Democrats' hysterics over Russian manipulation seems hypocritical. After all, Democrats had no problem whatsoever with President Barack Obama offering Putin "flexibility" in 2012 in exchange for a promise to loosen his pressure tactics. They cheered when Obama told Mitt Romney that he was delusional for embracing anti-Putin politics more appropriate to the 1980s. Now, Democrats are all hot and bothered about Putin's regime -- the same regime that Hillary Clinton handed a reset button, the same regime Obama allowed to take the lead in Syria, the same regime with which Obama meekly complied after Putin's takeover of Crimea.

Republicans are right: Yes, Democrats are awful hypocrites on Russia.

Here's the problem: So are Republicans. Trump questioned whether the Russians were behind the hacks at all. That's no surprise -- he spent most of the election cycle lathering up Putin's bare chest, congratulating him for his strength and equating his murder of journalists with some unspecified American sins. Trump then nominated Rex Tillerson to be secretary of state, a man who received the Order of Friendship from Putin in 2011.

So, what are Republicans doing during all of this? Capitulating. Former House Speaker Newt Gingrich calls the Tillerson pick wonderful -- the same Newt Gingrich who said in 2012 that Putin "represents a dictatorial approach that's very violent." (Of course, Gingrich now gives a lecture to the Heritage Foundation on the principles of Trumpism, so that's not much of a surprise.) Sean Hannity has accused anyone with questions about Russian hacking of simply wanting to undermine Trump. He said, "If all of these people care so much about these Russian allegations, then why didn't they feel the same way about Hillary Clinton's private server scandal?" We did! In fact, we spent years ripping Clinton apart. And now we'd like to know why Putin's hacking is all right. By the way, Hannity used to care about Russian interference and aggression. In March 2012, he called Putin a "huge problem," and in June 2013, he lamented that Putin was "laughing at the Obama admin's request to extradite Snowden back to the U.S." Now he wants Julian Assange, who is allegedly working with Putin, freed (in 2010 he wanted him jailed).

Here's the problem with the hypocrisy argument: You have to be nonhypocritical in order to make that charge. So long as Republicans are so intent on backing Trump's play that they act like hypocrites, it's going to be difficult to point out just how hypocritical Democrats are.

Obama Tries to Define Away Reality, but Reality Wins

December 21, 2016

Last Friday, President Obama gave his last press conference as commander in chief. Undeterred by his would-be successor's devastating loss to Donald Trump in the presidential election, unswayed by Republicans' complete domination of Congress, state legislatures and governor mansions, he maintained his cool and collected self-aggrandizement. Why not? According to Obama, Obama has been a major success.

Perhaps the most hilarious moment of delusion came when he talked about terrorism. "Over the past eight years, no foreign terrorist organization has successfully executed an attack on our homeland that was directed from overseas," Obama stated. He then continued, saying no attack has been executed "in a rainstorm with the attacker driving a tractor with one hand, drinking a Miller High Life with the other and wearing a clown nose."

To be fair, Obama didn't add those final qualifiers. But he might as well have. In order to define away the problem of terrorism that has grown dramatically worldwide on his watch, he simply spoke of terrorism as a problem of organized groups within defined territories. That's not how modern terrorism works. Terrorist groups can recruit without formal structures and can operate as independent cells within various countries.

Just three days after Obama's statements, an alleged jihadi plowed a truck into a Christmas market in Berlin; the same day, a Turkish terrorist murdered the Russian ambassador to Turkey. These latest attacks aren't outliers. In the past several years, we've seen terrorist attacks in Turkey, Germany, Belgium, Great Britain, Canada and Australia.

This sort of terrorism isn't relegated to foreign countries, of course. Here is an incomplete list of radical Islam-related terror attacks and attempts on American soil under Obama: shootings of American military recruiters in Little Rock, Arkansas; the massacre at Fort Hood; the Boston Marathon bombing; an attempted bombing of the airport in Wichita, Kansas; hatchet attacks on New York City police officers; attempted shootings at the "Draw Muhammad" event in Garland, Texas; the attacks on military recruiters in Chattanooga, Tennessee; the massacre at the San Bernardino Inland Regional Center; the Orlando nightclub shooting; the New York and New Jersey bombings; and the Ohio State University car attack.

Obama still thinks he can cover his abysmal record with closely drawn definitions of terrorism. It's the equivalent of President Bill Clinton saying he's been faithful to his wife except for certain areas, like sex. It's technically true so far as it goes, but it doesn't go very far.

Americans know that, and they reacted to Obama's consistent lying-by-omission by electing Trump, a man who needs little evidence to jump to conclusions. Obama is so careful to avoid spotting fact patterns that he simply omits inconvenient data points. Trump is so eager to spot fact patterns that he simply includes convenient non-data points. But Americans would rather have Trump's jump-to-conclusions mentality than Obama's avoid-conclusions-at-all-cost mentality -- Trump's mentality may lead to mistakes, but those mistakes are less likely to cost Western lives.

So Obama can hawk his faux sophistication on terrorism as much as he wants. If Democrats want to ensure that Republicans continue to win elections, they ought to follow his lead.

Obama's Skewed Moral Universe

December 28, 2016

President Barack Obama likes to see himself as a moral leader. "The arc of the moral universe is long," Obama likes to say, quoting Martin Luther King Jr, "but it bends toward justice." According to Obama, Obama is a genteel representative of decency and good grace, a man pointing America toward a broader vision, a fellow questing for social justice and contextual consideration.

In reality, he's a narcissistic fool. And like Burgess Meredith's character in "The Twilight Zone," he will be left standing in the ruins, bewailing the fates that abandoned him, leaving no worshipful admirers upon whom to lean.

Obama's legacy is one of failure all around the world. He leaves office with a genocide in Syria on his record -- a genocide he pledged to prevent, and then tolerated and finally lamented, mourning the fates while blithely ignoring his own cowardice. Libya, meanwhile, remains a full-scale disaster area, with tens of thousands of refugees from that failed campaign swamping Europe, along with those fleeing Syria, and his leftist European allies paying the political price.

Iran, the world's leading state sponsor of terrorism, stands on the brink of a nuclear dawn, its pockets filled with billions of dollars, its minions ascendant from Tehran to Aleppo to Beirut. Obama made that happen with nearly a decade of appeasement and a willingness to abandon freedom-minded Iranians to the tender mercies of the mullahs.

Meanwhile, Russia has only expanded its reach and influence, invading the sovereign nation of Ukraine and seizing Crimea to the deafening silence of the Obama administration. Russia has flexed its muscle in Kaliningrad, where it has stocked missiles, and in Syria, where it has assured Syrian President Bashar Assad's continued dominance.

China has grown its sphere of influence across the South China Sea, putting American allies from Taiwan and Japan to the Philippines directly under its thumb. Thanks to Obama's military cuts, China believes that it can bully American allies into embracing Chinese supremacy in international waters -- and it may be right. Simultaneously, Obama continues to drive America into debt, and the Chinese are large buyers of that outstanding debt.

The communist Cubans have been re-enshrined; so have the socialist Venezuelan authorities. The Islamic State group remains an international threat, and western capitals have been struck by Islamic terror time and again, to Obama's teeth-gnashing and general inaction.

But at least Obama is truly putting his focus where it's necessary: on declaring that our only ally in the Middle East, Israel, has no historic claim to its own existence and threatening Jews with sanctions for building bathrooms in East Jerusalem.

Obama came into office amidst grand promises to restore America's place in the world. Unless our place is the outhouse, he's failed. But at least he feels good about his accomplishments, even if thousands have died -- and thousands more will die -- in order to ensure his moral stature in his own mind.

About the Author

Ben Shapiro was born in 1984. He entered the University of California Los Angeles at the age of 16 and graduated summa cum laude and Phi Beta Kappa in June 2004 with a Bachelor of Arts degree in Political Science. He graduated Harvard Law School cum laude in June 2007.

Shapiro was hired by Creators Syndicate at age 17 to become the youngest nationally syndicated columnist in the United States. His columns are printed in major newspapers and websites including *The Riverside Press-Enterprise* and the *Conservative Chronicle*, Townhall.com, ABCNews.com, WorldNetDaily.com, Human Events, FrontPageMag.com, FamilySecurityMatters.com. His columns have appeared in *The Christian Science Monitor, Chicago Sun-Times, Orlando Sentinel, The Honolulu Advertiser, The Arizona Republic, Claremont Review of Books* and RealClearPolitics.com. He has been the subject of articles by *The Wall Street Journal, The New York Times*, The Associated Press, and *The Christian Science Monitor*; he has been quoted on "The Rush Limbaugh Show," "The Dr. Laura Show," at CBSNews.com, in the *New York Press, The Washington Times*, and *The American Conservative*.

The author of the national best-sellers, "Brainwashed: How Universities Indoctrinate America's Youth," "Porn Generation: How Social Liberalism Is Corrupting Our Future," and "Project President: Bad Hair and Botox on the Road to the White House." Shapiro has appeared on hundreds of television and radio shows around the nation, including "The O'Reilly Factor," "Fox and Friends," "In the Money," "DaySide with Linda Vester," "Scarborough Country," "The Dennis Miller Show," "Fox News Live," "Glenn Beck Show," "Your World with Neil Cavuto," "700 Club," "The Laura Ingraham Show," "The Michael Medved Show," "The G. Gordon Liddy

Show," "The Rusty Humphries Show," "The Lars Larson Show," "The Larry Elder Show," The Hugh Hewitt Show" and "The Dennis Prager Show."

Shapiro is married and runs Benjamin Shapiro Legal Consulting in Los Angeles.

AND WE ALL FALL DOWN
is also available as an e-book
for Kindle, Amazon Fire, iPad, Nook and
Android e-readers. Visit
creatorspublishing.com to learn more.

o o o

CREATORS PUBLISHING

We publish books.
We find compelling storytellers and
help them craft their narrative,
distributing their novels and collections
worldwide.

o o o

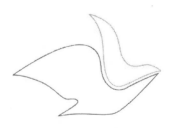

Made in the USA
Middletown, DE
03 August 2018